STO   NONFICTION   Sept. 14, 1976

5-24-76

Frozen Delights

Diana Collier and Nancy Goff

THOMAS Y. CROWELL COMPANY
New York   Established 1834

Copyright © 1976 by Diana Collier and Nancy Goff

Illustrations by Edward Linnartz
Designed by Abigail Moseley

Manufactured in the United States of America

Library of Congress Cataloging in Publication Data

Collier, Diana, 1942-
　　Frozen delights.

　　Includes index.
　　1.　Ice cream, ices, etc.　2.　Desserts, Frozen.
I.　Goff, Nancy, joint author.　II.　Title.
TX795.C64　　　641.8162　　　75-42494

ISBN 0-690-01097-4

1 2 3 4 5 6 7 8 9 10

Acknowledgments

Diana Collier would like to thank her contributors, tasters, and criticizers—Raj and Madeline; Mother; Mark, Elena, and Wiltold; Marvin; Evelyn; Sue and Ken, Carol, Hilda, and Erich; Irma and Alfred; Les Fabian, who used his worldwide resources to secure a recipe; and Oscar and Christopher, who enjoyed our failures as well as our successes.

Nancy Goff wishes to express much appreciation to her husband, Bob, and children, Jonathan and David, for their patience during the many hours of preparation. Many thanks to Connie Dormire for the loan of her old cookbook collection, to Marcia Sill for her many suggestions; to her mother for her Caribbean contributions, to her father for his good Jamaican rum, and to the tasters, who endured the bad with grace and enjoyed the good.

Contents

Contents

Introduction

Everyone loves ice cream. But imagine the possibility of delicious, rich, creamy-smooth, velvety-tasting ice cream from your own refrigerator freezer. *Frozen Delights* will help make the wish a reality.

This is the only book devoted solely to the still-freeze method of making ice cream. The technique is simple and uses convenient modern equipment, generally available in the contemporary kitchen. There's no need for rock salt, ice chipping, rigorous churning, and a lot of extra equipment.

Furthermore, this kind of homemade ice cream is delicious, nutritious, adaptable to all kinds of flavors, and of a higher quality than almost all commercial ice creams. It is sobering to realize that there is no legal requirement that commercial ice cream makers reveal the full list of ingredients in their ice cream. So even if you want to avoid additives, substitute ingredients, artificial flavors and colors, and other perhaps more harmful chemicals and emulsifiers, you can't if you buy your ice cream.*

We use only basic ingredients in our recipes, such as milk, cream, eggs, fruits, nuts, and natural flavorings. In some recipes we add certain processed materials, such as condensed and evaporated milk, dried fruit, chocolate, cream of tartar, gelatin, wine, and liqueur, but we avoid entirely artificial coloring, chemical emulsifiers, or "ice cream powders." We also suggest less sugar in many of our recipes than in the standard ones we have seen.

Many of the recipes are original, others are new and improved versions of old favorites, and two are interesting recipes taken directly from old cookbooks.

The scope of the more than 300 recipes in this book ranges from simple ice cream to more sophisticated frozen delights such as baked Alaskas, meringue desserts, frozen pies, ice cream cakes, sponge layers, and bombes. Also included are parfaits, soufflés, mousses, popsicles, sundaes, sodas, malts, milkshakes, floats, frozen cocktails, punches, marquises, spooms, and granités.

The recipes make from 1 pint to 2 quarts of ice cream or other frozen delicacy and generally require only a minimum amount of freezer space. Naturally, if you have a large freezing facility you can multiply the suggested amounts and make more. Making ice cream at home is a gastronomical treat worthy of children and gourmets alike.

---

*Possible additives to your favorite container of ice cream might be furcelleran, calcium sulfate, mono and diglycerides, polysorbates 65 and 80, sodium cargoxymethyl- cellulose, cellulose, dioctyl sodium sulfosuccinate, tetrasodium pryophosphate, sodium hexametaphosphate, calcium oxide and hydroxide, and magnesium oxide and hydrox- ide—just to name a few.

Notes on the History
of Frozen Desserts

According to Paul Dickson, in *The Great American Ice Cream Book* (to which we refer you for a detailed and amusing discussion of the history of ice cream in America), and according to other sources, ice cream evolved from the early practice of chilling wines and juices. The first stage of the evolution was the creation of primitive water ices. Then chilled milk and cream mixtures ultimately became ice cream.

Today, with modern refrigeration, it is easy to have a cold drink. But in the past, in most of the world, ice was a luxury item available to only the élite.

In the Bible, King Solomon is reported to have drunk chilled wines. On the other hand, the Greek physician Hippocrates warned against cold drinks, claiming they were a health hazard—a cold drink was believed to be a shock to the constitution that could result in death. This theory is still present among the folk of Europe and America, who can still be heard recounting elaborate second- and third-hand stories of horrible examples. Somehow, though, these examples never seem to involve the eating of ice cream.

Greek and Roman slaves prepared chilled drinks and fruit punches for their masters. It is said that the emperor Nero had slave runners bring snow from the mountains, which was then flavored with fruit juices, honey, and wines, thus creating "Italian ice."* These ices were served between highly seasoned courses during banquets so that the diners could cool and refresh their jaded palates.

Pliny the Elder agreed with Hippocrates that iced drinks were a health hazard, but for sanitary reasons. Seneca protested the practice of chilling by ice because of the expense. In that period snow was packed in straw-lined pits, where it then solidified into ice. It was later discovered that boiled water buried in the snow would turn to a very

---

*For a richer dessert add whipped cream. Whip ¾ cup heavy cream until soft peaks form. Add 2 Tbsp sugar and continue whipping until soft peaks begin to form. Quickly fold in whipped cream. If using sherbet as part of a layered dessert omit whipped cream.

---

clear ice. But the discussion, and the feasting, ended with the fall of the Roman Empire. The art of ice-making disappeared in Europe.

Not until hundreds of years later was it revived, with information from other parts of the world. Marco Polo is reported to have brought back to Italy the Oriental custom of eating water ices, which was also prevalent in the Middle East. The word "sherbet" comes from *sharbah*, the Arabic word for drink. Since the Muslims do not drink alcoholic beverages, sherbet, an icy sweet, was served in pearwood bowls and sipped from spoons. This was a popular refreshment for a sultan and his harem. In the Middle East sherbet is still served, a special symbol of hospitality. The sherbet of the Middle East is much like the ices in this book.

It is thought that the iced refreshment of Marco Polo was combined with milk and cream to make the first early ice cream in Italy. By the sixteenth century the Italians, who loved chilled drinks, discovered that saltpeter mixed with snow surrounding containers of boiled water produced a quick freeze. Italian ice creams, like many other arts of the Renaissance, found their way to other countries.

In 1533 the fourteen-year-old bride of Henri II, Catherine de Médicis, gets credit for bringing the secret of ices and sherbets to the court of France. According to Mr. Dickson, however, there is documentation that puts an ice creamlike dish in England during the fifteenth century at the coronation feast of Henry V, over a hundred years before its arrival in France.

But frozen desserts were still reserved for the élite until the reign of Louis XIV, when a Sicilian named Francesco Procopio dei Coltelli opened the Café Procope in Paris and served ice cream and sherbets to the so-called masses. Gradually other establishments appeared, each creating their own house specialties—hence such traditional frozen desserts as Biscuit Tortoni.

The art of freezing mixtures had advanced sufficiently by 1747 so that Mrs. Hanna Glasse could write in her British cookbook *The Art of Cookery Made Easy*:

> Take two Pewter Basons, one larger than the other; the inward one must have a close Cover, into which you are to put your Cream, and mix it with Raspberries or whatever you like best, to give it a Flavor and a Colour. Sweeten it to your Palate; then cover it close, and set it into the larger Bason. Fill it with Ice and a Handful of Salt; let it stand in this Ice three Quarters of an Hour, then uncover it, and stir the Cream well together; cover it close again and let it stand Half an Hour longer, after that turn it to your Plate . . .

Although the means for making ice cream were not yet widely

known during the early settlement of America, there is at least one reference to it in the eighteenth century—as being served at the table of Governor William Bladen of Maryland. And certainly the early Americans did crave cold drinks and ice. They soon devised their own ways for preserving winter ice. The European method of digging a hole in the ground, and covering it with a roof, was modified to an above-ground structure with double walls and doors called an ice house. Many of the early nineteenth-century mansions had their own ice houses.

In the early 1800s Americans even began exporting ice, first to the Caribbean. The industry grew to such proportions that large clipper ships carried thousands of tons of ice from the United States to tropical climates.

In nineteenth-century homes ice began to be considered a necessity, not a luxury. Large jugs of iced water were expected on every table. Horse-drawn ice wagons delivered chunks of ice to be placed in a wooden metal-lined ice box in the home.

Ice cream making did not evolve much, however, until 1846, when Nancy Johnson invented the hand-cranked ice cream freezer, which produces churn-freeze ice cream. Modern hand-cranked or electric ice cream freezers for home use have advanced little since then. This machine typically consists of a wood bucket with a metal pail inside. Crushed ice and rock salt are put between the bucket and pail, producing a freezing brine of low temperature. A crank or motor turns a paddle, or "dasher," inside the metal pail to stir the ice cream as it freezes, preventing crystallization. Since the whole process can be somewhat messy, it is traditionally done outside.

In the early 1800s the process for mechanical refrigeration was also discovered. It was found that a volatile liquid like ether or ammonia would produce intense cold if allowed to vaporize under low pressure. This is the principle of a modern refrigerator. However, it was not until the 1860s that refrigeration on a large scale became technically possible. Large commercial refrigeration devices were available to make ice for ice houses, railroad refrigeration cars, and large commercial freezers, but it was another fifty years before the first mechanical household refrigerator was developed.

The combination of the churn-freeze method and mechanical freezing equipment produced the vast American and worldwide commercial ice cream industry.

Around 1920 commercial production of the mechanical home refrigerator began. At a price of nine hundred dollars the early refrigerator was beyond the purchasing power of most of the population. However, as production rose, and the price came down, the refrigerator became an essential household appliance by the 1930s.

Although there is little documented information on the origin of still-freeze ice cream in America, there are references found in early cookbooks to ice cream made without an ice cream maker. In the 1896 edition of the *Fannie Farmer Cook Book* references are made to still-freeze desserts. A custard is prepared and whipped cream and/or beaten egg whites are folded in. The mixture is placed in a container with a tight-fitting lid. The container is then immersed in a bucket filled with rock salt and ice and the bucket is covered with newspapers or an old piece of carpet. The bucket is set in the shade for anywhere from two to five hours. Thus the early days of still-freeze ice cream required the same salt and ice mixture to freeze the ice cream as churn-frozen ice cream.

With the advent of mechanical refrigeration in the home the basic method of making still-frozen ice cream was modified. The freezing compartment of the refrigerator replaced the ice-and-salt-filled bucket. Ice cube trays replaced the tightly covered pail. Recipes for refrigerator tray ice cream and sherbet began to appear in the 1930s and 1940s editions of the *Fannie Farmer Cook Book*. Collections of regional recipes and magazine collections published during this period refer to homemade refrigerator tray ice cream and milk sherbet.

Since that time various cookbooks have contained a few recipes for "refrigerator tray" ice cream. In the *Encyclopedia of World Cookery* by Elizabeth Campbell, published in England, recipes for still-freeze ice cream and sherbet from several countries are included. France is famous for a "Bombe Glacée," a rich molded dessert, and Peach Melba, a half peach filled with a scoop of vanilla ice cream and covered with a sieved raspberry purée. In Hungary refrigerator tray ice cream is made with whipped cream, chocolate, and coffee. In Italy very rich ice cream is made from eggs, heavy cream, and fruit. The mixture is frozen in a refrigerator tray and stirred every half hour.

In this book we have compiled recipes using the still-freeze technique available for centuries; there's no need for a special ice cream maker. We have refined still-freeze ice cream recipes and developed recipes for other frozen desserts so that you can share our delight in delicious frozen desserts made at home with your regular kitchen equipment, and without the bother of salt, ice, and churning.

We hope you will regard this book, the first as far as we know devoted entirely to the systematic study and development of still-freeze desserts, as a departure in the history of ice cream as important today as the introduction of churn-freeze ice cream was in 1847.

Know Your Freezer

Understanding your freezing facility and its capabilities is very important in making still-freeze ice cream. And that freezing capacity is probably responsible if your frozen dessert is freezing up more quickly or slowly than our recipes indicate.

The chest freezer is the most economical to operate, because the cold air escapes only from the top portion of the freezer when it is opened. Since its temperature range is from 0° to 30° below 0° (all temperatures in the book are in Fahrenheit) this unit is ideal for making ice cream. Your frozen dessert will freeze up very quickly and last a long time, though it will also take a longer time to ripen.

Most upright freezers have one door, like many refrigerators, and are handy to use though not very cheap to run, because when the door is opened cold air escapes from all levels and the unit has to work hard to bring the temperature back down again. An upright freezer is excellent for making ice cream, since its temperature range is around 0°.

Another kind of freezer is part of a two-door combination refrigerator-freezer. On these units it is very important to set the unit at its coldest while making ice cream. This coldness is relative and will differ according to the make and condition of your refrigerator-freezer. After the ice cream is made the control may be turned back to a normal setting.

Regardless of what kind of refrigerator-freezer you have, don't forget what happens if your unit is described as "frost-free." This phrase means that the freezer goes through defrosting cycles. When it is going through a cycle the freezer temperature will rise for 10 minutes or so. This temperature rise may not be good for storing ice cream, which may start ripening, then refreeze, resulting in crystallization or shrinkage. There is nothing to be done about it except eat up all that great ice cream soon after making it.

Two-door units, having a freezer in one section and refrigerator in the other, will have a freezer temperature range of 10° to 0°. Ice cream will freeze up relatively fast and last pretty well. The freezing time in the recipes in this book is written with this kind of unit in mind.

A single-door refrigerator having a freezer compartment with an interior door closing off the unit from the rest of the refrigerator will have a temperature range of 20° or higher. If you are using this kind of unit to make ice cream, allow more freezing time than indicated in our recipes. Ice cream will store moderately well for a few days in such a freezer compartment, but not for any great length of time, since these units are not "true freezers"—that is, the temperature does not drop down to the zero degree range.

Diana's friend Lee, in her delightful one-room apartment, has something called a compact refrigerator with a freezing space capable of holding 2 refrigerator ice trays and 1 or 2 frozen food packages. This too will make ice cream! The ice cream may, however, require a good deal more time to freeze up than that suggested in the recipes and the ripening time may be shorter.

After testing and assessing your freezing facility, change the recipes accordingly. Initial freezing may take less time or it may take more. Know what your unit can do.

Should you not have a mechanical freezing facility, don't despair. We refer you to a recipe from *The White House Cook Book* (1900) entitled "Ice-Cream Without a Freezer."

Beat the yolks of eight eggs very light, and add thereto four cupfuls of sugar, and stir well. Add to this, little by little, one quart of rich milk that has been heated almost to boiling, beating all the while; then put in the whites of eight eggs beaten to a stiff froth. Then boil the mixture in a pail set inside another containing hot water. Boil about fifteen minutes or until it is as thick as a boiled custard, stirring steadily meanwhile. Pour into a bowl to cool. When quite cold, beat into it three pints of rich sweet cream and five teaspoonfuls of vanilla, or such other flavoring as you prefer. Put it into a pail having a close-fitting cover and pack in pounded ice and salt,—*rock salt*, not the common kind,—about three-fourths ice and one-fourth salt. When packed, before putting the ice on top of the cover, beat the custard as you would batter, for five minutes steady; then put on the cover and put the ice and salt over it, and cover the whole with a thick mat, blanket or carpet and let it stand for an hour. Then carefully uncover and scrape from the bottom and sides of the pail the thick coating of frozen custard, making every particle clear, and beat again very hard, until the custard is a smooth, half-congealed paste. Do this thoroughly. Put on the cover, ice, salt and blanket, and leave it for five or six hours, replenishing the ice and salt if necessary . . .

Freezing

Understanding the freezing process also helps you make good ice cream. There are three stages: the mixture cools to its freezing point; it solidifies; and then the temperature of the mixture gradually drops to that of the freezer.

The solidification phase is the concern in the making of ice cream. During this time the mixture is turning from a liquid or soft state to a solid or firm state. The temperature remains constant. The freezing starts at the outside or exposed area of the container, bottom (where it is in contact with the freezer shelf), side surfaces, and top; then it works toward the center.

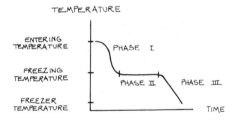

When the outside, bottom, and side surfaces of ice cream are frozen and the middle is soft, it's time for the second beating or stirring. Large frozen lumps, pieces, or ice crystals are broken up and mixed with the softer, partially frozen parts, resulting in a smooth product.

This second beating or stirring also redistributes any nuts or fruit that have settled to the bottom, depending on the density of the mixture. Further, particularly when beaten egg whites have been used, the mixtures separate, the heavier settling to the bottom, and it is necessary to reincorporate the two. Sometimes a third beating or stirring is necessary to achieve a uniformly smooth product; and in that case the recipes will suggest it.

If, while you are making bread, feeding the baby, making business calls, cutting the lawn, cleaning the house, or hitting a few golf balls, the mixture freezes too solidly before the second stirring, all is not lost. Nancy likes to leave the container out at room temperature until some of the solid softens and it becomes workable. Diana prefers to let it soften in the refrigerator. With Nancy's method it will melt more quickly and with Diana's more uniformly. Do whatever you prefer and then proceed with the recipe.

Ice crystals are often a problem in still-freeze ice cream. Crystallization can be reduced, though not eliminated entirely, by choice and proportion of ingredients. In churn-freeze ice cream the situation isn't quite as crucial, since the mixture is constantly in motion.

Ice crystals form when water, or a watery mixture, freezes and the water molecules stick together. If the substance is just water, ice results. In ice cream some of the other ingredients, such as sugar, heavy cream, egg yolks, egg whites, and gelatin, act as emulsifiers to prevent or reduce the formation of ice crystals by keeping the water molecules separate. The greater the concentration of such other ingredients the less likely it is that the water molecules will stick to one another. Also, the recommended stirrings or beatings break up any crystals that may have formed.

For example, in the diagram the sugar molecules separate the water molecules. As more sugar is added fewer ice crystals will form. But be careful, particularly when creating your own recipes. Too much sugar will prevent the mixture from freezing and create a syrupy mess.

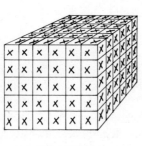

ICE CUBE

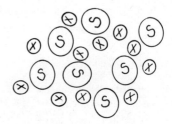

X - WATER MOLECULE
S - SUGAR MOLECULE

SUGAR MOLECULES PREVENT SOLID CRYSTALS FROM FORMING. WATER WILL NOT "STICK" TO SUGAR.

Equipment

Most of the recipes in this book can be made with ordinary, multi-purpose kitchen equipment. We are not recommending any equipment that will be used only for making ice cream, except the popsicle and individual ice cube molds.

Freezing facility (page 7)
2 sets of mixing bowls
2 sets of wooden spoons, different sizes (one set for cooking; second set for making bread, pastry, ice cream)
Standard measuring cups: 1/4 cup, 1/3 cup, 1/2 cup, 1 cup, 2 cups, 1 quart
Measuring spoons: 1/4 tsp, 1/2 tsp, 1 tsp, 1 Tbsp
2 rubber scrapers or spatulas
Long-handled stirring spoon
Wire whisks, large and small
Rotary beater
Hand-held electric beater
Electric mixer
Blender
Ice crusher
Grater

Knives: paring; heavy-duty 10-inch; and long, sharp thin-bladed
Cake server
Ice cream scoops
Cake tester, broom straw, or wooden toothpick
Food mill
Sieves, fine and coarse
Double boiler, preferably stainless steel, enamel, or glass
Saucepans of different sizes, preferably stainless steel, enamel, or
   glass
Baking or cookie sheet
7½-inch flan ring or pie plate
9-inch flan ring or pie plate
Cake pans: 8-inch diameter, 9-inch diameter, 9-by-13-inch rectan-
   gular
Soufflé dishes: 4, 6, and 8 cups
Molds: 4, 6, and 8 cups
Popsicle molds
Freezer containers (page 28)
Refrigerator trays
Individual ice cube molds
Pastry tube
Large glass punch bowl (4 to 5 quarts)
Serving platter or plate
Oven-proof serving platter or plate
Wooden board
Glasses: parfait, sherbet, champagne, and 14-oz
2 linen tea towels
Aluminum foil
Plastic wrapping
Waxed paper

 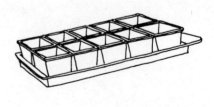

Ingredients

MILK AND CREAM

Milk as an ingredient in the recipes in this book is the homogenized pasteurized milk commonly available in New York and New Jersey, the proving ground for these recipes. Such milk must contain a minimum of 3.25 percent butterfat to be qualified under the laws of those states to be called "milk."

If there is any way you can get pasteurized (but not homogenized) milk, you might prefer it on the grounds that the less processing the better.

If you have milk that is not homogenized, stir it throughly before using it to distribute the butterfat. Diana remembers her mother carefully removing some of the "cream" from the top of the milk bottle for her father's morning coffee before shaking it to distribute the butterfat evenly.

Certified raw milk (sometimes available at your local dairy or health food stores) or milk from your own healthy cow will also have to be stirred before using to distribute the butterfat.

Light cream has a butterfat content of 18 percent. It is becoming less available in some areas. According to a dairyman source, Half and Half is supplanting light cream. The minimum butterfat content of *Half and Half* is supposed to be 10.5 percent; however, we have seen containers claiming butterfat content of 18 percent as well. When this is the case light cream and Half and Half may be used interchangeably in our recipes.

Heavy cream has a 36 percent butterfat content and adds richness and smoothness to ice cream. This is the cream to use for whipping.

Skimmed milk has had almost all of the butterfat removed.

Sweetened condensed milk is a canned product consisting of concentrated whole milk with sugar added. Milk has been reduced to 40

---

percent of its original volume in this product, which is quite useful in making ice cream.

Evaporated milk is homogenized whole milk reduced to 50 percent of its original volume; it has a butterfat content of 8 percent. Evaporated milk is said to be more easily digested than homogenized fresh milk. It has many uses in making ice cream.

Buttermilk sold in dairy departments of stores today is skimmed milk that has had a culture of bacteria added. It is then kept in a warm place until it thickens. At this stage it is similar to yogurt in appearance. After being stirred it is sold as buttermilk.

Old-fashioned buttermilk was produced when fully soured whole milk was churned. After the butterfat was separated from the milk the residue was called buttermilk. If this type is available to you, it has a fine flavor and is quite suitable to use in recipes calling for buttermilk.

Yogurt is a sour milk product widely available in the United States. If you wish you can make it yourself, either with a kit purchased for the purpose, or from a culture available at health food stores. A good description of how to make yogurt at home can be found in Jean Hewitt's *The New York Times Natural Foods Cookbook*.

Dairy *sour cream* is milk with an 18 percent butterfat content, usually pasteurized, homogenized, and soured by the addition of a culture to give it a pleasant and distinctively tart flavor.

WHIPPED CREAM

The butterfat content of whipping cream (heavy cream) for ice cream should be at least 36 percent to reduce crystallization. Whipped cream

adds lightness, smoothness, richness, and calories to ice cream, and we love it.

In whipping heavy cream we recommend that the bowl and beaters as well as the cream be chilled for best results. Don't attempt to use the blender in whipping cream or you will make butter! A wire whisk is good, as is a rotary beater; a hand-held electric beater is excellent, an electric mixer possible. Diana's 1940s vintage but terrific Kitchen-Aid makes butter but Nancy's 1967 Hamilton Beach works very well indeed. Diana usually uses a small electric beater while Nancy prefers a wire whisk and a large bowl to whip cream.

When whipping cream by hand or machine start out at a low speed and gradually increase it, rotating the bowl to incorporate air. As with egg whites, heavy cream is softly whipped when the cream starts to but doesn't hold peaks; instead it falls back on itself when the beater is lifted out of the bowl. If nuts, liqueur, fruit, or sugar are to be added whip only until soft peaks form. If cream is to be added directly to custard or any other mixture, whip until either soft peaks or stiff peaks form, depending on the recipe.

When stiff peaks have just formed, *stop*. Otherwise, the cream will become granular and you may have butter. (Actually, it's pretty good butter!)

Other ingredients must be cold before folding in whipped cream or all your work will be for naught—the cream will deflate.

If the cream gets too warm it will not whip up properly; therefore, a good idea for a hot day or if using a wire whisk is to set the bowl containing cream in a larger one containing ice and water. Then the cream will whip up immediately.

WHIPPED EVAPORATED MILK

Cookbooks specify many different ways to whip evaporated milk, some more complicated than others.

We recommend emptying the contents into a bowl and placing the bowl and the beaters to be used in the coldest part of the refrigerator for approximately half an hour.

Remove bowl and beaters from refrigerator and whip until you reach the consistency suggested in the recipe.

Should your kitchen be very warm, set the chilled bowl with milk into a larger bowl containing ice and water. Whip until the right consistency, and use as directed.

EGGS

The recipes in this book were tested using "large" eggs (approximately 2 oz. each liquid measure or 12 eggs = 24 oz) at room temperature. To use eggs of another size see Substitutions. Do not use even slightly cracked eggs in ice cream recipes.

Whole eggs and *egg yolks* can be treated in a similar manner. If beating eggs for a custard, sugar or sweetening can be added either at the beginning or near the end of beating.

Beating eggs for a custard can easily be done with a wire whisk, rotary egg beater, hand-held electric beater, or electric mixer at medium speed. The eggs and yolks should be beaten until they become frothy and light in color. The sugar need not be completely dissolved, since it will dissolve when the custard is cooked. For custards, egg yolks alone will produce a smoother product than whole eggs.

To beat whole eggs or egg yolks for uncooked ice cream, frozen pies, or soufflés, it is very desirable to use an electric mixer. At least 5 minutes of beating at high speed is needed, and few cooks are dedicated enough to beat for half an hour or more by hand to achieve the same effect.

First beat the eggs or yolks until they have increased in volume and thickened slightly. Add the sugar or sweetening in a thin stream or 1 tablespoon at a time while still beating. Continue to beat until the eggs are much lighter in color and the volume has expanded even more. The eggs will appear to be very thick and sticky, and strands falling from lifted beater will remain visible for several seconds on the surface of the mixture. Taste to make sure the sugar is completely dissolved, with no granules. Do not worry about overbeating.

Egg whites are a whole different thing. They are used to add volume and lightness to ice cream. In our recipes we usually suggest that egg whites be beaten until soft peaks form; sugar is then added, and the whites are beaten further until they hold stiff peaks and are smooth and glossy. The egg whites must be at room temperature or they won't rise enough. If the recipe calls for a tablespoon of sugar, just add it and continue beating; but if more is to be added, do so in a thin stream, beating all the while. When the sugar is added and the mixture beaten further, the appearance of the egg whites changes: they become smooth, glossy, and hold very stiff peaks.

A little bit of cream of tartar adds acidity to the stiffly beaten egg whites, thus reducing their tendency to "leak" or become granular. We recommend using a stainless steel or glass bowl instead of copper, aluminum, or plastic for this operation.

Egg whites will not beat properly if there is any foreign matter in the whites, such as egg yolk, water, cream, etc. Use care in separating the white from the yolk and make sure the beater is clean and dry. It is possible to beat the egg whites and then beat the heavy cream with the same beaters, *but it won't work the other way around.*

After egg whites are stiffly beaten they may be folded into a hot or cold mixture without losing their stiffness and body—unlike whipped cream, which dissolves when it comes in contact with anything hot.

We like using wire whisks with custard and chocolate to gain smoothness and do not wish to discourage the use of a whisk in beating egg whites. It is long, hard work, however, and using an electric mixer or hand-held electric beater is very satisfactory. Start the machine at a slow speed and gradually increase it, rotating the bowl to force air into the mixture. The egg whites are softly beaten when they do not hold peaks but fall back on themselves when the beater is lifted out of the bowl. Add sugar and beat until the beater holds the egg whites and stiff peaks form. Taste a bit to make sure the sugar is dissolved—there should be no granular taste. If there is, continue beating until the egg whites taste smooth. This can take as long as an additional 5 minutes.

For best results, use immediately after beating. However, beaten egg whites may be loosely covered and stored in the refrigerator up to half an hour before use.

In making ice cream you will find that a lot of egg whites accumulate. Put them in a freezer container, cover tightly, and freeze until you are ready to make sherbet, baked Alaska, or a meringue dessert.

Before using, allow egg whites and container to defrost in the refrigerator. Then measure out what you need, bring to room temperature, and use. Two egg whites equal between 1/4 and 1/3 cup.

SUGAR

Raw sugar is unrefined cane sugar, light beige in color. This sugar has a very mild flavor all its own but lends a slightly different flavor and texture to frozen desserts than granulated white sugar when used.

Turbinado sugar is a partly refined sugar similar to raw sugar in texture, color, and taste. Both blend well with the flavors in many recipes.

Granulated white sugar is a highly refined product made from cane or beet sugar. This sugar is pure white in color and has little distinctive flavor beyond its sweetness. It blends very well in frozen desserts, enhancing the fruit, chocolate, and other flavorings.

Confectioners' sugar is finely ground granulated sugar with 3 percent cornstarch added. Use confectioners' sugar only when specified in the recipe.

Light- and dark-brown sugar as manufactured in the United States are granulated white sugar with molasses added. The dark brown has more molasses added than the light brown, so its flavor is stronger. Keep them in tightly closed containers to avoid hard lumps. If brown sugar becomes rock hard, add a whole apple to the tightly closed container and the sugar will soften in a day or two. When used in frozen desserts the flavors of these sugars blend unobtrusively with the flavors of the other ingredients.

Molasses is made from the juice of sugar cane. We recommend unsulphured, milder-flavored molasses for the recipes in this book.

Light corn syrup is a liquid sweetener made from cornstarch. It has a very mild flavor that blends well with other flavors used in frozen desserts.

Dark corn syrup is light corn syrup to which caramel syrup has been added. It should be used only when the flavor of the syrup is desired as part of the flavor of the frozen dessert.

Pure maple syrup is made from the sap of sugar maple trees. The syrup has a strong, distinctive flavor and should be used to sweeten only when a maple flavor is called for. We do not recommend using any of the artificially flavored syrups or those that are only partially pure maple syrup.

Honey is used in frozen desserts for its distinctive flavor and nutritive value. It is sweeter than sugar when used in frozen desserts and should be used only when its specific flavor is desired. Honey varies considerably from one kind to another, depending on the bees and flowers, so it is best to experiment to find out which is your favorite. Try blueberry honey.

GELATIN

Gelatin is sometimes used in recipes to give a smooth texture to the dessert. It retards excessive crystallization and is used in making popsicles, water ices, some sherbets, and some ice creams to make them less icy.

We recommend only the unflavored gelatin. To use, sprinkle the amount needed into cold water or other cold liquid in a small saucepan or bowl. Stir and set aside so that the gelatin can soften. Place liquid and gelatin over low heat and stir until granules melt and are no longer visible. Remove from heat and use as directed.

Since gelatin becomes firm at a higher temperature than the freezing point of water, it is a useful ingredient in any frozen dessert that is made in a mold and then unmolded. The gelatin helps the unmolded dessert keep its shape when brought to the table for serving.

VANILLA BEAN

Vanilla bean and vanilla extract differ so much in taste that we regard them as two separate flavors. Nevertheless, we do use them as substitutes—for instance, in our recipes you can always substitute 1 teaspoon vanilla extract for 1 inch of vanilla bean.

When using vanilla bean, cut off the required amount, slice in half lengthwise, scrape out the black powder (vanilla), and beat with the egg yolks. If you want to use vanilla bean in recipes not requiring eggs, add the black powder to milk or liquid used in recipe.

If using vanilla bean in other types of recipes, the powder inside the bean is usually added to the liquid and then to the body of the recipe, unless otherwise indicated.

EXTRACTS

The extracts used in this book are vanilla extract, made by mashing vanilla beans or pods in a 35 percent alcohol solution; almond extract, made from oil of almonds in a 30 percent alcohol solution; and mint extract (see below).

For a full flavor any extract used in custard-based ice cream should be added to the custard after it has been cooked and cooled slightly, unless otherwise indicated in the recipe. Extracts can also be beaten into egg whites, but the egg whites must then be used immediately, since the addition of an extract tends to deflate the whites. We also add extracts to whipped cream with excellent results.

When using extracts in any other mixture, add only when it is cool.

Extracts should be used sparingly, as a little bit goes a long way.

MINT EXTRACT

Makes 1 cup of mint extract to be used as directed.

1 cup water
½ cup fresh mint leaves or 10 to 15 dried mint leaves

Stir fresh or dried mint leaves into 1 cup water in small saucepan. Bring water to a boil, cover, and remove from heat. Let mint leaves steep for half an hour. Strain the liquid into a small bowl to remove the leaves. Pour extract into small jar, cover tightly, and store in refrigerator.

BREWING STRONG COFFEE

Grind up 2 to 3 rounded tablespoons Italian roast coffee beans in a blender or coffee grinder. After grinding, this will measure just under 1/4 cup and will make a very strong half cup of coffee.

Commercially ground coffee can also be used. Use two heaping coffee measures, or 5 Tbsp ground coffee. However, we recommend the Italian roast coffee because it tastes less bitter when cold.

Spoon the ground coffee into a filter, or a strainer lined with cheesecloth, muslin, or filter paper, and set over a measuring cup. Heat water to boiling. Pour a little more than 1/2 cup water over coffee grounds to make 1/2 cup strong coffee. Should you need more coffee, increase the amounts proportionately.

Instant coffee may also be used. But be aware of the different taste produced, often experienced as a bitter aftertaste when used in ice cream. Some people can detect whenever instant coffee or some artificial substitute has been used. Try not to sacrifice taste for convenience.

COCONUTS

Diana uses coconut in many of her recipes but recommends using only unsweetened dried or fresh coconut, not the canned, sweetened variety.

Whole coconuts are available in many grocery stores and are easy to open. Look it over first to see if there are any cracks. If so, put it back and take another one. Also shake it to make sure there is liquid. If there isn't, your coconut may be old, dried out inside, or sour, and it's then of little use.

It's also possible to find dried finely grated packaged unsweetened coconut in many health food or Indian stores.

To open a fresh coconut, first preheat your oven to 350°. Use an ice pick or screwdriver and punch holes in two of the "eyes" on the end of the coconut. Then, drain off the liquid, which is a delicious drink by itself.

Put the coconut in the oven on a tray or in a shallow pan for 20 minutes. Carefully remove the hot coconut from the oven. Usually the shell has cracked. If it hasn't, hit it with a hammer until it does. Then pull or wedge it apart the best way you can.

Now, while the coconut is still hot, insert a strong, thin knife between the meat and the shell and separate the two. It's easier to handle the pieces when cool but not as easy to separate the meat from the shell.

Then, cut off the inner brown skin. If you want to eat it raw, now is a good time!

For finely grated coconut drop a few pieces at a time into a blender and blend until it's as fine as you want it.

For a coarser batch, grate against coarse part of grater. Watch your fingers when you get to the little pieces! Those are the ones Diana usually reserves for the blender.

In the recipes requiring coconut Diana has indicated "finely grated . . ." but feel free to substitute a coarser variety. After all, these are your ice cream creations and they should be made to your taste.

Grated coconut can be used immediately or dried; but don't keep freshly grated coconut in refrigerator more than a day or two—it will develop mold.

To dry, put the grated coconut in a shallow pan and place this either in the sun for a few days or in the oven at very low temperature (200° to 250°), shaking pan from time to time, for 20 minutes. Watch it carefully, since you don't want to toast it.

Grated dried coconut can be easily stored in plastic bags, plastic containers, or jars, in the cupboard, refrigerator, or wherever. Once it's dried, no mold will appear.

In an emergency it is possible to use the sweetened variety. Soak the required amount in a great deal of water, rinsing several times to remove as much sweetening as possible. Drain and remove excess water by squeezing the coconut in paper towels. Dry it quickly in the oven at the lowest temperature, just as you would for fresh coconut.

CARAMELIZED NUTS

When used in ice cream caramelized nuts give a sweet taste and crunchy texture. In addition, they can be chopped and used as a topping on sundaes or banana splits. Here's how to make them.

3/4 cup almonds, walnuts, pecans, or other nuts
1/3 cup granulated sugar
2 Tbsp water

Oil a 9-inch round cake pan with vegetable oil. Spread 3/4 cup nuts in a single layer in the cake pan.

Place ⅓ cup sugar with 2 Tbsp water in a small saucepan. Cook sugar and water over high heat, swirling pan to dissolve sugar. Continue boiling sugar water, swirling pan occasionally, until syrup turns an amber color. Quickly pour syrup over nuts and stir to coat evenly. Set aside to cool.

Break up nuts and place in a tightly covered container.

Caramelized nuts may be stored in a tightly covered container in the freezer for months. If the container is not tightly covered the nuts will absorb moisture and become soggy.

CANDIED CITRUS RIND

Candied citrus rind can be found in grocery stores but here's an easy recipe for making your own.

Grated rind from one lemon, orange, or lime
Granulated sugar

Finely grate the rind from a lemon, orange, or lime, being careful to grate only that part of rind that has color—the white part underneath is too bitter for these recipes. Measure out amount of rind and place in small container. Add the same amount of granulated sugar to the rind and stir thoroughly. Sugar is added to citrus rind to sweeten it and to avoid a bitter taste when rind is used in ice cream or sherbet.

Cover tightly and store in refrigerator until ready to use. The rind will keep for several months.

Hints

COOKING CUSTARD

The secret of delicious smooth custard is to have the right cooking temperature and stir, stir, stir.

In the top portion of a double boiler, over simmering water, heat the milk and cream until either lukewarm or hot but not boiling, depending on recipe. Then remove from heat and set aside.

Using an electric mixer or large wire whisk, beat the egg yolks with sugar and any other ingredients specified in the recipe, such as cornstarch, vanilla bean, or liqueur, until the mixture is frothy and light yellow in color. The sugar doesn't have to be completely dissolved, since it will do so as the custard cooks. The addition of cornstarch to the eggs acts as a stabilizer to help prevent curdling when the custard cooks.

In a thin stream pour one third or all (depending on recipe) of the milk into the beaten egg yolk mixture, stirring all the while. Don't set top of double boiler back over simmering water. Set aside. The milk will warm the egg yolks sufficiently to again reduce the chance of curdling.

Pour warm egg and milk mixture back into top of double boiler, place over simmering water, and cook, stirring, stirring, stirring, until custard thickens. Careful attention to stirring, scraping of all surfaces of the pot, and heat from the simmering but not boiling water are extremely important or your custard may curdle and lumps form; the whole thing can be spoiled. If the custard looks as though it is getting too hot, quickly lift the top of the double boiler off the water until it cools, BUT KEEP STIRRING.

When the custard has thickened, remove from heat and continue to stir until it cools slightly and steam has escaped.

Chill in refrigerator until ready for use. If the custard is not to be used immediately, allow to cool before covering and storing; otherwise condensation may form and make the custard watery. Custard is at its best in its first 24 hours, so use it promptly.

What to do if:
Milk gets too hot while heating. Remove from heat, take off the film, pour the milk into a bowl, and wash out the pot. Then continue with the recipe.

Lumps form or custard curdles. Remove from heat and strain. If it is thick enough, continue with the recipe. If not, beat another egg yolk, slowly beat in a little warm custard and then add the yolk and custard back to the main mixture. Continue as before, stirring constantly.

After curdling, if the taste is off, discard and start again.

If you don't have a double boiler, don't despair. Use a pot with a heavy-gauge or thick bottom over low direct heat. Compensate in the cooking time for the thickness of the pot, which will retain heat after the pan is removed from the burner. But just keep stirring.

Remember! As soon as the custard starts to thicken, remove from heat. Continue stirring. If custard has not become thick enough, return to heat, continuing to stir, a few moments longer; then remove again when it looks thick enough. Continue to stir until cool. Proceed with recipe.

MELTING CHOCOLATE

In the recipes in this book we use unsweetened chocolate, semi-sweet chocolate, chocolate bars (Swiss and others), and chocolate chips, melted, chopped, grated, or shaved. Chopping, grating, and shaving chocolate is not very difficult, but melting chocolate can be.

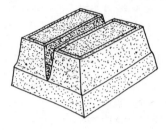

If chocolate is melted at too high a temperature, it will burn. To avoid this we recommend using very low heat, regardless of method chosen.

If you use an electric stove it is possible to melt the required amount of chocolate by itself in a saucepan directly on the burner on a "warm" setting. Check it often to make sure the chocolate doesn't burn at the edges before melting completely.

It is also possible to melt chocolate directly on the burner using a gas stove over a *very* low flame, but you must watch the chocolate constantly. When Diana uses this method she is forever lifting the pot off the burner when it appears to be getting too hot, waiting for the chocolate to cool slightly, and then setting it back on for a few more moments.

Nancy likes to melt chocolate by placing the required amount by itself in a small metal bowl and then setting the bowl in a saucepan or larger bowl containing very hot water. She then sets it aside to let the chocolate melt. If necessary the pot can be set on the stove over low heat. But don't let the water boil or there will be the possibility of the chocolate "tightening" (see below).

Chocolate may also be melted in the top of a double boiler over simmering, not boiling water. If the chocolate is to be melted by itself the water should not be boiling, because then steam forms and rises around the top portion of the double boiler, condenses into the chocolate, and causes it to tighten. If only a few drops of liquid get into chocolate while it is melting the fat separates from the cocoa, causing a chalky or "tightened" product to form. Unsweetened chocolate has the greatest tendency to tighten; semi-sweet chocolate appears to have enough other ingredients added to reduce its tendency to tighten, thus making it easier to melt. However, this tightening won't happen if the chocolate is melted with a good deal more than a few drops of water, coffee, butter, or any other liquid. *But don't stir this liquid in until the chocolate is completely melted!*

After the chocolate is melted, stir liquid and chocolate together with wire whisk until smooth. You now can add small amounts of other ingredients, such as custard or beaten egg whites. Stir thoroughly with wire whisk and add some more. Continue to add in this fashion until a smooth product results. If too much is added at one time lumps may form. If so, warm the chocolate slightly and continue to stir until lumps disappear.

If the chocolate tightens, it can be restored by adding one or two tablespoons of an odorless, tasteless cooking oil such as corn oil. Stir with wire whisk until chocolate is smooth again; and proceed with the recipe.

If the chocolate burns, or turns dark at the edges, throw it away and start over.

FRUITS

Fruit is one of the best sources of flavor in ice cream. However, large pieces of fruit can become icy lumps after freezing, because they have a high water content and form a nucleus for crystallization. For best results, purée or finely chop the fruit, steep it in sugar for an hour or more to bring out the fullest flavor, then add as directed by the recipe.

RIPENING

When we say "allow ice cream to ripen or temper..." we're referring to the amount of time necessary to let the frozen dessert soften sufficiently to be served and enjoyed. If the dessert is too cold much of the subtle flavor is lost. The dessert should be firm but not like a rock.

This time is approximate, since it depends on the temperature of your freezing facilities (see page 7), how many times you open and close the door, the age of the ice cream, ingredients in the ice cream, the size and shape of the container used, etc. For example, most pies and soufflés containing a good deal of alcohol can be served directly from the freezer or left at room temperature for 5 to 10 minutes; other types of frozen desserts need from 10 minutes to 2½ hours. Furthermore, the shape of the container will affect the freezing and ripening time. If the container is long and flat like a refrigerator tray the time will be much less than if the container is deep.

Mr. Dickson defines this point of ripeness or "dippability" to be when the ice cream is firm enough to cut easily and soft enough so that pressure need not be applied when filling a dipper. This state is supposed to lie between 8° and 12° F. However, we have found that a practical way to test for ripeness is to stick a knife down through the ice cream. If the knife goes in with some difficulty, but all the way through, it's just right. If not, put it back into the refrigerator and test again in a few minutes.

We recommend that you let the ice cream soften in the refrigerator so that it softens uniformly and doesn't become mushy and soft around the edges (particularly important when using molds). Pies are the exception to the rule. They ripen best at room temperature.

STORING

Since homemade ice cream has no preservatives or artificial emulsifiers, it may not keep as long as some commercial ice creams. Store homemade ice cream in a tightly covered container with as little air as possible between the lid and the ice cream. A piece of aluminum foil or plastic wrap can be placed down on top of the ice cream and then the lid put on. This double protection discourages the formation of ice crystals on the surface of the ice cream.

The bowl used in preparing ice cream may be used for storing it too. Cover the surface of the ice cream with aluminum foil or plastic wrap. Place a plate on top of the bowl if you can.

Plastic containers are handy for storing ice cream, but clean them thoroughly so there is no odor from other foods. If you intend to make a good deal of homemade ice cream buy some new containers and reserve them only for ice cream.

Refrigerator ice trays are also very good to use in making ice cream, since the mixture will freeze up much more quickly because of

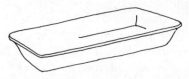

the greater exposed surface area. Cover tightly with refrigerator tray lids, aluminum foil, or plastic wrap. If you intend to use ice trays for freezing ice cream, we suggest purchasing some especially for that purpose.

When storing molded ice cream such as parfaits, mousses, or sherbet in sherbet or champagne glasses, make a cone out of aluminum foil and set it on top.

When freezing and storing sponge cakes, carefully wrap with aluminum foil or plastic wrap.

With larger cake creations, wrap as best you can with aluminum foil or plastic wrap, or cover with a cake cover made out of plastic, glass, or aluminum.

MOLDS AND UNMOLDING

Many shapes of molds are available to use in making frozen desserts—round, square, heart-shaped, rectangular, timbale-shaped, etc. In this book we have experimented with copper molds with tin linings, tin molds, aluminum molds, glass and plastic molds, and found them all satisfactory.

To unmold ice cream, ice, or sherbet, dip mold in lukewarm water up to 1 minute, depending on the thickness and composition of the mold. For example, a copper mold with a tin lining will need the full minute, while a thin plastic mold will require only a few seconds. Place serving dish upside down on top of mold and invert. If dessert doesn't unmold promptly, repeat procedure. Quickly place unmolded dessert back in freezer 10 minutes or longer to firm up. Most desserts may require refrigerator ripening time before serving.

Another way to mold is to line the mold form completely with foil or strips of foil, letting it or them extend a bit over the rim. Pack the mold as usual. After the mold is dipped and inverted to unmold, pull gently on the foil; the ice cream should slip out of the container very easily. Peel off foil and return the dessert to the freezer to firm up 10 minutes or longer.

A third way, if you are still having difficulties, is to oil the mold with an odorless, colorless vegetable oil such as corn oil before packing in the ice cream. Unmold as indicated above.

Use a mold only if you are planning to unmold a dessert, as it is difficult to serve directly from the mold. Individual recipes indicate which are suitable for molding.

SERVING ICE CREAM

It's always pleasant to see ice cream served attractively rather than having the freezer container set on the table and the ice cream served directly from it. If you are serving ice cream directly from the container, do so away from the table. Place scoops of ice cream into sherbet glasses, champagne glasses, bowls or parfait glasses and serve plain or topped with whipped cream, and nuts or fruit.

Of course, molded desserts or baked Alaskas should be brought to the table in all their splendor. Cut and serve at the table.

A nice touch is to serve a glass of water with your dessert. When Diana lived in Europe she always appreciated the glass of water that was served along with her dessert, or soda, even though she may have been having tea or coffee as well. That glass of water cleared the palate for enjoyment of the dish.

DECORATING CAKES AND PIES

Tear off a piece of waxed paper about 20 inches long. Fold in half. Roll into a cone with the folded edge forming the tip. Tape the cone with masking tape. Fill with icing and squeeze gently to make patterns on the surface of the pie or cake.

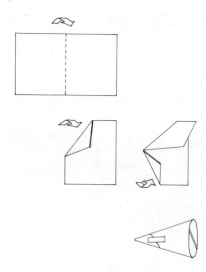

Definitions

These definitions of the different types of desserts will help you determine the application of the techniques suggested in the following sections.

An ice cream is made from a cooked egg yolk custard to which a flavoring and whipped cream have been added.

A French parfait is a lighter ice cream having an uncooked beaten egg yolk custard base with sugar water and gelatin to which a flavoring and whipped cream have been added.

A soufflé is a very sweet, rich, smooth, airy "ice cream" made from beaten egg yolks, beaten egg whites, and whipped cream.

A mousse is a molded dessert having a thick base or purée with whipped cream and beaten egg whites combined to give it lightness.

A sherbet is a very light, airy dessert made with beaten egg whites only (no yolks) and a flavoring.

A milk sherbet is a sherbet to which milk has been added, making it slightly heavier.

An ice is a light, refreshing, frozen dessert made from sugar water, gelatin, and fruit juices or fruit purée.

A popsicle is a combination of fruit juices, fresh or frozen, and gelatin molded around a handle for holding.

A baked Alaska is a cake base, ice cream filling, and meringue covering. The Alaska is then cooked to brown the meringue.

A meringue dessert is a crisp meringue base filled with ice cream and sauce, and covered with whipped cream.

A frozen pie is a cookie crust with a smooth creamy frozen filling.

An ice cream cake is alternate layers of cake and ice cream and frosted with whipped cream.

A sponge layer is a light, bland, firm cake.

A bombe is a molded combination of different ice creams, sherbets, mousses, and ices.

A *sundae* is an ice cream, sherbet, mousse, or ice with sauce or syrup and topping.

A *soda* is a milk drink with sauce or syrup, milk or cream, ice cream, carbonated soda, and an optional topping.

A *float* is a drink with soda or coffee and ice cream.

A *milkshake* is a sweet milk drink made with milk, various flavorings, and ice cream beaten together in a blender.

A *malted milk* is a milk drink made with milk, malted milk powder, and ice cream, beaten together in a blender.

A *spoom* is a frozen alcoholic drink made with sherbet and wine or liquor.

A *granité* is a frozen alcoholic drink made with sugar water, fruit juices or fruit purée, and wine or liqueur.

A *marquise* is a frozen alcoholic ice creamlike concoction made with wine or liquor.

A *punch* is a frozen alcoholic drink with sugar water, fruit juices or purée, wine or champagne, and liqueur.

A *frozen cocktail* is a frozen alcoholic drink with fresh or concentrated fruit juices, liquor, and crushed ice, and is made in a blender.

Ice Creams

Vanilla ice cream in some form is the basis for many recipes in this book. The only important change from one vanilla ice cream recipe to another is the richness of the custard base. This base can be made with heavy cream, half cream and half milk, light cream, Half and Half, whole milk, or skimmed milk. The amount of egg yolks can also vary, changing the richness and lightness of the basic ice cream. Then flavoring is added and you have a whole different thing: Chocolate Ice Cream, Nougat Ice Cream, Banana Nut Ice Cream, Blueberry Ice Cream, Brazil Nut Ice Cream, Peppermint Stick Ice Cream, Rum Raisin Ice Cream, and so on.

Since we feel you should learn to make vanilla ice cream first, we have started with several vanilla ice cream recipes; then the rest of the ice creams follow in alphabetical order.

If you have made ice cream the still-freeze way before, you may wish to skip the introduction until later and turn immediately to your favorite recipe. For those of you not familiar with the making of ice cream in this fashion, read the introduction first, since it fully explains the procedures just briefly described in the recipes for ice cream.

FRENCH VANILLA ICE CREAM

Makes about 1½ quarts of very rich and creamy ice cream with an unusual flavor.

    1 cup milk
    ½ cup heavy cream
    4 egg yolks
    ½ cup granulated sugar
    1 tsp cornstarch
    2-inch piece of vanilla bean
    1½ cups heavy cream
    1 Tbsp rum

Combine 1 cup milk and ½ cup heavy cream in top of double boiler and heat, over simmering water, until lukewarm. Set aside.

In medium-sized bowl, using electric mixer or wire whisk, beat together 4 egg yolks, ½ cup sugar, and 1 tsp cornstarch until thick and light yellow in color. Cut off a 2-inch piece of vanilla bean, slice it in half lengthwise, scrape out black powder inside, and add this to egg yolks and sugar. Discard the remaining bean bark. Beat a few moments longer.

Slowly pour warm cream into beaten egg yolks and sugar, stirring all the while. Scrape mixture back into top of double boiler and cook, over simmering water, stirring constantly, until custard thickens. Remove from heat and continue to stir a few moments until custard cools slightly.

Chill in refrigerator.

Whip 1½ cups heavy cream until soft peaks form. Add 1 Tbsp rum and whip a moment longer. Remove chilled custard from refrigerator. Fold in whipped cream. Scrape vanilla cream into freezer container, cover, and freeze for 1 hour.

Remove from freezer, uncover, stir to break up frozen pieces, and leave in original container or scrape into serving dish. Cover again and freeze until firm.

Before serving, allow ice cream to ripen in refrigerator 30 minutes.

VANILLA VELVET

Makes 1 quart of an ice cream with a smooth velvety texture suitable for serving by itself or in a combination.

⅔ cup condensed milk
2 cups heavy cream
½ tsp vanilla extract

In medium-sized mixing bowl combine ⅔ cup condensed milk, 2 cups heavy cream, and ½ tsp vanilla extract. Chill in refrigerator about ½ hour.

Remove and whip until cream forms stiff peaks.

Scrape into freezer container or serving dish, cover, and freeze until firm.

Allow ice cream to ripen in refrigerator 30 minutes before serving.

HIGH PROTEIN VANILLA ICE MILK

Makes a little more than 1 quart. This recipe shows that you can make an excellent "ice cream" without using any cream.

    1 13-oz can evaporated milk
    1 cup skimmed milk
    4 egg yolks
    1/4 cup granulated sugar
    1 Tbsp cornstarch
    1 1/2-inch piece of vanilla bean

Open the can of evaporated milk, pour into medium-sized bowl, and place in coldest part of refrigerator at least 1 hour.

In top of double boiler heat 1 cup skimmed milk over simmering water to just under boiling. Set aside.

Beat 4 egg yolks with 1/4 cup sugar and 1 Tbsp cornstarch until thick, pale yellow in color, and sugar is dissolved. Cut off a 1 1/2-inch piece of vanilla bean. Cut in half lengthwise and scrape out black powder. Add this to egg yolks and beat mixture a few moments longer. Discard the remaining bean bark.

In a thin stream pour hot milk into beaten egg yolks, beating all the while. Then pour back into top of double boiler and cook custard over simmering water, stirring constantly, until thick (about 20 to 30 minutes). Remove from heat and continue to stir until custard cools slightly.

Chill in refrigerator 30 minutes. Place beaters in refrigerator with evaporated milk to chill.

Place 1 tray of ice cubes in large bowl with 2 cups water. Remove bowl containing evaporated milk and beaters from refrigerator. Set bowl containing milk in larger bowl with icy water. Whip with chilled beaters until stiff peaks form.

Remove custard from refrigerator. Scrape into whipped milk and fold one mixture into the other.

Scrape mixture into freezer container, cover, and freeze 1 1/2 hours.

Remove from freezer, uncover, stir to break up frozen pieces, cover again, and freeze until firm.

Allow ice cream to ripen in refrigerator 10 to 20 minutes before serving.

VANILLA ICE CREAM

Makes 1 quart. Delicious, lower in calories and not as rich as the French Vanilla Ice Cream. Remains soft and makes good cones for children.

1/4 cup evaporated milk, chilled
2 egg whites
1/4 cup granulated sugar
4 egg yolks
2 Tbsp granulated sugar
1/4 cup heavy cream
1 Tbsp vanilla extract

Chill can of evaporated milk for at least 1/2 hour.

In medium-sized bowl beat 2 egg whites until frothy. Slowly beat in 1/4 cup sugar and continue beating until whites are smooth and glossy, and sugar has dissolved. Chill in refrigerator.

In a small bowl beat 4 egg yolks until very thick, light yellow in color, and greatly increased in volume. Gradually add 2 Tbsp sugar and continue beating until the yolks resemble mayonnaise. Chill in refrigerator.

Combine 1/4 cup chilled evaporated milk with 1/4 cup heavy cream in a small bowl. Using clean beaters whip milk and cream until soft peaks are formed. Stir in 1 Tbsp vanilla extract.

Remove chilled bowls of beaten egg white and beaten egg yolks from refrigerator. Quickly fold whipped yolks into whipped whites until fully incorporated. Then fold in whipped milk and cream.

Scrape mixture into freezer container, cover tightly, and freeze. This ice cream remains soft and will be ready to serve in about 4 hours.

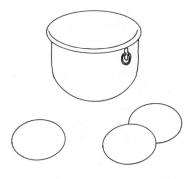

ALMOND MACAROON ICE CREAM

Makes 1½ pints of a crunchy, honey-sweet ice cream that fully lives up
to its name.

    1 cup milk
    ½ cup heavy cream
    3 egg yolks
    ½ cup honey
    ½ tsp arrowroot
    1-inch piece of vanilla bean
    6 homemade almond macaroons (page 106),
        broken up and toasted
    2 Tbsp sliced almonds, broken up and toasted
    ½ cup heavy cream

In the top of double boiler heat together over simmering water 1
cup milk and ½ cup heavy cream until hot but not boiling. Set aside.

Using electric mixer beat together in medium-sized bowl 3 egg
yolks, ½ cup honey, and ½ tsp arrowroot until mixture is lemon-
colored.

Cut off a 1-inch piece of vanilla bean, slice in half lengthwise,
scrape out black powder, and add to egg yolks. Beat until thoroughly
incorporated.

In a thin stream add hot milk to beaten egg yolk mixture, beating
all the while. Pour back into top of double boiler and cook over
simmering water, stirring constantly, until custard has thickened.
Remove from heat and continue to stir for a few moments until custard
cools slightly.

Chill custard in refrigerator.

Preheat oven to 300°. Break up 6 macaroons (about 1 cup) and 2
Tbsp sliced almonds into shallow roasting pan. Toast in oven about 10
minutes, checking and shaking pan from time to time. Remove and
cool. (Diana sticks pan in freezer while preparing cream.)

Whip ½ cup heavy cream until it forms soft peaks. Fold in cooled
macaroons and almonds. Remove chilled custard from refrigerator
and fold in whipped cream mixture.

Scrape into freezer container, cover, and freeze about 1½ hours.

Remove from freezer, uncover, stir to break up frozen lumps,
leave in freezer container or pour into serving dish or mold, cover
again, and freeze until firm.

Allow to ripen in refrigerator 45 to 60 minutes before serving.

APRICOT ICE CREAM

Makes 1 quart of ice cream with a distinct but not overpowering apricot flavor.

3/4 cup dried apricots
Water
1/4 cup heavy cream
1/2 cup milk
2 egg yolks
1/4 cup granulated sugar
1/2 tsp cornstarch
3/4 cup heavy cream
1/4 tsp almond extract

Place 3/4 cup dried apricots and enough water to cover them in a saucepan. Heat to boiling. Remove from heat and set aside for 30 minutes, to allow the apricots to soften.

Combine 1/4 cup heavy cream and 1/2 cup milk in top of double boiler and heat over simmering water to lukewarm. Set aside.

In a small bowl beat 2 egg yolks, 1/4 cup sugar, and 1/2 tsp cornstarch until the yolks are lemon colored. Slowly pour the warmed milk into the egg yolks, stirring all the while. Pour custard back into top of double boiler and cook over simmering water until custard thickens. Chill in refrigerator.

Drain apricots, reserving liquid. Place apricots in the blender and blend at high speed, adding just enough apricot liquid (about 1/4 to 1/2 cup) to make a rough paste. The apricots should be in very small chunks.

Whip 3/4 cup heavy cream until soft peaks are formed.

Remove chilled custard from refrigerator. Stir in apricots and 1/4 tsp almond extract. Fold in whipped cream. Scrape mixture into freezer container, cover tightly, and freeze for 1 hour, or until partially frozen around edges of container.

Remove ice cream from freezer, stir thoroughly to break up frozen pieces, leave in original container or scrape into serving dish, cover, and return to freezer for 3 hours, or until firm.

Before serving, allow the ice cream to ripen in the refrigerator for 30 minutes.

APRICOT-FLAVORED FRUIT ICE CREAM

Makes about 1½ quarts of a good sweet-tart apricot-pineapple ice cream.

    1 16-oz can whole or sliced apricots in heavy syrup
    1 cup canned pineapple chunks in heavy syrup
    Juice of 1 orange
    Juice of 2 lemons
    2 tsp unflavored gelatin
    ½ cup light-brown sugar, with lumps broken up
    1½ cups heavy cream

Drain fruit. Reserve apricot and pineapple juice in medium-sized bowl (about 1 cup).

Squeeze juice from 1 orange and 2 lemons. Mix with reserved juices. Stir in 2 tsp gelatin and set bowl containing juices over hot water. Stir, from time to time, to dissolve gelatin. Add ½ cup brown sugar, with lumps broken up.

Chop finely apricots and pineapple and add to fruit juices. Chill in refrigerator about 1½ hours.

Whip 1½ cups heavy cream until it forms soft peaks. Remove slightly jelled fruit mixture from refrigerator. Fold in whipped cream.

Cover bowl and freeze for 2 hours.

Remove from freezer, stir to break up any ice particles, cover again, and freeze for another 2 hours.

Remove again from freezer, stir, and pour into freezer container or mold, cover again and return to freezer until firm.

Allow ice cream to ripen in refrigerator for 30 minutes before serving.

AVOCADO-JAVA ICE CREAM

Makes over 1 quart of a rich and satisfying ice cream. The avocado and coffee enhance each other's flavor while each remains distinct.

½ cup strong coffee, made from Mocha-Java dark-roast beans
1 cup light cream
3 egg yolks
¼ cup granulated sugar
½ tsp arrowroot
Juice of ½ lime
1 large, smooth-skinned Florida avocado
1 cup heavy cream

Brew ½ cup strong coffee from finely ground Mocha-Java dark-roast coffee beans; if these beans are unavailable, use espresso coffee.

In top of double boiler heat 1 cup light cream over simmering water to just under boiling. Pour in coffee and then set aside.

Beat 3 egg yolks with ¼ cup sugar and ½ tsp arrowroot until thick and light yellow in color. Slowly pour hot cream and coffee into beaten egg yolks, beating all the while. Then pour mixture back into top of double boiler and cook custard over simmering water until thick, stirring constantly.

Remove from heat, but continue to stir until custard cools slightly. Chill in refrigerator 30 minutes.

Squeeze juice from half a lime and put juice into blender. Cut large avocado into chunks and put them into blender with the lime juice. Blend until a purée and pour into medium-sized bowl.

Whip 1 cup heavy cream until stiff peaks form. Set aside.

Remove chilled custard from refrigerator. Stir until smooth and add to avocado purée. Stir one mixture into the other. Fold in whipped cream. Cover bowl and freeze for 2 hours.

Take out of freezer, uncover, stir to break up frozen pieces, and beat until smooth. Pour into freezer container or serving dish or mold, cover, and freeze until firm.

Allow ice cream to ripen 45 to 60 minutes in refrigerator before serving.

BANANA-NUT ICE CREAM

Makes 1½ quarts of delicious banana-flavored, not too sweet, ice cream with the crunchy taste of walnuts.

1 cup Half and Half
4 egg yolks
½ cup corn syrup
1 tsp arrowroot
2-inch piece of vanilla bean
1 cup heavy cream
Pinch of salt
2 medium-sized very ripe bananas (about 1 cup)
½ cup walnuts, broken up

In the top of a double boiler heat 1 cup Half and Half until lukewarm. Set aside.

In medium-sized bowl beat together 4 egg yolks, ½ cup corn syrup, and 1 tsp arrowroot with electric mixer until thick and pale yellow in color.

Cut off a 2-inch piece of vanilla bean, slice it in half lengthwise, scrape out powder, and add this to beaten egg yolks and syrup. Beat until well mixed.

In a thin stream pour warmed cream into egg yolk and syrup mixture, beating all the while.

Pour mixture back into top of double boiler and cook, over simmering water, stirring constantly, until custard starts to thicken, about 10 minutes. Remove from heat. Continue to stir until custard cools slightly. Chill in refrigerator.

Whip 1 cup heavy cream with a pinch of salt until it forms soft peaks. Remove chilled custard from refrigerator and pour into bowl containing whipped cream. Fold one into the other. Then cover and place in freezer for 1 hour.

Mash or blend 2 very ripe medium-sized bananas (about 1 cup). Break up ½ cup walnuts.

Remove partially frozen ice cream, uncover, break up icy pieces, and beat until smooth. Fold in mashed bananas and walnuts. Scrape into freezer container or serving dish, cover again, and freeze until firm.

Allow ice cream to ripen 45 minutes in refrigerator before serving.

BLUEBERRY ICE CREAM

Makes 1½ pints of an excellent seasonal treat.

1 pint fresh blueberries
¼ cup water
½ cup granulated sugar
Juice of ½ lemon
1 cup light cream
2 egg yolks
2 Tbsp granulated sugar
½ tsp arrowroot
1 cup heavy cream
1 tsp vanilla extract
Blueberry Syrup (page 186)

Carefully wash and remove the stems from 1 pint fresh blueberries. Pour into 3-quart stainless-steel pot with ¼ cup water and ½ cup sugar. Bring to a boil and then simmer over low heat for 10 minutes, stirring from time to time. Press berries through a fine sieve or blend in blender until a purée.

Squeeze juice from ½ lemon. Add to blueberry purée. Set aside in refrigerator.

In the top of double boiler heat 1 cup light cream over simmering water until hot, but not boiling. Set aside.

Beat 2 egg yolks together with 2 Tbsp sugar and ½ tsp arrowroot until thick and pale yellow in color. Slowly add hot cream, beating all the while. Then pour mixture back into top of double boiler and cook custard over simmering water until thick, stirring constantly. Remove from heat and continue to stir until it has cooled slightly.

Chill in refrigerator 30 minutes.

Whip 1 cup heavy cream until soft peaks form. Add 1 tsp vanilla extract and whip a moment longer.

Take out chilled custard and blueberry purée from refrigerator. Scrape custard into medium-sized bowl. Fold in whipped cream, then the purée. Cover bowl and place in freezer 1 hour.

Remove bowl from freezer, uncover, stir to break up frozen pieces, pour into freezer container or serving dish, cover, and freeze until firm.

Allow ice cream to ripen 1 hour in refrigerator before serving. Garnish with a Blueberry Syrup topping.

BRANDIED BING CHERRY ICE CREAM

Makes about 1½ quarts. There can be no substitute for the memorable blend of brandied Bing cherries and cream.

1½ cups Half and Half
⅓ cup light-brown sugar, with lumps broken up
4 egg yolks
½ tsp arrowroot
¼ tsp salt
1½ cups brandied Bing cherries
1 cup heavy cream

In the top of double boiler heat over simmering water 1½ cups Half and Half until just under boiling. Set aside.

Using electric mixer, beat together ⅓ cup brown sugar, with the lumps broken up, 4 egg yolks, and ½ tsp arrowroot until thick and light in color. Stir in ¼ tsp salt.

In a thin stream pour hot Half and Half into beaten egg yolks and sugar, beating all the while.

Return to top of double boiler and cook custard over simmering water, stirring constantly until thick. Remove from heat but continue to stir a few moments longer until custard starts to cool slightly. Then chill in refrigerator about 30 minutes.

Drain liquid from a jar of brandied cherries into a small bowl. Coarsely chop enough cherries to measure 1½ cups. Set aside. Return remaining cherries to jar with their liquid.

Using medium-sized bowl whip 1 cup heavy cream until it forms soft peaks. Stir in chopped brandied cherries. (Add more brandy now if you wish a stronger flavor.)

Remove chilled custard from refrigerator and fold in whipped cream and cherries. Cover container and freeze for 1 hour.

Remove ice cream from freezer, uncover, stir to break up frozen lumps and redistribute cherries. Leave in original container or pour into serving dish or parfait glasses. Cover and return to freezer until firm.

Allow ice cream to ripen in refrigerator 1 to 1½ hours before serving.

BRAZIL NUT ICE CREAM

Makes a little more than 1½ pints. A bland, sweet ice cream flavored mainly by the nuts.

1½ cups milk
½ cup granulated sugar
1 tsp arrowroot
2 whole eggs
1 tsp vanilla extract
½ cup Caramel Syrup (page 184)
¾ cup Brazil nuts, coarsely chopped
½ tsp salt
½ cup heavy cream

In top of double boiler heat 1½ cups milk over simmering water to lukewarm. Set aside.

In medium-sized bowl mix together ½ cup sugar with 1 tsp arrowroot. Stir in up to ½ cup warm milk until a smooth paste forms. Beat 2 whole eggs with wire whisk until light yellow in color. Add to paste and beat until smooth. Slowly add rest of warm milk to egg mixture, beating all the while.

Scrape mixture back into top of double boiler and cook over simmering water, stirring constantly, until custard thickens. Remove from heat but continue to stir a few moments until custard cools slightly. Stir in 1 tsp vanilla extract and ½ cup Caramel Syrup. Chill in refrigerator for 30 minutes.

Coarsely chop enough Brazil nuts to measure ¾ cup. Stir in ½ tsp salt. Set aside.

Whip ½ cup heavy cream until stiff peaks form. Remove custard from refrigerator and fold in whipped cream. Pour into freezer container, cover, and freeze for 1 hour.

Remove from freezer, uncover, stir to break up icy particles, and beat until smooth. Fold in chopped Brazil nuts. Cover container and freeze for another hour.

Remove from freezer, uncover, and stir to break up icy particles and redistribute the nuts. Scrape into freezer container, serving dish, or mold, cover, and freeze until firm.

Allow ice cream to ripen 30 to 45 minutes in refrigerator before serving.

BUTTERMILK ICE CREAM

Makes 1½ pints of sweet-sour almond-flavored ice cream.

> 2 egg yolks
> ¼ cup granulated sugar
> 1 tsp cornstarch
> 1 cup buttermilk
> ½ tsp almond extract
> ½ cup heavy cream

In a small bowl beat 2 egg yolks, ¼ cup sugar, and 1 tsp cornstarch with wire whisk until egg yolks are light in color. Beat in 1 cup buttermilk. Pour beaten egg yolks and buttermilk mixture into top of double boiler and cook over simmering water, stirring constantly, until custard thickens. Remove from heat and stir until custard starts to cool. Stir in ½ tsp almond extract.

Place custard in refrigerator to chill.

Whip ½ cup heavy cream until it forms stiff peaks. Remove chilled custard from refrigerator. Fold whipped cream into custard. Scrape mixture into freezer container, cover tightly, and place in freezer for 1½ hours or until partially frozen.

Remove from freezer, uncover, and stir thoroughly. Leave in freezer container or scrape into serving dish, cover tightly, and freeze for 3 hours or until firm.

Allow ice cream to ripen in refrigerator for 45 minutes before serving.

BUTTER PECAN ICE CREAM

Makes 2 quarts of deliciously rich, sweet ice cream.

1/2 cup heavy cream
1 cup milk
4 Tbsp butter
4 egg yolks
1/2 cup granulated sugar
1 tsp cornstarch
1 tsp vanilla extract
1 cup pecans, chopped
3 Tbsp dark corn syrup
2 egg whites
2 Tbsp granulated sugar
1 cup heavy cream

Warm 1/2 cup heavy cream, 1 cup milk, and 4 Tbsp butter in top of double boiler over simmering water until the butter melts.

Combine 4 egg yolks, 1/2 cup sugar, and 1 tsp cornstarch in small mixing bowl. Using wire whisk, beat until ingredients are frothy and light yellow in color.

Slowly pour a third of the warmed cream into egg yolks, stirring all the while. Pour both eggs and cream back into top of double boiler and cook over simmering water until custard thickens. Remove from heat and stir in 1 tsp vanilla extract. Place in refrigerator to cool for 30 minutes.

Chop enough pecans to fill 1-cup measure. In a small bowl combine pecans with 3 Tbsp dark corn syrup. Set aside.

Beat 2 egg whites until soft peaks are formed. Slowly beat in 2 Tbsp sugar and continue beating until very stiff peaks are formed. Set aside.

Whip 1 cup heavy cream until soft peaks are formed. Set aside.

Remove custard from refrigerator and stir in pecans. Fold in beaten egg whites, then the whipped cream. Scrape mixture into freezer container, cover tightly, and place in freezer for 2 hours.

Remove from freezer, uncover, and stir thoroughly to break up frozen pieces. Leave in container or scrape into serving dish, cover again, and freeze for 5 hours or until firm.

Allow ice cream to ripen in refrigerator for 1 hour before serving.

This ice cream does not keep longer than 1 week and is best if served within 3 days.

BUTTERSCOTCH PECAN ICE CREAM

Makes 1½ quarts of a mellow, smooth ice cream with fried buttered nuts.

> ½ cup pecans, chopped
> 2 Tbsp butter
> 4 egg yolks
> ¼ cup light-brown sugar, with lumps broken up
> ¼ cup dark corn syrup
> 1 tsp cornstarch
> 1 13-oz can evaporated milk
> 1½ cups heavy cream

Chop enough pecans to measure ½ cup.

Melt 2 Tbsp butter in a small skillet and gently fry the pecans until slightly browned. Use very low heat to avoid burning the butter. Set aside.

In top of double boiler beat together with a wire whisk 4 egg yolks, ¼ cup brown sugar, with lumps broken up, ¼ cup dark corn syrup, and 1 tsp cornstarch until light yellow in color. Add evaporated milk and stir thoroughly.

Place top of double boiler over simmering water and cook until custard thickens, stirring constantly. Remove from heat and stir to cool. Stir in nuts and butter. Place in refrigerator to chill.

Whip 1½ cups heavy cream until soft peaks form. Remove chilled custard from refrigerator. Fold whipped cream into chilled custard.

Scrape mixture into freezer container, cover tightly, and freeze until frozen around the edges of the container. Remove from freezer, uncover, and stir thoroughly to break up frozen particles and redistribute nuts throughout ice cream. Leave in container or scrape into serving dish, cover, and freeze for 4 hours or until firm.

Allow ice cream to ripen in refrigerator for 1 hour before serving.

CAPPUCCINO ICE CREAM

Makes 1 quart of coffee ice cream with a taste of chocolate and brandy based on a drink Diana experienced on a recent Braniff flight to Dallas.

$1/2$ cup strong Italian coffee (page 21)
1 cup milk
$1/2$ cup heavy cream
$1/4$ tsp cinnamon
$1/2$ oz or $1/2$ square unsweetened chocolate
4 egg yolks
$1/2$ cup dark-brown sugar, with lumps broken up
$1/2$ tsp arrowroot
1 cup heavy cream
1 Tbsp dark-brown sugar, with lumps broken up
$1/2$ cup Cognac

Brew $1/2$ cup coffee using Italian roast coffee beans.

In top of double boiler combine 1 cup milk, $1/2$ cup heavy cream, $1/4$ tsp cinnamon, and $1/2$ oz chocolate. Slowly heat over simmering water until chocolate has melted. Pour in coffee. Stir and set aside.

Using electric mixer beat together in medium-sized bowl 4 egg yolks, $1/2$ cup dark-brown sugar, with the lumps broken up, and $1/2$ tsp arrowroot. Beat until mixture is thick and pale yellow in color.

In a thin stream pour heated milk mixture into beaten egg yolks and sugar, beating all the while. Then pour entire mixture back into top of double boiler and cook slowly over simmering water, stirring constantly, until custard has thickened. Remove from heat and continue to stir a few moments longer until custard has cooled slightly. Chill in refrigerator 1 hour.

Whip 1 cup heavy cream with 1 Tbsp brown sugar, with lumps broken up, until it forms soft peaks. Add $1/2$ cup Cognac and beat a few moments longer.

Remove chilled custard from refrigerator. Fold in whipped cream and Cognac, cover, and freeze for 2 hours.

Remove ice cream from freezer, uncover, stir to break up frozen pieces, scrape into freezer container or serving dish or mold, cover again, and freeze until firm.

Allow ice cream to ripen in refrigerator $1 1/2$ to 2 hours before serving.

CARAMEL ICE CREAM

Makes 1½ pints. Somewhat sweet vanilla ice cream that tastes very good with fruits or nuts on top.

1½ cups milk
⅓ cup granulated sugar
1 tsp arrowroot
1 whole egg
½ tsp vanilla extract
½ cup Caramel Syrup (page 184)
½ cup heavy cream

In top of double boiler heat 1½ cups milk over simmering water to just under boiling. Set aside.

In medium-sized bowl mix together ⅓ cup sugar and 1 tsp arrowroot. Stir in up to ½ cup of heated milk until a smooth paste forms. Slightly beat 1 egg and add to paste. Beat mixture until smooth. Slowly add remaining hot milk to egg mixture, beating all the while.

Scrape mixture back into top of double boiler and cook over simmering water, stirring constantly, until custard thickens. Remove from heat and continue to stir a few moments until custard cools slightly. Stir in ½ tsp vanilla extract and ½ cup caramel syrup.

Chill in refrigerator for 30 minutes.

Whip ½ cup heavy cream until stiff peaks form. Remove custard from refrigerator and fold in whipped cream. Pour into freezer container, cover, and freeze for 1 hour.

Remove from freezer, uncover, stir to break up icy particles, and beat until smooth. Scrape back into freezer container or into serving dish, cover, and freeze until firm.

Allow to ripen 30 minutes in refrigerator before serving.

CHOCOLATE ICE CREAM

Makes 1½ quarts. Rich, velvet-smooth ice cream that is just barely enough.

1 cup milk
½ cup heavy cream
4 egg yolks
½ cup granulated sugar
1 tsp cornstarch
½ tsp vanilla extract
1½ oz unsweetened chocolate
1 Tbsp water
1 cup heavy cream
1 Tbsp granulated sugar

Combine 1 cup milk and ½ cup heavy cream in top of double boiler and heat to lukewarm over simmering water. Set aside.

In medium-sized bowl using electric mixer or wire whisk beat together 4 egg yolks, ½ cup sugar, and 1 tsp cornstarch until thick and light yellow in color.

Slowly pour warm milk into beaten egg yolk mixture, stirring all the while. Scrape back into top of double boiler and cook custard over simmering water, stirring constantly, until thick. Remove from heat and continue to stir a few moments longer until slightly cool. Stir in ½ tsp vanilla extract. Set aside.

Place 1½ oz chocolate in small saucepan with 1 Tbsp water and melt over very low heat. When chocolate has melted, whip with small wire whisk until chocolate and water form a smooth paste. Add 2 Tbsp custard and beat until smooth. Add 3 Tbsp more custard and beat until smooth. Add 5 more Tbsp and beat again until smooth. Scrape combined chocolate and custard into rest of custard and beat with large wire whisk until smooth and uniformly blended.

Chill in refrigerator.

Whip 1 cup heavy cream until soft peaks form. Add 1 Tbsp sugar and whip a moment longer. Remove chilled chocolate custard from refrigerator, scrape into whipped cream, and fold one mixture into the other. Cover bowl and freeze for 1 hour.

Remove from freezer, uncover, stir to break up frozen pieces, scrape into freezer container or serving dish, cover, and freeze until firm.

Allow ice cream to ripen 45 minutes in refrigerator before serving.

CHOCOLATE BALLS

Makes 6 sweet crunchy balls.

1½ pints Chocolate Ice Cream (page 51)
2 oz semi-sweet chocolate curls
½ cup finely chopped pecans

Make the Chocolate Ice Cream. While it's freezing prepare chocolate curls. Using a vegetable peeler, carefully shave curls off a solid piece of chocolate. Chop the pecans finely, to measure ½ cup. Combine the chocolate curls and chopped pecans in a small flat bowl. Place in refrigerator until ready to use.

Place small dessert dishes or a 9-by-13-inch pan lined with waxed paper in freezer.

When chocolate ice cream is firm enough to form balls (if a knife can be inserted with difficulty), remove ice cream from freezer and chocolate pecan mixture from refrigerator. Using an ice cream scoop or large spoon, form a ball of ice cream and roll ball in chocolate pecan mixture. Place ball in dessert dish or pan in freezer. Repeat until all balls are formed.

Balls will firm up in 1 hour. Cover tightly until ready for use. They will keep for about 24 hours.

Allow balls to ripen at room temperature for 15 minutes before serving. If the day is hot, allow only 5 minutes.

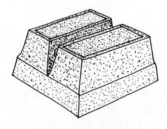

CHOCOLATE-ALMOND ICE CREAM

Makes 1 quart almond-flavored ice cream, which is a good filling for a chocolate sponge cake.

1½ oz semi-sweet chocolate
½ cup heavy cream
⅝ cup milk
3 egg yolks
4½ Tbsp granulated sugar
¾ tsp cornstarch
5 tsp rum
¾ cup chopped caramelized almonds (page 22)
1 cup plus 2 Tbsp heavy cream

Melt 1½ oz semi-sweet chocolate in metal bowl placed either in very hot water or on "warm" burner of electric stove. Set aside.

In top of double boiler warm ½ cup heavy cream and ⅝ cup milk over simmering water. Set aside.

In small bowl, using a wire whisk, beat 3 egg yolks until frothy and lemon-colored. Beat in 4½ Tbsp sugar and ¾ tsp cornstarch. Slowly pour in a third of the warmed milk and cream, stirring all the while.

Pour eggs and milk back into rest of milk in top of double boiler. Slowly cook over simmering water, stirring constantly, until custard thickens. Stir in melted chocolate. Remove from heat and place in refrigerator to chill, about 30 minutes.

Remove chilled custard from refrigerator. Stir in 5 tsp rum and ¾ cup chopped caramelized almonds.

Whip 1 cup plus 2 Tbsp heavy cream until soft peaks form. Fold whipped cream into cold custard. Scrape into freezer container, cover tightly, and place in freezer for 1½ hours or until custard is frozen around the edges.

Remove from freezer, uncover, and stir thoroughly to break up any frozen pieces and to make sure almonds are evenly distributed. Leave in original container or scrape into serving dish, cover tightly, and freeze until firm (about 3 hours).

Allow ice cream to ripen for 30 minutes in refrigerator before serving.

CHOCOLATE CHIP ICE CREAM

Makes 1½ quarts of chocolate chip ice cream at its best.

3/4 cup heavy cream
3/4 cup milk
4 egg yolks
1/2 cup granulated sugar
1 tsp cornstarch
2 tsp vanilla extract
2 oz semi-sweet Swiss chocolate, finely chopped
1½ cups heavy cream

Combine ¾ cup heavy cream and ¾ cup milk in top of double boiler and heat to lukewarm over simmering water. Set aside.

In small bowl, using a wire whisk, beat together 4 egg yolks, ½ cup sugar, and 1 tsp cornstarch until light yellow in color.

Slowly pour a third of the warmed cream into beaten egg yolks, stirring all the while. Pour mixture back into top of double boiler and cook over simmering water until the custard thickens. Remove from heat and continue to stir a few moments longer. Stir in 2 tsp vanilla extract. Place custard in refrigerator to chill for 30 minutes.

Finely chop 2 oz semi-sweet Swiss chocolate.

Remove cold custard from refrigerator and stir in chopped chocolate.

Whip 1½ cups heavy cream until soft peaks form; then fold into custard. Scrape mixture into freezer container, cover tightly, and place in freezer for 1½ hours or until frozen around edges of container.

Remove ice cream from freezer and stir thoroughly to break up frozen pieces. Cover and return to freezer for 4 hours or until firm.

Allow ice cream to ripen in the refrigerator for 30 minutes before serving.

This ice cream can be kept for 1 week.

CHOCOLATE-HAZELNUT ICE CREAM

Makes 1½ pints of deliciously nutty ice cream that is quick and simple since it can be made in the blender.

    ⅔ cup hazelnuts (blended makes about 1 cup)
    1 cup heavy cream
    ¼ cup dark-brown sugar
    ½ cup water
    1 3-oz Swiss bittersweet chocolate bar (or your favorite chocolate
        bar), broken up
    3 egg yolks

Pour ⅔ cup hazelnuts into a blender and blend until finely chopped.

Whip 1 cup heavy cream until it forms soft peaks. Fold in hazelnuts. Set aside in refrigerator.

Heat together, stirring, ¼ cup brown sugar and ½ cup water in a small saucepan until sugar is dissolved. Remove from heat and set aside.

Break up the Swiss chocolate into small pieces and put into blender. Pour in the hot sugar water. Blend until chocolate is dissolved and mixture is smooth and syrupy (a few moments).

Take off top and let cool for 5 minutes. Then add 3 egg yolks and blend a few moments longer.

Remove whipped cream mixture from refrigerator and scrape into medium-sized bowl. Pour in chocolate-egg yolk mixture from blender. Fold whipped cream into chocolate.

Cover and freeze for 1½ hours.

Remove from freezer, uncover, stir to break up frozen pieces, scrape into freezer container or serving dish, cover again, and freeze until firm.

Allow ice cream to ripen 1 hour in refrigerator before serving.

CHOCOLATE-PECAN ICE CREAM

Makes 1 quart of rich, nutty ice cream, delicious in a baked Alaska.

2½ oz semi-sweet Swiss chocolate
1 cup milk
½ cup heavy cream
4 egg yolks
6 Tbsp granulated sugar
1 tsp cornstarch
½ tsp vanilla extract
1 cup pecans, finely chopped
1 cup heavy cream
1 Tbsp granulated sugar

Melt 2½ ounces semi-sweet chocolate in a small saucepan placed over a warm burner or in a large bowl filled with very hot water. Set aside.

In top of double boiler heat 1 cup milk and ½ cup heavy cream over simmering water to lukewarm.

Combine 4 egg yolks, 6 Tbsp sugar, and 1 tsp cornstarch in a small bowl and beat with a wire whisk until smooth and light yellow in color.

Slowly pour a third of the warm cream into beaten egg yolks, stirring all the while. Pour mixture into top of double boiler and cook over simmering water until custard thickens, stirring constantly.

Add melted chocolate to custard and stir with a wire whisk to thoroughly combine chocolate. At first small specks of chocolate will form. Continue stirring, the flecks will melt, and the custard will turn darker.

Remove from heat and stir until custard cools slightly. Add ½ tsp vanilla extract. Place custard in refrigerator to chill for 30 minutes.

Finely chop enough pecans to measure 1 cup.

Whip 1 cup heavy cream until soft peaks form. Add 1 Tbsp sugar and whip a few moments longer. Fold in chopped pecans.

Remove chilled custard from refrigerator and fold in whipped cream. Scrape into freezer container, cover tightly, and freeze until frozen around edges of container (about 2 hours).

Remove ice cream from freezer, uncover, and stir thoroughly to break up any large lumps. Leave in container or scrape into serving dish, cover, and freeze for 4 hours or until firm.

Allow ice cream to ripen in refrigerator for 30 minutes before serving.

CHOCOLATE VELVET

Makes 1½ quarts of smooth, rich, easy chocolate ice cream that is great soft or firm.

1/3 cup homemade Chocolate Syrup (page 186)
2/3 cup condensed milk
2 cups heavy cream
1/4 tsp vanilla extract

In a medium-sized bowl pour 1/3 cup homemade Chocolate Syrup, 2/3 cup condensed milk, 2 cups heavy cream, and 1/4 tsp vanilla extract.

Place bowl containing ingredients and beater in back of refrigerator for 30 to 45 minutes or until thoroughly chilled.

Remove chilled materials from refrigerator. Whip cream until it forms stiff peaks. Scrape into freezer container or serving dish, cover tightly, and freeze until firm.

Allow to ripen up to 30 minutes in refrigerator before serving.

COCONUT-VANILLA-ALMOND ICE CREAM

Makes 1½ quarts of very chewy and mildly sweet ice cream that is a fusing of the sea and the desert.

3 Tbsp butter, melted
½ cup sliced almonds
⅓ cup freshly grated dried coconut (page 21)
1 cup milk
1 cup heavy cream
5 egg yolks
½ cup Turbinado sugar
1 tsp arrowroot
1-inch piece of vanilla bean
1 cup heavy cream
1 Tbsp Turbinado sugar

Melt 3 Tbsp butter over low heat. Sauté ½ cup sliced almonds in 1 Tbsp of the melted butter until they start to turn brown. Remove from heat. To drain off burned butter, scrape nuts onto paper towel and then into small bowl.

Wipe out pan with paper towel to use again. Put the other 2 Tbsp melted butter into the skillet. Add ⅓ cup dried coconut. Stir and sauté until slightly browned. Scrape into nuts and set aside to cool.

In top of double boiler combine 1 cup milk and 1 cup heavy cream. Heat over simmering water to just under boiling. Set aside.

In medium-sized bowl with electric mixer beat together 5 egg yolks, ½ cup Turbinado sugar, and 1 tsp arrowroot until mixture is thick and light in color.

Cut off a 1-inch piece of vanilla bean, slice it in half lengthwise, scrape out black powder, and add this to egg yolks. Beat until thoroughly incorporated. Discard the remaining bean bark.

Pour hot milk in a thin stream into beaten egg yolks and sugar, beating all the while. Pour back into top of double boiler and slowly cook custard over simmering water, stirring constantly, until it thickens. Remove from heat and continue to stir a few moments longer.

Chill the custard in refrigerator for 30 minutes.

Whip 1 cup heavy cream with 1 Tbsp Turbinado sugar until it forms soft peaks. Stir in cooled sautéed almonds and coconut. Remove custard from refrigerator. Fold whipped cream mixture into chilled custard.

Pour into freezer container and freeze for 1 hour.

Remove from freezer, stir to break up frozen particles, leave in original container or pour into a serving dish, cover again, and return to freezer until firm.

Allow ice cream to ripen 45 minutes in refrigerator before serving.

COFFEE ICE CREAM

Makes 1½ quarts of an ice cream greeted with pleasure at every test.

1 cup milk
½ cup heavy cream
½ cup very strong fresh coffee (page 21)
5 egg yolks
½ cup light brown sugar, with lumps broken up
1 tsp cornstarch
½ cup heavy cream
1 tsp light-brown sugar, with lumps broken up
1 Tbsp rum

In the top of double boiler heat together over simmering water 1 cup milk and ½ cup heavy cream until hot but not boiling. Add ½ cup very strong fresh coffee. Set aside.

Using electric mixer and large bowl beat together 5 egg yolks, ½ cup light-brown sugar, with lumps broken up, and 1 tsp cornstarch, until thick and light yellow in color.

Add hot milk and coffee in a thin stream to beaten eggs and sugar, beating all the while. Return to top of double boiler and cook custard over simmering water, stirring constantly, until thick. Remove from heat and continue to stir a few moments longer until custard cools slightly.

Chill custard in refrigerator for 30 minutes.

Whip ½ cup heavy cream until it forms soft peaks. Add 1 tsp light-brown sugar, with the lumps well broken up, and 1 Tbsp rum. Continue to whip until stiff peaks form.

Remove chilled custard from refrigerator. Fold whipped cream into chilled custard. Cover and freeze for 1 hour.

Remove from freezer, uncover, stir to break up frozen pieces, leave in freezer container or scrape into serving dish, cover again, and return to freezer until firm.

Allow ice cream to ripen in refrigerator 1 hour before serving.

CINNAMON-APPLEJACK ICE CREAM

Makes 1½ quarts of rich ice cream laced with applejack and chunks of apples.

> ½ cup heavy cream
> 1 cup milk
> 4 egg yolks
> ½ cup granulated sugar
> 1 tsp cornstarch
> ¼ cup applejack or apple brandy
> 1 large apple
> ¼ tsp cinnamon
> 2 tsp granulated sugar
> 1½ cups heavy cream

Place ½ cup heavy cream and 1 cup milk in top of double boiler over simmering water and heat to lukewarm. Set aside.

In a small bowl using a wire whisk beat 4 egg yolks, ½ cup sugar, and 1 tsp cornstarch until egg yolks are light yellow in color. Slowly pour a third of the warm milk into egg yolks, stirring all the while.

Scrape mixture back into top of double boiler and cook over simmering water until custard thickens, stirring constantly.

Remove custard from heat and stir in ¼ cup applejack or apple brandy. Place in refrigerator to chill for 30 minutes.

Wash, core, peel, and chop a large apple into very small pieces. Wrap pieces in cheesecloth or paper towel and squeeze tightly to remove as much moisture as possible. Combine apple bits with ¼ tsp cinnamon and 2 tsp sugar.

Remove chilled custard from refrigerator. Stir in the chopped apple. Whip 1½ cups heavy cream until soft peaks form and fold into the custard. Scrape mixture into freezer container, cover tightly, and place in freezer for 1½ hours.

Remove ice cream from freezer, uncover, and stir thoroughly to break up any large ice crystals. Leave in container or scrape into serving dish, cover again, and freeze for 4 hours or until firm.

Allow ice cream to ripen in refrigerator for 30 minutes before serving.

This ice cream keeps about 1 week.

CRÈME DE MENTHE ICE CREAM

Makes 1½ quarts of smooth, very sweet ice cream, delicious with chocolate cake in a baked Alaska.

   ³/₄ cup heavy cream
   ³/₄ cup milk
   4 egg yolks
   1 tsp cornstarch
   ½ cup granulated sugar
   ½ cup Crème de Menthe
   1½ cups heavy cream

Combine ³/₄ cup heavy cream and ³/₄ cup milk in top of double boiler and warm over simmering water. Set aside.

Beat together 4 egg yolks, 1 tsp cornstarch, and ½ cup sugar with a wire whisk until light yellow in color.

Slowly pour a third of the warm milk and cream into egg yolks, stirring all the while. Scrape mixture back into remaining milk in top of double boiler and cook over simmering water until custard thickens, stirring constantly. Remove from heat and continue to stir a little to cool custard. Stir in ½ cup Crème de Menthe.

Place custard in refrigerator to chill.

Whip 1½ cups heavy cream until soft peaks form.

Remove custard from refrigerator. Fold whipped cream into chilled custard.

Scrape mixture into freezer container, cover tightly, and freeze for 1½ hours or until frozen around the edges of the container. Remove ice cream from freezer, uncover, and stir thoroughly. Leave in container or scrape into serving dish, cover, and freeze for 4 hours or until firm.

Allow ice cream to ripen in refrigerator for 30 minutes before serving.

DRAMBUIE ICE CREAM

Makes 1½ quarts of sweet Scotch-flavored ice cream.

¾ cup heavy cream
¾ cup milk
4 egg yolks
½ cup light-brown sugar, with lumps broken up
1 tsp cornstarch
6 Tbsp Drambuie
1½ cups heavy cream

Combine ¾ cup heavy cream and ¾ cup milk in top of double boiler and heat to lukewarm over simmering water. Set aside.

In a small bowl using a wire whisk beat together 4 egg yolks, 1 tsp cornstarch, and ½ cup brown sugar with lumps broken up until mixture is pale yellow in color.

Slowly pour a third of the warm milk and cream into egg yolks, stirring all the while. Scrape mixture back into remaining milk in top of double boiler and cook over simmering water until custard thickens, stirring constantly. Remove from heat and stir to cool.

Stir in 6 Tbsp Drambuie. Place custard in refrigerator to chill.

Whip 1½ cups heavy cream until soft peaks form. Remove chilled custard from refrigerator and fold in the whipped cream.

Scrape mixture into freezer container, cover tightly, and freeze for 1½ hours or until frozen around the edges of the container. Remove ice cream from freezer, uncover, and stir thoroughly to break up frozen pieces. Leave ice cream in freezer container or scrape into serving dish, cover, and return ice cream to freezer for 4 hours or until firm.

Allow ice cream to ripen in refrigerator for 1 hour before serving.

FIG ICE CREAM

Makes 1 pint of chewy ice cream good when made with imported Turkish dried figs.

½ cup finely chopped dried figs
2 egg whites
2 Tbsp dark-brown sugar, with lumps broken up
½ cup heavy cream

Finely chop enough figs to measure ½ cup. Set aside.

In a small bowl beat 2 egg whites until soft peaks form. Beat in 2 Tbsp brown sugar with lumps broken up, and continue beating until egg whites hold stiff peaks. Beat in chopped figs. At first lumps of figs will form, but as the mixture is beaten the lumps separate.

Place mixture in refrigerator to chill.

Whip ½ cup heavy cream until soft peaks form. Remove chilled egg white mixture from refrigerator and fold in the whipped cream. Scrape mixture into freezer container or serving dish, cover tightly, and place in freezer for 2 hours or until firm.

Since this ice cream remains soft, it can be served directly from freezer.

GINGER ALE ICE CREAM

Makes about 2 quarts of ice cream with a heightened ginger flavor. You will enjoy it if you particularly like ginger ale.

3 cups light cream
10 egg yolks
3/4 cup light-brown sugar, with lumps broken up
1 tsp arrowroot
1/2 tsp vanilla extract
1/2 cup crystallized ginger, finely chopped
1 cup ginger ale
1 1/2 cups heavy cream

In the top of double boiler heat over simmering water 3 cups cream until hot but not boiling. Set aside.

In a large bowl using electric mixer beat together 10 egg yolks, 3/4 cup brown sugar, with lumps broken up, and 1 tsp arrowroot until thick and light yellow in color.

In a thin stream add hot cream to egg mixture, beating all the while. When well mixed pour back into top of double boiler and cook custard over simmering water, stirring constantly, until custard thickens. Remove from heat and continue to stir a few moments longer until custard starts to cool. Stir in 1/2 tsp vanilla extract.

Chill custard in refrigerator (about 1/2 hour).

Finely chop enough crystallized ginger to measure 1/2 cup, and scrape into 1 cup ginger ale. Set aside.

Whip 1 1/2 cups heavy cream until stiff. Fold in chopped ginger and ginger ale.

Remove chilled custard from refrigerator and fold into whipped cream mixture.

Cover and freeze 1 1/2 hours.

Remove ice cream from freezer, uncover, and stir to break up frozen pieces and redistribute ginger. Scrape into a freezer container or serving dish, cover again, and return to freezer until firm.

Allow ice cream to ripen 1 1/2 hours in refrigerator before serving.

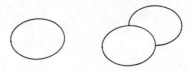

GINGER-PEAR ICE CREAM

Makes 1½ pints. This is a richly flavored, moderately sweet ice cream that satisfies well in small servings.

2 to 2½ cups fresh, ripe pears, sliced (about 3 pears)
2 Tbsp confectioners' sugar
¼ tsp lime juice
1 cup light cream
2 egg yolks
2 Tbsp confectioners' sugar
½ tsp arrowroot
1 tsp crystallized ginger
½ cup heavy cream
1 Tbsp confectioners' sugar

Wash, peel, core, and slice enough pears to make 2 to 2½ cups. Put pear slices into medium-sized bowl and sprinkle with 2 Tbsp sugar. Squeeze enough lime juice to make ¼ tsp. Add to pear slices and gently stir fruit until evenly covered with sugar and juice. Set aside in refrigerator at least 1 hour.

Using top of double boiler heat 1 cup light cream over simmering water until hot, but not boiling. Set aside.

Beat 2 egg yolks, 2 Tbsp sugar, and ½ tsp arrowroot with a wire whisk until thick and pale yellow in color. In a thin stream pour hot cream into beaten egg yolks, beating all the while. Then pour mixture back into top of double boiler and cook over simmering water, stirring constantly, until thick. Remove from heat and continue to stir until custard cools slightly.

Finely chop enough crystallized ginger to make 1 teaspoon. Stir into warm custard. Set custard in refrigerator to chill (about 30 minutes).

Remove sugared pears from refrigerator and pour into blender. Blend until a purée. Pour into medium-sized bowl.

Whip ½ cup heavy cream with 1 Tbsp confectioners' sugar until stiff peaks form. Remove chilled custard from refrigerator and fold into pear purée, then fold in whipped cream. Cover and freeze 2 hours.

Take out of freezer, uncover, break up frozen pieces, beat until smooth, and pour into freezer container or serving dish or mold. Cover and return to freezer until firm.

Allow ice cream to ripen in refrigerator 1 hour before serving.

HARVEY'S BRISTOL CREAM ICE CREAM

Makes 1½ pints. The flavor from the sweet sherry is brought out in the ice cream.

 3/4 cup heavy cream
 3/4 cup milk
 4 egg yolks
 1 tsp cornstarch
 1/2 cup granulated sugar
 1/2 cup Harvey's Bristol Cream sherry
 1½ cups heavy cream

Combine 3/4 cup heavy cream and 3/4 cup milk in top of double boiler and heat to lukewarm over simmering water. Set aside.

Using a wire whisk beat together 4 egg yolks, 1 tsp cornstarch, and 1/2 cup sugar until light yellow in color.

Slowly pour a third of the warm milk and cream into the beaten egg yolks, stirring all the while. Scrape mixture back into remaining milk in top of double boiler and cook over simmering water, stirring constantly, until custard thickens. Remove from heat and stir to cool.

Stir in 1/2 cup Harvey's Bristol Cream. Place custard in refrigerator to chill.

Whip 1½ cups heavy cream until soft peaks form. Remove chilled custard from refrigerator and fold in the whipped cream.

Scrape mixture into freezer container, cover tightly, and place in freezer for 1½ hours or until frozen around the edges of container. Remove ice cream from freezer, uncover, and stir thoroughly to break up any frozen pieces. Leave in container or scrape into serving dish, cover, and return to freezer for 4 hours or until firm.

Allow ice cream to ripen in refrigerator for 30 minutes before serving.

HONEY ALMOND ICE CREAM

Makes 1½ quarts of a heavenly smooth ice cream with nuts. It is good with Honey Cream (page 180).

½ cup heavy cream
1 cup milk
4 egg yolks
1 tsp cornstarch
½ cup honey
½ tsp almond extract
4½ oz almonds, chopped
2 Tbsp honey
1½ cups heavy cream

Combine ½ cup heavy cream and 1 cup milk in top of double boiler and heat to lukewarm over simmering water. Set aside.

In a small bowl using wire whisk beat 4 egg yolks and 1 tsp cornstarch until light yellow in color. Stir in ½ cup honey. Slowly pour half of the warmed milk into beaten egg yolks, stirring all the while. Scrape mixture back into top of double boiler and cook over simmering water, stirring constantly, until custard thickens. Remove from heat. Stir in ½ tsp almond extract.

Place custard in refrigerator to chill.

Chop 4½ oz almonds. Combine with 2 Tbsp honey. Remove chilled custard from refrigerator. Stir in honeyed almonds.

Whip 1½ cups heavy cream until soft peaks form. Fold whipped cream into custard. Scrape mixture into freezer container, cover tightly, and place in freezer for 1 hour or until partially frozen. Remove from freezer, uncover, and stir thoroughly to break up any ice crystals and redistribute almonds. Leave in freezer container or scrape into serving dish, cover, and return to freezer for 4 hours or until firm.

Allow ice cream to ripen in refrigerator for 45 minutes before serving.

This ice cream will keep for 2 weeks in a tightly covered container.

HONEY-STRAWBERRY ICE CREAM

Makes about 1 quart. This delicately honey-flavored ice cream reminded our friends of rhubarb.

2 tsp unflavored gelatin
1/4 cup cold milk
1 pint fresh strawberries
Juice of 1/2 lemon
4 egg yolks
1/3 cup honey
1 cup cream
1/4 tsp salt

In a small container soften 2 tsp gelatin in 1/4 cup cold milk. Set over hot water to melt gelatin. Stir occasionally and set aside.

Wash and hull 1 pint strawberries. Pour into blender. Squeeze juice from half a lemon and add to strawberries; then blend 30 seconds. Set aside.

In medium-sized mixing bowl using electric mixer beat 4 egg yolks with 1/3 cup honey until thick and pale yellow in color. Slowly pour warmed milk and gelatin into beaten egg yolks and honey, beating all the while. Fold in puréed strawberries.

Chill custard in refrigerator 30 minutes.

Whip 1 cup heavy cream with 1/4 tsp salt until stiff peaks form. Remove chilled strawberry custard from refrigerator and fold in whipped cream.

Cover bowl tightly and freeze 1 hour.

Take out of freezer, uncover, and stir to break up frozen pieces. Scrape ice cream into freezer container, serving dish, or mold, cover, and freeze until firm.

Allow ice cream to ripen in refrigerator 1 hour before serving.

IRISH COFFEE ICE CREAM

Makes 1½ quarts. A good dessert for a winter dinner party.

½ cup very strong coffee (page 21)
1 cup milk
½ cup heavy cream
5 egg yolks
1 tsp cornstarch
½ cup granulated sugar
½ cup Irish whiskey
1½ cups heavy cream
1 Tbsp granulated sugar

Prepare ½ cup very strong coffee. Set aside to cool.

Combine 1 cup milk and ½ cup heavy cream in top of double boiler and heat to lukewarm over simmering water.

In a small bowl using a wire whisk beat together 5 egg yolks, 1 tsp cornstarch, and ½ cup sugar until egg yolks are frothy and pale yellow in color.

Slowly stir in a third of the warmed milk and cream into egg mixture. Scrape eggs and milk back into top of double boiler and cook over simmering water, stirring constantly, until custard thickens. Remove from heat and continue to stir until custard cools slightly. Stir in prepared coffee and ½ cup Irish whiskey. Place custard in refrigerator to chill.

Whip 1½ cups heavy cream until soft peaks form. Whip in 1 Tbsp sugar. Remove chilled custard from refrigerator and fold in the whipped cream. Scrape mixture into freezer container, cover tightly, and freeze for approximately 1½ hours.

Remove ice cream from freezer, uncover, and stir thoroughly to break up any large ice crystals. Leave in freezer container or scrape into serving dish, cover, and freeze for 4 hours or until firm.

Allow ice cream to ripen in refrigerator for 1 hour before serving.

LEMON ICE CREAM

Makes 2 pints of unsweet ice cream with the great taste of lemon. Try this recipe with limes as a substitute; it is also delicious.

    Grated rind of 4 lemons
    Juice of 4 lemons
    1 cup light-brown sugar, with lumps broken up
    2 cups heavy cream

Grate the rind of 4 lemons and set aside.

Squeeze juice from grated lemons into small bowl, removing pits. Add 1 cup brown sugar, with lumps broken up, to juice. Stir and set aside.

In medium-sized bowl whip 2 cups heavy cream until it forms soft peaks. Add grated lemon rind, brown sugar, and lemon juice and whip a few moments longer.

Cover and freeze for 1 hour.

Remove ice cream from freezer, uncover, and stir to break up frozen pieces. Scrape into freezer container or serving dish, cover again, and freeze until firm.

Allow ice cream to ripen in refrigerator 10 minutes before serving.

LEMON LIME ICE CREAM

Makes 1 pint of smooth sweet-tart ice cream.

    Juice of ½ lime
    Juice of 1 lemon
    ½ tsp candied grated lime rind (page 23)
    ½ tsp candied grated lemon rind (page 23)
    2 egg whites
    ¼ tsp cream of tartar
    ½ cup granulated sugar
    ½ cup heavy cream

Squeeze the juice from half a lime and 1 lemon. Pour into cup. Add ½ tsp candied lime rind and ½ tsp candied lemon rind. Set aside.

In a 1½-quart mixing bowl beat 2 egg whites and ¼ tsp cream of tartar until soft peaks form. Slowly beat in ½ cup sugar and continue beating until egg whites hold very stiff peaks and are smooth and glossy. Sugar should be completely dissolved.

Stir in juices and rind. Place in refrigerator to chill.

Beat ½ cup heavy cream until soft peaks form. Remove chilled beaten egg whites from refrigerator. Fold whipped cream into egg whites. Scrape mixture into freezer container or serving dish, cover, and freeze for 2 hours.

This ice cream remains soft and can be served directly from freezer. It will keep for 1 month in a tightly covered container.

MAPLE WALNUT VELVET

Makes 1½ pints of a simple to make sweet ice cream that has a creamy velvet texture. Diana feels pure maple syrup is particularly good in it.

⅓ cup condensed milk
1½ cups heavy cream
¼ tsp vanilla extract
¼ cup pure maple syrup
½ cup English walnut pieces (canned)

In medium-sized bowl combine ⅓ cup condensed milk, 1½ cups heavy cream, and ¼ tsp vanilla extract. Thoroughly chill in refrigerator (about 30 to 45 minutes).

Remove and whip until cream forms soft peaks. Add ¼ cup maple syrup and whip a few moments longer until cream holds stiff peaks. Fold in ½ cup English walnut pieces.

Scrape into freezer container or serving dish, cover, and freeze until firm.

Allow ice cream to ripen 30 minutes in refrigerator before serving.

MACADAMIAN NUT ICE CREAM

Makes 1½ quarts of an ice cream based on recipe secured for us from Hawaii by Leslie Fabian of Dean Witter & Co.

¾ cup milk
¾ cup heavy cream
4 egg yolks
½ cup granulated sugar
1 tsp cornstarch
2-inch piece of vanilla bean
1½ cups heavy cream
1 Tbsp granulated sugar
1 Tbsp brandy
1½ cups Macadamian nuts, coarsely chopped

Combine ¾ cup milk and ¾ cup heavy cream in top of double boiler and heat to just under boiling. Set aside.

In medium-sized bowl using electric mixer beat together 4 egg yolks, ½ cup sugar, 1 tsp cornstarch, and the black vanilla powder scraped from inside a 2-inch piece of vanilla bean until thick and light yellow in color.

Slowly pour hot milk into beaten egg yolk mixture, stirring all the while. Scrape back into top of double boiler and cook custard over simmering water, stirring constantly, until thick. Remove from heat and continue to stir a few moments longer until slightly cool. Put custard in refrigerator to chill.

Coarsely chop 1½ cups Macadamian nuts.

Whip 1½ cups heavy cream with 1 Tbsp sugar until soft peaks form. Stir in 1 Tbsp brandy and the coarsely chopped nuts.

Remove cooled custard from refrigerator and scrape into whipped cream. Fold one mixture into the other. Cover bowl and place in freezer 1½ hours.

Remove from freezer, uncover, stir to break up any frozen pieces and redistribute the nuts, cover again, and freeze another 1½ hours.

Remove from freezer again, uncover, stir to redistribute nuts, scrape into freezer container or serving dish, cover, and freeze until firm.

Allow to ripen in refrigerator 30 to 40 minutes before serving.

MINCEMEAT ICE CREAM

Makes 1½ quarts of very rich ice cream—a holiday dessert.

    1 9-oz package dried concentrated mincemeat
    2 Tbsp brandy
    2 Tbsp granulated sugar
    1 cup water
    1 tsp cornstarch
    1 cup milk
    4 Tbsp butter
    4 egg yolks
    ½ cup granulated sugar
    1 tsp cornstarch
    1½ cups heavy cream

Combine concentrated mincemeat, 2 Tbsp brandy, 2 Tbsp sugar, 1 cup water, and 1 tsp cornstarch in a small saucepan. Boil mixture for 3 minutes and set aside to cool.

Heat 1 cup milk and 4 Tbsp butter in top of double boiler over simmering water until butter melts. Remove from heat and set aside.

In small bowl using wire whisk beat 4 egg yolks, ½ cup sugar, and 1 tsp cornstarch until light yellow in color. Slowly pour warm milk into beaten egg yolks, stirring all the while. Scrape mixture back into top of double boiler and cook over simmering water, stirring constantly, until custard thickens. Remove from heat and stir in prepared mincemeat. Put custard in refrigerator to chill.

Whip 1½ cups heavy cream until soft peaks form. Remove chilled custard from refrigerator and fold in the whipped cream.

Scrape mixture into freezer container, cover tightly, and place in freezer for 2 hours or until ice cream is frozen around the edges of container. Remove ice cream from freezer, uncover, and stir thoroughly to break up any frozen pieces. Leave in freezer container or scrape into serving dish, cover tightly, and return to freezer for 4 hours or until firm.

Allow ice cream to ripen in refrigerator for 10 minutes before serving.

This ice cream will keep for 1 month in a tightly covered container.

MINT CHOCOLATE CHIP ICE CREAM

Makes 1½ quarts of natural mint ice cream flavored with crunchy chocolate chips.

  ¾ cup heavy cream
  ¾ cup milk
  4 egg yolks
  ½ cup granulated sugar
  1 tsp cornstarch
  ½ cup homemade mint extract (page 20)
  3 oz mini semi-sweet chocolate chips
  1½ cups heavy cream

Combine ¾ cup heavy cream and ¾ cup milk in top of double boiler and heat to lukewarm over simmering water.

In small bowl using wire whisk beat together 4 egg yolks, ½ cup sugar, and 1 tsp cornstarch until egg yolks are frothy and lemon-colored.

Slowly stir in a third of the warmed milk and cream into the egg mixture. Scrape eggs and milk back into top of double boiler and cook over simmering water until custard thickens, stirring constantly. Remove from heat and continue to stir until custard cools slightly. Stir in ½ cup homemade mint extract. Place custard in refrigerator to chill.

Remove custard from refrigerator and stir in 3 oz mini semi-sweet chocolate chips.

Whip 1½ cups heavy cream until soft peaks form. Fold into prepared custard and scrape mixture into freezer container, cover tightly, and freeze for approximately 1½ hours.

Remove ice cream from freezer, uncover, and stir thoroughly to break up large ice crystals and redistribute chocolate chips. Leave in freezer container or scrape into serving dish, cover, and freeze for approximately 4 hours or until firm.

Allow ice cream to ripen in refrigerator for 1 hour before serving.

Ice Creams

MINTED PEAR ICE CREAM

Makes 1½ pints of pear-flavored ice cream that has a slight tang from the mint liqueur.

    2 to 2½ cups fresh, ripe pears, sliced
    ¼ tsp lime juice
    2 Tbsp confectioners' sugar
    1 cup Half and Half
    2 egg yolks
    2 Tbsp confectioners' sugar
    ½ tsp arrowroot
    ½ cup heavy cream
    1 Tbsp Crème de Menthe

Wash, peel, core, and slice enough pears to make 2 to 2½ cups. Pour pears into medium-sized bowl. Squeeze enough lime juice to measure ¼ tsp and add to fruit. Sprinkle 2 Tbsp confectioners' sugar over fruit and stir until fruit is well covered with juice and sugar. Set aside in refrigerator at least 1 hour.

In top of double boiler heat 1 cup Half and Half over simmering water until hot but not boiling. Set aside.

Beat 2 egg yolks with 2 Tbsp confectioners' sugar and ½ tsp arrowroot until thick and pale yellow in color. In a thin stream add hot cream to beaten egg yolks, stirring all the while. Then pour back into top of double boiler and cook custard over simmering water, stirring constantly, until thick. Remove from heat and continue to stir until custard cools slightly.

Chill custard in refrigerator 30 minutes.

Remove chilled sugared pears from refrigerator. Pour into blender and blend until a purée. Pour into medium-sized bowl.

Whip ½ cup heavy cream until soft peaks form. Add 1 Tbsp Crème de Menthe and whip a moment longer.

Remove custard from refrigerator and scrape into pear purée. Fold in the whipped cream. Cover and freeze 2 hours or until frozen around the edges of the container. Take out of freezer, uncover, and stir to break up frozen pieces. Beat until smooth. Scrape into freezer container or serving dish, cover, and freeze until firm.

Allow ice cream to ripen 45 minutes in refrigerator before serving.

MOLASSES ICE CREAM

Makes 1½ pints of a smooth, mellow-flavored ice cream that is wonderful on a cold day.

    2 egg yolks
    1 Tbsp molasses
    3 Tbsp light corn syrup
    1 small can evaporated milk (5.3 oz)
    ¾ cup heavy cream

Beat 2 egg yolks in small bowl using wire whisk until egg yolks are thick and light yellow in color. Add 1 Tbsp molasses, 3 Tbsp light corn syrup, and contents from 1 small can of evaporated milk and beat until well mixed. Scrape mixture into top of double boiler and cook over simmering water, stirring constantly, until custard thickens. Remove from heat, continuing to stir until custard cools slightly.

Place custard in refrigerator to chill.

Whip ¾ cup heavy cream until soft peaks form.

Remove chilled custard from refrigerator. Fold whipped cream into custard, scrape into freezer container, cover tightly, and place in freezer until partially frozen (about 1 hour).

Remove from freezer, uncover, stir thoroughly to break up frozen pieces, leave in container or scrape into serving dish, cover again, and return to freezer until firm.

Allow ice cream to ripen in refrigerator for 30 minutes before serving.

NOUGAT ICE CREAM

Makes 1½ pints of a great nutty ice cream that takes a long time to eat.

1 cup milk
2 egg yolks
¼ cup granulated sugar
¼ tsp arrowroot
¼ tsp vanilla extract
⅓ cup each of pistachios, hazelnuts, English walnuts,
and almonds, chopped
¼ tsp salt
2 egg whites
1 cup heavy cream

In top of double boiler heat over simmering water 1 cup milk until hot but not boiling. Set aside.

In medium-sized bowl using electric mixer beat together 2 egg yolks, ¼ cup sugar, and ¼ tsp arrowroot until thick, pale yellow in color, and sugar is dissolved.

In a thin stream pour hot milk into beaten egg yolks and sugar, beating all the while.

Then pour mixture back into top of double boiler and cook custard over simmering water, stirring constantly, until custard is thick. Remove from heat and continue to stir a few moments longer until slightly cooled. Stir in ¼ tsp vanilla extract.

Chill custard in refrigerator 30 minutes.

Coarsely chop ⅓ cup each pistachios, hazelnuts, English walnuts, and almonds and put them in small bowl. Stir in ⅛ tsp of the salt and set aside.

Beat 2 egg whites with ⅛ tsp salt until stiff peaks form. Set aside.

Whip 1 cup heavy cream until stiff peaks form. Fold in assorted chopped nuts.

Remove chilled custard from refrigerator. Fold in the beaten egg whites and then the whipped cream with nuts.

Scrape mixture into freezer container, cover, and freeze for 1 hour.

Remove, uncover, stir to break up frozen pieces, leave in container or put in a serving dish, cover again, and return to freezer until firm.

Allow ice cream to ripen in refrigerator 1 hour before serving.

NUTTY FIG ICE CREAM

Makes 1 quart of ice cream that is quite nourishing.

⅔ cup dried organic Calmyrna figs, finely chopped
⅓ cup medium dry sherry
¾ cup walnuts, broken up
2 cups milk
6 egg yolks
½ cup Turbinado sugar
1 tsp arrowroot
6 egg whites
1 cup heavy cream
2 Tbsp Turbinado sugar

Using a very sharp knife, finely chop ⅔ cup figs and put in small mixing bowl. Pour ⅓ cup sherry over chopped figs. Stir and set aside.

Break up ¾ cup walnuts and set aside.

In top of double boiler heat over simmering water 2 cups milk to just under boiling. Set aside.

In medium-sized bowl beat together 6 egg yolks, ½ cup sugar and 1 tsp arrowroot until mixture is thick and light in color.

Slowly pour heated milk into egg yolks, beating all the while. Pour back into top of double boiler and cook slowly over simmering water, stirring constantly until custard thickens. Remove from heat and continue to stir, allowing custard to cool. Put in bowl and set aside.

In another medium-sized bowl beat 6 egg whites until stiff peaks form. Fold egg whites into custard.

Chill this mixture in refrigerator (about 1 hour).

Whip 1 cup heavy cream until it forms soft peaks. Fold in reserved walnuts and figs. Remove chilled custard from refrigerator and gently fold in whipped cream mixture. Cover and freeze until stiff around the edges (about 2 hours).

Remove from freezer, uncover, and stir to break up frozen pieces. Scrape into freezer container or serving dish, cover again, and return to freezer until firm.

Let ice cream ripen in refrigerator 45 minutes before serving.

ORANGE-PINEAPPLE ICE CREAM

Makes almost 1 quart of very sweet, soft ice cream with chunks of pineapple.

2 egg whites
1/8 tsp cream of tartar
1/3 cup granulated sugar
3/4 cup crushed canned pineapple, well drained
3 Tbsp concentrated frozen orange juice, thawed
1/2 cup heavy cream

In a medium-sized mixing bowl beat 2 egg whites with 1/8 tsp cream of tartar until soft peaks form. Slowly add 1/3 cup sugar and continue beating until egg whites are smooth and glossy and hold stiff peaks.

Thoroughly drain juice from can of crushed pineapple and measure out 3/4 cup pineapple. Fold crushed pineapple and 3 Tbsp concentrated orange juice into beaten egg whites. Place in refrigerator to chill.

Whip 1/2 cup heavy cream until soft peaks form. Remove chilled mixture from refrigerator. Quickly fold in the whipped cream. Scrape mixture into freezer container or serving dish, cover tightly, and freeze for 3 hours or until firm.

Ice cream will remain soft and can be served directly from freezer.

PAPAYA ICE CREAM

Makes about 1½ pints. A way of turning this bland tropical fruit into an exciting delight.

2 small ripe papayas (size of medium avocado)
⅔ cup light-brown sugar, with the lumps broken up
Juice of 2 limes
1 cup heavy cream
1 Tbsp confectioners' sugar

Wash 2 small papayas, cut in half, and scoop out the seeds. Scoop meat out of shell and place in blender with ⅔ cup light-brown sugar with the lumps broken up. Squeeze juice from 2 limes and add to fruit in blender. Blend mixture until puréed.

Whip 1 cup heavy cream until soft peaks form. Add 1 Tbsp confectioners' sugar and whip a moment longer. Pour purée into whipped cream and fold one mixture into the other. Cover bowl and place in freezer 1 hour.

Remove from freezer, uncover, stir to break up frozen pieces, beat until smooth, scrape into freezer container or serving dish, cover again, and freeze until firm.

Allow ice cream to ripen in refrigerator 45 to 60 minutes before serving.

PEACHES AND CREAM

Makes 1 quart of moderately sweet peach ice cream with chopped almonds.

1½ cups fresh peaches, chopped (1 lb)
½ cup light-brown sugar, with lumps broken up
¼ tsp lime juice
2 Tbsp sliced almonds
1½ cups heavy cream

Wash, peel, and chop about 1 lb peaches or enough to measure 1½ cups. Put in blender. Add ½ cup light-brown sugar with lumps broken up and ¼ tsp lime juice. Blend until puréed.

Finely chop enough sliced almonds to measure 2 Tbsps. Set aside.

In medium-sized bowl whip 1½ cups heavy cream until it forms soft peaks. Fold in chopped almonds. Pour in peach purée and fold one mixture into the other.

Cover and freeze for 1 hour.

Remove from freezer, uncover, stir to break up frozen pieces. Pour into freezer container or serving dish, cover again, and return to freezer until firm.

Allow ice cream to ripen 1 hour in refrigerator before serving.

PEACHES AND SOUR CREAM

Makes 1½ quarts mildly sweet, really refreshing peachy peach ice cream.

3 cups fresh peaches, diced or mashed (2 lbs)
½ cup light-brown sugar, with lumps broken up
¼ tsp lemon juice
3 cups sour cream
⅓ cup heavy cream

Wash, peel, and dice or mash enough peaches to measure 3 cups (about 1½ to 2 lbs). Place in small bowl.

Stir ½ cup light-brown sugar with the lumps broken up, or removed, into peaches. Then stir in ¼ tsp lemon juice. Let sit i refrigerator about 1 hour to allow sugar and lemon juice to bring out flavor of fruit.

Scoop 3 cups sour cream into medium-sized bowl. Stir in ⅓ cup heavy cream until smooth. Fold in fruit until evenly distributed. Cover tightly and put in freezer for 1 hour.

Remove, uncover, and stir to break up icy particles and redistribute peaches. Pour into freezer container or serving dish, cover again, and return to freezer until firm.

Allow ice cream to ripen in refrigerator 1½ hours before serving.

PEPPERMINT STICK ICE CREAM

Makes 1½ quarts. A favorite of Nancy's children, especially when served with warm Fudge Sauce (page 180).

½ cup crushed peppermint candies or candy canes
1 cup milk
½ cup heavy cream
4 egg yolks
½ cup granulated sugar
1 tsp cornstarch
1 tsp vanilla extract
1½ cups heavy cream

Place candy between 2 sheets of waxed paper and, using a rolling pin, crush enough candy to measure ½ cup.

Combine 1 cup milk and ½ cup heavy cream in top of double boiler and heat to lukewarm over simmering water. Set aside.

In small bowl, using a wire whisk, beat together 4 egg yolks, ½ cup sugar, and 1 tsp cornstarch until light yellow in color.

Slowly pour a third of the warmed cream into beaten egg yolks, stirring all the while. Pour mixture back into top of double boiler and cook over simmering water, stirring constantly, until the custard thickens. Remove from heat and continue to stir a few moments longer. Stir in 1 tsp vanilla extract and crushed candy. Place custard in refrigerator for 30 minutes to chill.

Whip 1½ cups heavy cream until soft peaks form. Remove custard from refrigerator and fold in the whipped cream. Scrape mixture into freezer container, cover tightly, and place in freezer for 1½ hours or until frozen around edges of container.

Remove ice cream from freezer, uncover, and stir thoroughly to break up frozen pieces. Cover again and return to freezer for 5 hours or until firm.

Allow ice cream to ripen in the refrigerator for 30 minutes before serving.

Top with warm Fudge Sauce, if you like.

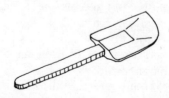

PINEAPPLE ICE CREAM

Makes 1 quart of moderately sweet, pineapple-and-citrus-flavored ice cream.

2 tsp unflavored gelatin
1/4 cup milk
1 1/4 cups crushed canned pineapple, well drained
Juice of 1/2 lemon
Juice of 1/2 lime
4 egg yolks
2 Tbsp light-brown sugar, with lumps broken up
1 cup heavy cream

Stir 2 tsp gelatin into 1/4 cup cold milk in a small metal bowl. Place in larger bowl containing hot water and let sit until gelatin melts.

Thoroughly drain juice from a large can of crushed pineapple and measure out 1 1/4 cups of the pineapple. Save any leftover pineapple and juice for another use. Squeeze juice from half a lemon and half a lime. Combine juice and pineapple in small bowl. Set aside.

In a medium-sized bowl beat 4 egg yolks until yolks are thick and light yellow in color. Beat in 2 Tbsp light-brown sugar, with lumps broken up, and continue beating until mixture resembles mayonnaise. Stir in melted gelatin. Fold in the pineapple and juices. Place in refrigerator to chill for 30 minutes.

Whip 1 cup heavy cream until soft peaks form. Remove pineapple and egg mixture from refrigerator. Fold whipped cream into mixture, scrape into freezer container or serving dish, cover, and freeze for 4 hours or until firm.

Allow ice cream to ripen in refrigerator for 30 minutes before serving.

PISTACHIO ICE CREAM

Makes 1½ pints of superb crunchy ice cream, thick with nuts.

⅜ cup heavy cream
⅜ cup milk
2 egg yolks
½ tsp cornstarch
¼ cup granulated sugar
½ cup natural pistachio nuts, coarsely chopped
1 tsp vanilla extract
½ tsp almond extract
¾ cup heavy cream

Combine ⅜ cup heavy cream and ⅜ cup milk in top of double boiler and heat over simmering water until lukewarm. Set aside.

In a small bowl using wire whisk, beat together 2 egg yolks, ½ tsp cornstarch, and ¼ cup sugar until light yellow in color.

Shell and chop enough pistachio nuts to measure ½ cup. Set aside.

Slowly pour warm milk into egg yolks, stirring all the while. Pour mixture back into top of double boiler and cook over simmering water, stirring constantly, until custard thickens. Remove from heat and continue to stir until slightly cool.

Stir in 1 tsp vanilla extract and ½ tsp almond extract. Stir in chopped pistachio nuts. Place custard in refrigerator to chill.

Whip ¾ cup heavy cream until soft peaks form. Remove chilled custard from refrigerator and fold in the whipped cream, trying to distribute nuts evenly.

Scrape mixture into freezer container, cover tightly, and freeze for 1 hour or until frozen around the edges of container. Remove ice cream from freezer, uncover, and stir thoroughly to break up frozen pieces and redistribute nuts throughout ice cream. Leave in container or scrape into serving dish, cover, and return to freezer for 3 hours or until firm.

Allow ice cream to ripen in refrigerator for 1 hour before serving.

PISTACHIO-ALMOND ICE CREAM

Makes 1 quart of a firm-bodied, mildly sweet ice cream that is very filling.

2 cups milk
6 egg yolks
2/3 cup light-brown sugar, with lumps broken up
1/2 tsp arrowroot
3/4 cup natural pistachio nuts, finely chopped
1/3 cup blanched and slivered almonds, finely chopped
1 cup heavy cream

In the top of double boiler heat over simmering water 2 cups milk until hot but not boiling. Set aside.

Using electric mixer beat together in medium-sized bowl 6 egg yolks, 2/3 cup light-brown sugar, with lumps broken up, and 1/2 tsp arrowroot until thick and pale yellow in color. In a thin stream add hot milk to egg yolk mixture, beating all the while, until well mixed.

Pour back into top of double boiler and cook custard over simmering water, stirring constantly, until very thick. Remove from heat and continue to stir a few moments longer to cool.

Chill custard in refrigerator 30 minutes.

Shell and finely chop enough pistachios to measure 3/4 cup and finely chop 1/3 cup blanched and slivered almonds. Mix the nuts and set aside.

Whip 1 cup heavy cream until it holds soft peaks. Fold in the nuts.

Remove chilled custard from refrigerator and fold in the whipped cream and nuts.

Scrape mixture into freezer container, cover, and freeze for 1 1/2 hours.

Remove from freezer, uncover, stir to break up any frozen particles and redistribute the nuts, leave in freezer container or scrape into serving dish, cover again, and freeze until firm.

Allow ice cream to ripen 2 1/2 hours in refrigerator before serving.

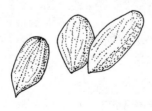

PLAIN BUTTER PECAN ICE CREAM

Makes 1½ pints. This is what commercial Butter Pecan pretends to be.

1 cup milk
2 egg yolks
⅓ cup light-brown sugar, with lumps broken up
¼ tsp arrowroot
¼ tsp vanilla extract
1 cup pecans, finely chopped
3 Tbsp butter, melted
1 cup heavy cream
Pinch of salt

In the top of double boiler over simmering water heat 1 cup milk to just under boiling. Set aside.

Using electric mixer in medium-sized bowl beat together 2 egg yolks, ⅓ cup light-brown sugar with lumps broken up and ¼ tsp arrowroot until thick and light in color.

In a thin stream pour hot milk into beaten egg yolks and sugar, beating all the while.

Pour mixture back into top of double boiler and cook very slowly over simmering water, stirring constantly, until custard thickens. Remove from heat and continue to stir until custard starts to cool. Stir in ¼ tsp vanilla extract. Chill in refrigerator 30 minutes.

Finely chop enough pecans to make 1 cup. Melt 3 Tbsp butter in small skillet and sauté pecans until they start to turn brown. Remove from heat and cool. (Diana sticks them in the freezer until she is ready.)

Whip 1 cup heavy cream with pinch of salt until it forms soft peaks. Fold in cooled pecans. Remove chilled custard from refrigerator. Fold whipped cream mixture into cooled custard. Scrape into freezer container, cover, and place in freezer for 1 hour.

Remove from freezer, uncover, stir to break up frozen pieces, pour back into freezer container or serving dish, cover again, and return to freezer until firm.

Allow ice cream to ripen in refrigerator 1½ hours before serving.

PRUNE ICE CREAM

Makes 1 quart of smooth, rich ice cream, especially for the prune lover.

3/4 cup dried, pitted prunes
1/2 cup water
1/4 cup orange juice, fresh or frozen
2 egg whites
1/2 cup granulated sugar
3/4 cup heavy cream

Place 3/4 cup dried pitted prunes and 1/2 cup water (or enough to cover prunes) in small saucepan. Heat to boiling, remove from heat, cover, and set aside 30 minutes for prunes to soften.

Squeeze enough orange juice to measure 1/4 cup. Pour into blender.

When prunes are soft, drain them, reserving liquid. Add prunes to orange juice in blender and blend at high speed until puréed. If prunes do not immediately form a smooth purée, add 1/4 cup of reserved prune liquid and blend again. If necessary, add a little more juice and blend again until purée is fairly smooth. Set aside.

In small bowl beat 2 egg whites until soft peaks are formed. Slowly beat in 1/2 cup sugar and continue beating until egg whites are smooth, glossy, and hold very stiff peaks. Fold prune purée into egg whites and place in refrigerator to chill.

Whip 3/4 cup heavy cream until soft peaks form. Remove chilled prune mixture from refrigerator and fold in the whipped cream. Scrape cream into freezer container or serving dish, cover tightly, and place in freezer for 2 hours or until firm enough to serve.

This ice cream remains soft and can be served directly from freezer.

PUMPKIN ICE CREAM

Makes 1 quart of a light, spicy ice cream resembling pumpkin pie.

1 small can evaporated milk (5.3 oz)
2 egg yolks
1/2 cup light-brown sugar, with lumps broken up
1/4 tsp powdered ginger
1/2 tsp powdered cinnamon
1/4 tsp powdered nutmeg
1 cup fresh (see below) or canned pumpkin purée
2 egg whites
1/8 tsp salt
1/8 tsp cream of tartar

Combine evaporated milk, 2 egg yolks, 1/2 cup light-brown sugar with lumps broken up, 1/4 tsp ginger, 1/2 tsp cinnamon, and 1/4 tsp nutmeg in top of double boiler. Using a wire whisk beat the ingredients until smooth. Place top over simmering water and cook until custard thickens, stirring constantly.

Remove from heat. Stir in 1 cup pumpkin purée. Set aside.

In medium-sized bowl beat 2 egg whites, 1/8 tsp salt, and 1/8 tsp cream of tartar until stiff peaks are formed. Fold beaten egg whites into pumpkin custard. Scrape into freezer container or serving dish, cover tightly, and freeze until firm (about 3 hours).

Serve directly from freezer.

This ice cream is best if eaten within 1 week.

To cook fresh pumpkin, select a medium-sized milk, or eating, pumpkin, not the jack-o'-lantern variety, since it is too stringy. This pumpkin is almost white and looks like a big squash. If in doubt ask the grocer.

Slice pumpkin in half and scoop out the inner pulp and seeds. Place halved pumpkin in large roasting pan with cut side down. Since water is given off as the pumpkin cooks the pan must have a depth of at least 1 inch. If one pan is not big enough for pumpkin halves to lie flat, use two. Bake at 350° about 1 hour or until the pumpkin is tender and pierces easily with a fork. Turn pumpkin halves over and allow to cool.

When pumpkin has cooled, scrape the pulp away from the skin and purée in blender or put through a food mill.

Pumpkin purée may be frozen for later use in a tightly covered container. It will keep about 6 months.

RASPBERRY ICE CREAM

Makes 1 quart of tangy, smooth, colorful ice cream.

2 tsp unflavored gelatin
1/4 cup milk
2 10-oz packages frozen raspberries, thawed
4 egg yolks
2 Tbsp light-brown sugar, with lumps broken up
1 cup heavy cream

Stir 2 tsp gelatin into 1/4 cup cold milk in small metal bowl. Place the bowl in a larger one containing hot water. Set aside until gelatin melts.

Thaw and drain 2 10-oz packages frozen raspberries. Place berries in a small bowl and mash with fork. Set aside.

In medium-sized bowl beat 4 egg yolks until the yolks are thick, light yellow in color, and have increased in volume. Add 2 Tbsp light-brown sugar with lumps broken up and beat until mixture resembles mayonnaise. Stir in melted gelatin, then the mashed berries. Chill mixture in refrigerator for 30 minutes.

Whip 1 cup heavy cream until soft peaks form. Remove mixture from refrigerator and fold in the whipped cream. Scrape into freezer container and freeze until firm (about 4 hours).

Allow ice cream to ripen in refrigerator for 30 minutes before serving.

RUM RAISIN ICE CREAM

Makes 2 quarts of smooth, rich, rum-flavored ice cream.

3/4 cup raisins
1 cup water
1 cup heavy cream
1 cup milk
6 egg yolks
3/4 cup granulated sugar
1-inch piece of vanilla bean
1 1/2 tsp cornstarch
1/4 cup Appleton Special Jamaican rum
2 cups heavy cream
2 Tbsp granulated sugar

In a small saucepan heat 3/4 cup raisins and 1 cup water to boiling. Remove from heat and set aside to cool.

Combine 1 cup heavy cream and 1 cup milk in top of double boiler and heat over simmering water to lukewarm. Set aside.

In a small bowl, using a wire whisk, beat together 6 egg yolks, 3/4 cup sugar, the powder from a 1-inch piece of vanilla bean, and 1 1/2 tsp cornstarch until egg yolks are light yellow in color.

Slowly pour a third of the warm milk and cream into egg yolks, stirring all the while.

Pour egg and milk mixture back into top of double boiler with remaining milk and cream. Cook custard, over simmering water, stirring constantly, until it thickens. Remove from heat and stir to cool.

Drain cooled raisins. Stir raisins and 1/4 cup rum into custard. Place custard in refrigerator to chill.

Whip 2 cups heavy cream until soft peaks form. Add 2 Tbsp sugar and whip a moment longer. Remove chilled custard from refrigerator. Fold whipped cream into custard, distributing raisins evenly throughout.

Place mixture in freezer container, cover tightly, and freeze until frozen around the edges of the container (about 2 hours).

Remove ice cream from freezer, uncover, stir thoroughly to break up frozen pieces and redistribute raisins, leave in original container or scrape into serving dish, cover, and return to freezer for 4 hours or until firm.

Allow ice cream to ripen in refrigerator for 1 hour before serving.

STRAWBERRY ICE CREAM

Makes 1 quart. This will particularly please those who prefer only moderately sweet desserts.

> 1 pint fresh strawberries, washed and hulled
> Juice of ½ lemon
> ½ cup granulated sugar
> 1 pint sour cream
> ¼ cup heavy cream
> ½ tsp salt

Wash and hull strawberries. Squeeze juice of half a lemon. Blend the strawberries in blender with lemon juice and ½ cup sugar until a purée.

In medium-sized bowl combine 1 pint sour cream with ¼ cup heavy cream. Stir in ½ tsp salt. Fold in puréed strawberries.

Leave mixture in the bowl or pour into freezer container. Cover tightly and freeze until firm.

When ice cream has begun to set, a little over 1 hour later, take out of freezer, uncover, stir to break up frozen lumps, cover again, and return to freezer until firm.

Allow ice cream to ripen in refrigerator 1 hour before serving.

STRAWBERRY-PEACH ICE CREAM

Makes 2 quarts of a good, interesting blend, devised after trying a disappointing commercial product.

1 quart strawberries
1/4 cup granulated sugar
2 cups peaches, cut up
1/4 cup granulated sugar
Juice of 1/2 lime
2 cups heavy cream
2 Tbsp Kirschwasser

Wash, hull, and slice 1 quart strawberries into medium-sized bowl. Sprinkle with 1/4 cup sugar, stir, and set aside.

Wash, peel, and cut up enough peaches to measure 2 cups. Pour into medium-sized bowl, sprinkle with 1/4 cup sugar, stir, and set aside beside strawberries to steep at least 1 hour.

Squeeze juice from half a lime and pour into blender. Add strawberries and peaches to blender, reserving 1/3 cup of each to be added later. Blend until fruit is a purée. Pour into large bowl and chill in refrigerator.

Whip 2 cups heavy cream until soft peaks form. Add 2 Tbsp Kirschwasser, and whip a moment longer.

Remove purée from refrigerator and fold in the whipped cream. Cover and freeze 1 1/2 hours.

Take out of freezer, uncover, stir to break up frozen pieces, and beat until smooth. Stir in reserved sliced strawberries and peaches. Pour into freezer container or 2-quart serving mold. Cover and freeze until firm.

Allow ice cream to ripen in refrigerator 1 hour before serving.

STRAWBERRY-RHUBARB ICE CREAM

Makes about 1½ quarts of a tart, refreshing ice cream that lingers wonderfully.

    4 cups rhubarb, cut into 1-inch pieces (1 lb)
    1 pint strawberries, hulled and sliced
    Juice of 1 orange
    Juice of 1 lemon
    ½ cup granulated sugar
    1 cup heavy cream
    ¼ tsp salt

Cut off leaves and small stems from rhubarb stalks. Wash and cut the stalks into 1-inch pieces. Set aside.

Wash, hull, and slice 1 pint strawberries. Set aside.

Squeeze juice from 1 orange and 1 lemon.

Combine rhubarb, strawberries, juice, and ½ cup sugar in 3-quart pot or top of double boiler. Cook over very low heat or simmering water, stirring from time to time, until rhubarb starts to get soft—is easily pierced by fork. Remove from heat immediately and chill in refrigerator or by setting pot in bowl of ice water. If rhubarb is over-cooked it gets very mushy and doesn't taste as good. Don't worry about the strawberries.

In small bowl whip 1 cup heavy cream with ¼ tsp salt until it forms stiff peaks. Remove chilled rhubarb and strawberries from refrigerator and pour into medium-sized bowl. Fold in the whipped cream. Cover tightly and place in freezer for 1 hour.

Remove from freezer, uncover, stir to break up icy pieces, pour into freezer container or a serving dish, cover again, and return to freezer until firm.

Allow ice cream to ripen in refrigerator 2 hours before serving.

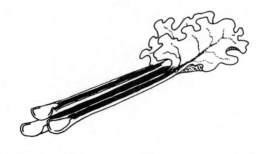

Ice Creams

SWEET POTATO ICE CREAM

Makes 1 quart of an ice cream that will provoke cries of delight or groans depending upon your tasters' feelings about sweet potatoes. Diana prefers to use the orange-fleshed sweet potato (yam) for this recipe.

    1 cup mashed sweet potato or yam
    ½ cup light-brown sugar, with lumps broken up
    2 egg whites
    ½ tsp salt
    1 cup heavy cream
    ¼ cup pumpkin seeds
    ¼ cup sunflower seeds

Peel, boil, and mash 1 (or more) large sweet potato. Stir in ½ cup light-brown sugar with lumps broken up. Set aside to cool.

Beat 2 egg whites until almost stiff. Add ½ tsp salt and beat a moment longer. Fold in the sweet potato mixture.

Whip 1 cup heavy cream until it forms soft peaks. Fold in ¼ cup pumpkin seeds and ¼ cup sunflower seeds. Fold into sweet potato and egg whites.

Cover and freeze the mixture for 1½ hours.

Remove from freezer, uncover, stir to break up frozen pieces and redistribute seeds, scrape into freezer container or serving dish, cover again, and freeze until firm.

Allow ice cream to ripen in refrigerator 2 hours before serving.

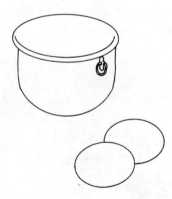

Ice Creams

VANILLA EGGNOG ICE CREAM

Makes 1½ quarts of ice cream, moderately sweet and reminiscent of the holiday season.

1 cup milk
½ cup heavy cream
7 egg yolks
½ cup light-brown sugar, with lumps broken up
½ tsp arrowroot
2-inch piece of vanilla bean
1½ cups heavy cream
½ cup brandy or rum

In top of double boiler heat together over simmering water 1 cup milk and ½ cup heavy cream until hot but not boiling. Set aside.

In large bowl using electric mixer beat together 7 egg yolks, ½ cup brown sugar with lumps broken up, and ½ tsp arrowroot until thick and pale yellow in color.

Cut off a 2-inch piece of vanilla bean, slice in half lengthwise, scrape out vanilla powder and add this to egg yolks and sugar (discard the remaining bean bark). Beat a few moments longer.

In a thin stream pour hot milk into egg yolks and sugar, beating all the while. Pour back into top of double boiler and cook slowly over simmering water, stirring constantly, until custard is thick. Remove from heat and continue to stir for a few moments until custard cools slightly.

Chill custard in refrigerator about 30 minutes.

In medium-sized bowl whip 1½ cups heavy cream until it forms soft peaks. Add ½ cup brandy or rum and whip a few moments longer or until stiff peaks form.

Remove chilled custard from refrigerator and scrape into whipped cream. Fold one into the other.

Cover and place in freezer for 1 hour.

Remove from freezer, uncover, stir to break up frozen pieces, pour into freezer container or serving dish, cover again, and return to freezer until firm.

Allow ice cream to ripen in refrigerator 30 minutes before serving.

WALNUT ICE CREAM

Makes 1 quart of a sweet rum-flavored dessert.

2 egg whites
1/4 tsp cream of tartar
1/2 cup granulated sugar
3/4 cup caramelized walnuts (page 22)
1 Tbsp rum
1 cup heavy cream

In a medium-sized mixing bowl beat 2 egg whites with 1/4 tsp cream of tartar until soft peaks form. Slowly beat in 1/2 cup sugar and continue beating until egg whites are smooth and glossy, hold stiff peaks, and the sugar has completely dissolved.

Pour 3/4 cup caramelized walnuts into blender and blend until pulverized.

Fold walnuts into beaten egg whites. Gently stir in 1 Tbsp rum. Place in refrigerator to cool (about 30 minutes).

Whip 1 cup heavy cream until soft peaks form. Remove cooled egg white mixture from refrigerator and fold in the whipped cream. Scrape mixture into freezer container or serving dish, cover tightly, and freeze for 3 hours. Ice cream remains soft and can be served directly from freezer.

This ice cream keeps for 1 month in a tightly covered container.

WHITE COFFEE VELVET

Makes 1 quart of an unusual coffee ice cream that doesn't look like coffee ice cream—it's white!

2/3 cup condensed milk
2 cups heavy cream
1 cup very strong Italian roast coffee (page 21)

In medium-sized bowl combine 2/3 cup condensed milk and 2 cups heavy cream. Thoroughly chill in refrigerator about 30 to 45 minutes.

Brew 1 cup very strong Italian roast coffee. Refrigerate until cool.

Remove chilled cream from refrigerator and whip until it forms soft peaks. Add the cooled coffee to the whipped cream in a thin stream, whipping all the while. Continue to whip until cream forms stiff peaks.

Fold into a freezer container or a serving dish, cover, and freeze until firm.

Allow ice cream to ripen in refrigerator 30 minutes before serving.

YOGURT ICE CREAM

Makes 1 quart of delicious honey-flavored ice cream that is relatively low in calories.

    2 eggs
    2/3 cup milk
    4 Tbsp honey
    2 8-oz containers plain yogurt
    4 oz nuts (optional)

In top of double boiler beat 2 eggs with wire whisk until frothy. Add 2/3 cup milk and beat until milk and eggs are well combined. Stir in 4 Tbsp honey.

Place top of double boiler over simmering water and cook custard until thickened, stirring constantly. Place custard in refrigerator to cool (about 30 minutes).

Remove cooled custard from refrigerator and stir in 2 8-oz containers plain yogurt and, if you wish, 4 oz of your favorite nuts. Scrape mixture into freezer container, cover tightly, and freeze.

After 1 hour remove ice cream from freezer, uncover, and stir thoroughly to break up frozen pieces. Cover tightly and return to freezer.

After 1 more hour remove ice cream from freezer again, uncover, and stir thoroughly to break up any ice crystals. Leave in original container or scrape into serving dish, cover tightly, and freeze for 2 more hours or until firm.

Allow ice cream to ripen in refrigerator for 30 minutes or until soft enough to serve.

French Parfaits, Mousses, and Soufflés

French Parfaits

A French parfait is very different from an American parfait in that it is simply ice cream made with a special method, while an American parfait is an elaborate frozen dessert consisting of alternate layers of ice cream and sauce.

There are two kinds of French parfaits: one uses uncooked egg yolks as an emulsifier while the other uses gelatin.

To prepare a parfait using an uncooked egg yolk base, combine sugar and water; boil; pour over beaten egg yolks, stirring until mixture is cool; fold in whipped cream; and freeze until firm.

To prepare a gelatin-based parfait, soften gelatin in cold water; boil combined juices or purée and sugar; stir into softened gelatin; chill mixture; whip until thick; fold in whipped cream; and freeze in serving mold or parfait glasses until firm.

French parfaits usually require 30 to 60 minutes in the refrigerator to ripen before serving.

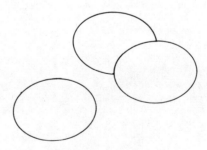

CHOCOLATE FRENCH PARFAIT

Makes 1½ pints. The strong chocolate flavor laces the light texture.

½ cup water
½ cup light-brown sugar
4 egg yolks
3 oz unsweetened chocolate
¼ cup water
1 cup heavy cream

Combine ½ cup water with ½ cup light-brown sugar in a small saucepan. Boil for 5 minutes over moderate heat.

Meanwhile beat 4 egg yolks until thick and light yellow in color. In a thin stream pour hot sugar water into beaten egg yolks, beating all the while. Continue to beat until mixture starts to cool.

In the top of a double boiler, melt 3 oz chocolate with ¼ cup water over simmering water. Don't stir.

When chocolate has melted, vigorously beat chocolate and water together with wire whisk until smooth. Remove from heat and beat in ½ cup egg mixture until smooth. Add ¼ cup more and beat again until smooth. Pour in rest of egg mixture and beat until chocolate and egg are well blended and smooth.

Set aside in refrigerator to cool for 30 minutes.

Whip 1 cup heavy cream until soft peaks form. Remove chocolate mixture from refrigerator and scrape into whipped cream. Fold one into the other. Scrape into freezer container, serving dish, or parfait glasses, cover, and freeze until firm.

Allow parfait to ripen 45 to 60 minutes in refrigerator before serving.

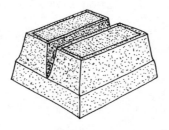

French Parfaits, Mousses, and Soufflés 101

COFFEE FRENCH PARFAIT

Makes 1½ quarts. An exceptionally satisfying way of using coffee.

⅓ cup ground coffee from Italian roast coffee beans, scant
¾ cup light-brown sugar
1 cup water
8 egg yolks
2½ cups heavy cream
1 tsp vanilla extract

Grind enough Italian roast coffee beans to measure a scant ⅓ cup.

In 1½-quart saucepan combine ¾ cup brown sugar with 1 cup water and bring to a boil. Add ground coffee and cook 5 minutes over very low heat. Remove from heat and pour through filter or fine sieve lined with cheesecloth. Set aside.

Beat 8 egg yolks with electric mixer until thick and light yellow in color. In a thin stream pour in hot filtered coffee, beating all the while. Continue to beat until mixture cools.

Place in refrigerator for 30 minutes.

Whip 2½ cups heavy cream with 1 tsp vanilla extract until soft peaks form. Remove cooled coffee mixture from refrigerator and pour into whipped cream. Vigorously fold one mixture into the other, since coffee has a tendency to settle to the bottom. Quickly pour into freezer container, serving dish, or parfait glasses, cover, and freeze until firm.

Allow parfait to ripen in refrigerator 30 to 45 minutes before serving.

GRAPE FRENCH PARFAIT

Makes 1½ pints of a light, delicious dessert—tends to be a favorite.

2 tsp unflavored gelatin
¼ cup cold water
Juice of 1 orange
Juice of ½ lime
¾ cup red grape juice
¼ cup granulated sugar
1 cup heavy cream

In medium-sized bowl sprinkle 2 tsp gelatin over ¼ cup cold water. Stir. Set aside for gelatin to soften.

Squeeze juice from 1 orange and ½ lime. Pour into saucepan with ¾ cup grape juice and ¼ cup granulated sugar. Heat to boiling and boil over moderate heat for 10 minutes. Pour into softened gelatin and stir until gelatin has melted. Set bowl in refrigerator 30 to 45 minutes until mixture cools and thickens.

Whip 1 cup heavy cream until soft peaks form.

Remove thickened juices from refrigerator and beat with electric mixer until stiff peaks form. Mixture should resemble stiffly beaten egg whites. Fold in the whipped cream. Scrape into freezer container, serving dish, or parfait glasses. Cover and freeze until firm.

Allow parfait to ripen in refrigerator 30 to 45 minutes before serving.

VANILLA FRENCH PARFAIT

Makes 1 pint, with a flavor reminiscent of ice cream parlors of long ago.

½ cup water
¼ cup granulated sugar
4 egg yolks
2-inch piece of vanilla bean
1 cup heavy cream

Combine ½ cup water with ¼ cup sugar in a small saucepan. Heat to boiling and boil over moderate heat for 5 minutes or until sugar has completely dissolved.

Meanwhile beat 4 egg yolks and the black vanilla powder scraped from a 2-inch split piece of vanilla bean until thick and light yellow in color.

In a thin stream pour hot sugar water into the eggs, beating all the while. Continue beating until mixture cools.

Place in refrigerator until mixture cools completely (about 30 minutes).

Whip 1 cup heavy cream until soft peaks form. Remove vanilla mixture from refrigerator and pour into whipped cream. Fold one mixture into the other. Scrape into freezer container, serving dish, or parfait glasses, cover, and freeze until firm.

Allow to ripen 45 to 60 minutes in refrigerator before serving.

Mousses

Mousses have a somewhat spongy consistency and can be very light and airy. They are made by mixing whipped cream or whipped cream and beaten egg whites with a not very liquid mixture of other ingredients; then they are frozen until firm. These desserts do not have to be stirred.

Mousses are excellent by themselves but also can be used in parfaits, bombes, baked Alaskas, sodas, and malteds.

These desserts are attractive when served from soufflé dish into sherbet glasses or served directly in sherbet glasses or demi-tasse cups.

BANANA MOUSSE

Makes 1½ pints of a light-brown banana concoction that is spright from the ginger.

    2 ripe bananas
    Juice of ½ lime
    ¼ cup dark-brown sugar, with lumps broken up
    3 egg whites
    ⅛ tsp cream of tartar
    1 Tbsp confectioners' sugar
    2 Tbsp crystallized ginger
    1 cup heavy cream

Break up 2 medium-sized bananas into blender. Squeeze juice from ½ lime and add to banana pieces with ¼ cup brown sugar with lumps broken up. Blend until a purée. Pour into medium-sized bowl and set aside.

Beat 3 egg whites with ⅛ tsp cream of tartar until soft peaks form.

Add 1 Tbsp confectioners' sugar and beat until thick, smooth, and glossy. Set aside in refrigerator.

Finely chop enough crystallized ginger to measure 2 Tbsp.

Whip 1 cup heavy cream until soft peaks form. Fold in the chopped ginger.

Remove beaten egg whites from refrigerator. Fold them into banana purée. Then fold in the whipped cream and ginger. Scrape into freezer container or serving dish, cover, and freeze until firm.

Allow to ripen 15 to 20 minutes in refrigerator before serving.

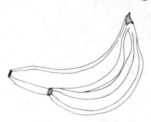

BISCUIT TORTONI

Makes about 1½ pints of a smooth and moderately sweet ice cream based on a recipe created by an Italian, Tortoni, who had one of the earliest ice cream parlors in Paris—in 1798.

6 homemade macaroons (page 106), broken up (about 1 cup)
⅓ cup egg whites
½ cup dark-brown sugar, with lumps broken up
1 cup heavy cream
2 Tbsp brandy

Break up 6 homemade macaroons into shallow roasting pan. Toast in preheated slow oven (250°) about 10 minutes, shaking pan 3 or 4 times. Set aside to cool.

Using electric mixer beat ⅓ cup egg whites and ½ cup dark-brown sugar with lumps broken up until mixture forms stiff peaks and is smooth and glossy. Fold in the toasted macaroons.

Whip 1 cup heavy cream in small bowl until it forms soft peaks. Add 2 Tbsp brandy and whip until stiff peaks form.

Fold whipped cream into beaten egg whites and macaroons. Scrape into freezer container or serving dish, cover, and freeze until firm.

Let the tortoni ripen in the refrigerator for 10 minutes before serving.

MACAROONS

Makes about 2 dozen cookies that are very different from the commercial variety. Six cookies, broken up, equal about 1 cup.

7 oz almond paste
1/2 cup granulated sugar
1/3 cup egg whites
2 Tbsp white flour
1/3 cup confectioners' sugar
1/4 tsp vanilla extract

In medium-sized bowl break up almond paste with your hands and then into finer pieces with pastry blender. Using electric mixer cream in 1/2 cup sugar. Add 1/3 cup egg whites and beat until mixture is a smooth liquid paste (about 10 minutes).

Using small bowl sift together 2 Tbsp flour and 1/3 cup confectioners' sugar. Add this sugar mixture to paste, a tablespoon at a time, beating all the while. Beat in 1/4 tsp vanilla extract.

Using teaspoon, drop thick batter onto well-greased cookie sheet 2 inches apart. Macaroons will spread out.

Cover and let stand from 5 minutes to 24 hours.

Bake in preheated slow oven (275° to 300°) for 45 to 60 minutes or until macaroons have turned light brown. Let cool on sheet about 10 minutes to set. Carefully remove from cookie sheet to cake rack with spatula to finish cooling.

Store in tightly closed tin.

CAFE MOUSSE

Makes a little more than 1 quart with a great coffee flavor—not too strong, not too weak.

1/2 cup water
1/2 cup granulated sugar
1/4 cup fresh coffee ground from Italian roast coffee beans
2 egg whites
1/8 tsp cream of tartar
Pinch of salt
1 tsp confectioners' sugar
1 1/2 cups heavy cream
1 tsp confectioners' sugar
1 tsp vanilla extract

In small saucepan combine 1/2 cup water with 1/2 cup sugar and 1/4 cup freshly ground Italian roast coffee. Heat to boiling and boil for 5 minutes over low heat. Pour through fine sieve lined with cheesecloth into 2-cup measure. Set aside to seep through.

Beat 2 egg whites with 1/8 tsp cream of tartar and a pinch of salt until stiff peaks form. Add 1 tsp confectioners' sugar and beat a moment longer. In a thin stream slowly add coffee, beating all the while. Set aside in refrigerator to cool 30 minutes.

In medium-sized bowl whip 1 1/2 cups heavy cream until soft peaks form. Add 1 tsp confectioners' sugar and 1 tsp vanilla extract; then continue whipping cream until stiff peaks form. Remove coffee and egg whites from refrigerator. Scrape the cooled egg white mixture into whipped cream and fold one mixture into the other. Immediately scrape into freezer container, serving dish, parfait glasses, or demitasse cups, cover, and freeze until firm.

Allow the mousse to ripen 15 minutes in refrigerator before serving.

CANTALOUPE MOUSSE

Makes 1 1/2 quarts of a fruit dessert mildly flavored with cantaloupe.

1 very ripe cantaloupe
Juice of 1/2 lime
Juice of 2 oranges or 1/2 cup orange juice
2 Tbsp granulated sugar
2 egg whites
1 Tbsp confectioners' sugar
1 cup heavy cream

Cut cantaloupe in half, scoop out the seeds, and then scoop out the meat. Put in blender. Squeeze juice from half a lime and 2 oranges and add it plus 2 Tbsp sugar to blender. Blend until puréed. Set aside in refrigerator.

Beat 2 egg whites until soft peaks form. Add 1 Tbsp confectioners' sugar and beat until thick, smooth, and glossy.

Whip 1 cup heavy cream until stiff peaks form.

Remove cantaloupe purée from refrigerator. Pour it into medium-sized bowl. First fold in the beaten egg whites, and then the whipped cream. Pour into freezer container or serving dish and freeze until firm.

Allow to ripen 10 to 20 minutes in refrigerator before serving.

CHOCOLATE MOUSSE

Makes 1 quart of a really superb dessert—light enough to float well in a chocolate soda.

2 oz semi-sweet chocolate
2 oz unsweetened chocolate
1/2 cup water
1/4 cup granulated sugar
3 egg whites
1/4 tsp cream of tartar
1 Tbsp confectioners' sugar
1 1/2 cups heavy cream
1 tsp confectioners' sugar
1/2 tsp vanilla extract

In top of double boiler melt 2 oz semi-sweet chocolate and 2 oz unsweetened chocolate with 1/2 cup water and 1/4 cup sugar over simmering water. Do not stir.

Meanwhile beat 3 egg whites with 1/4 tsp cream of tartar and 1 Tbsp confectioners' sugar until stiff peaks form.

When chocolate has melted, remove from heat, and beat with wire whisk until smooth. Scrape beaten egg whites into chocolate and fold them in fully. Set mixture in refrigerator to cool.

Whip 1 1/2 cups of heavy cream with 1 tsp confectioners' sugar until soft peaks form. Add 1/2 tsp vanilla extract and whip a moment longer. Remove chocolate egg whites from refrigerator and fold them into whipped cream. Immediately scrape into serving dish, freezer container, parfait glasses, or demi-tasse cups, cover, and freeze until firm.

Allow mousse to ripen 2 hours in refrigerator before serving.

COFFEE TORTONI BALLS

Makes 1 1/2 pints of ice cream based on yet another recipe by Tortoni, that Italian dessert wizard.

1/2 cup finely chopped sliced almonds
1/2 cup grated fresh coconut
1/3 cup very strong Italian roast coffee (page 21)

1/3 cup condensed milk
1 cup heavy cream
2 egg whites
1/4 cup dark-brown sugar, with lumps broken up
1 tsp vanilla extract

Preheat oven to 250°.

Finely chop enough sliced almonds to measure 1/2 cup. Combine with 1/2 cup grated fresh coconut in shallow roasting pan. Toast in oven about 10 minutes, shaking pan from time to time so that mixture doesn't burn. Set aside to cool.

Brew 1/3 cup very strong Italian roast coffee. Set aside in refrigerator to cool.

Combine 1/3 cup condensed milk and 1 cup heavy cream. Refrigerate until cold (about 45 minutes).

Beat together 2 egg whites and 1/4 cup brown sugar with lumps broken up until stiff peaks form. Fold 1/2 cup of cooled coconut-nut mixture into beaten egg whites, reserving rest to roll balls of ice cream in. Set aside in refrigerator.

Remove chilled cream mixture and coffee from refrigerator. Whip cream until it forms soft peaks. Then add coffee and whip until cream holds stiff peaks. Stir in 1 tsp vanilla extract.

Remove chilled beaten egg white mixture from refrigerator. Scrape this into cream and then fold until thoroughly mixed.

Cover and freeze in a medium shallow bowl until firm.

To make balls, allow ice cream to ripen in refrigerator about 20 minutes or just long enough so that the ice cream can be scooped out.

Line cookie sheet or shallow roasting pan with waxed paper. Put in freezer.

Remove bowl from refrigerator. Using ice cream scoop or large spoon, scoop out ball of ice cream, quickly form it with your hands, roll in remaining toasted coconut and nuts, and immediately place on lined pan in freezer to firm. Don't wait until all balls are formed but freeze as you go along.

Balls will freeze up again in about 30 minutes. When ready to serve, put the balls quickly into individual sherbet cups or in a cluster in large bowl.

If storing for any length of time balls must be covered in the freezer or the ice cream will crystallize. Ripen in refrigerator 20 minutes before serving.

KIWI MOUSSE

Makes 1½ pints of a bittersweet frozen delight. Kiwis, or "Chinese gooseberries," are a novel, newly available fruit.

1 cup kiwis, cut up (about 3 kiwis)
½ tsp lime juice
2 Tbsp light-brown sugar with lumps broken up
2 egg whites
2 Tbsp confectioners' sugar
1 cup heavy cream
2 Tbsp confectioners' sugar

Wash, peel, and cut into small pieces enough kiwis to measure 1 cup. Put through food mill into small bowl. If little black seeds have gone through mill also, press purée through a fine sieve into medium-sized bowl.

Squeeze enough lime juice to make ½ tsp and add it plus 2 Tbsp light-brown sugar with lumps broken up to the purée. Stir and set aside in refrigerator.

Beat 2 egg whites until soft peaks form. Add 2 Tbsp confectioners' sugar and beat until stiff peaks form and egg whites are smooth and glossy.

Whip 1 cup heavy cream with 2 Tbsp confectioners' sugar until stiff peaks form.

Remove chilled kiwi purée from refrigerator. Gently fold in first the beaten egg whites and then the whipped cream.

Carefully scrape mixture into freezer container, serving dish, or sherbet glasses. Cover and freeze until firm.

Allow to ripen in refrigerator 20 to 30 minutes before serving.

MANGO MOUSSE

Makes 1½ pints of a pale orange mousse. A nice, light dessert after a heavy meal.

1 very ripe mango
3 egg yolks
2 Tbsp granulated sugar
½ cup heavy cream

Peel and chop 1 mango. Place pieces in blender and blend to produce a fairly smooth purée. Set aside.

In a medium-sized bowl beat 3 egg yolks until very thick and volume has increased. This takes at least 5 minutes. Slowly beat in 2 Tbsp sugar and continue beating until ribbons falling from lifted beaters remain visible on the surface.

Fold in the mango purée.

Whip ½ cup heavy cream until soft peaks form.

Fold the whipped cream into the mango mixture. Scrape into individual serving dishes or one large dish, cover tightly, and freeze until firm (about 3 hours).

Allow mousse to ripen in refrigerator for 20 minutes before serving.

MOCHA MOUSSE

Makes 1 to 1½ pints of a dessert that is a must after a French or Italian meal.

½ cup very strong coffee (page 21)
2 oz semi-sweet chocolate
2 oz unsweetened chocolate
⅓ cup egg whites
4 Tbsp granulated sugar
1 cup heavy cream
2 Tbsp confectioners' sugar

Brew half a cup very strong coffee. Pour into top of double boiler and heat, over simmering water, with 2 oz semi-sweet chocolate and 2 oz unsweetened chocolate until chocolate has melted. Do not stir. Remove from heat. Just before adding the egg whites whip with wire whisk until chocolate and coffee blend together to form a smooth paste.

Using electric mixer beat ⅓ cup egg whites until soft peaks form. Beat in 4 Tbsp sugar, a tablespoon at a time. Continue to beat until egg whites hold stiff peaks and are smooth and glossy.

Add beaten egg whites to warm chocolate mixture, ½ cup at a time, and beat mixture with wire whisk until smooth. Set aside in refrigerator to cool for 15 minutes.

Whip 1 cup heavy cream until soft peaks form. Add 2 Tbsp confectioners' sugar and whip until stiff peaks form. Remove cooled mocha-chocolate mixture from refrigerator and fold in the whipped cream.

Scrape into freezer container or serving dish, cover, and freeze until firm (about 4 hours).

Allow mousse to ripen in refrigerator 30 to 45 minutes before serving.

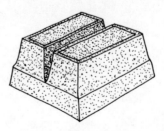

NUTTY COGNAC MOUSSE

6 portions or 1½ pints of a very sophisticated "eggnog" with an enhanced Cognac flavor.

6 egg yolks
½ cup light-brown sugar, with lumps broken up
½ cup Cognac
½ cup walnuts, broken up
6 egg whites
½ cup heavy cream

In medium-sized bowl with electric mixer beat together 6 egg yolks and ½ cup brown sugar, with lumps broken up, until thick and light in color.

Scrape mixture into top of double boiler and cook over simmering water, stirring constantly, until mixture is very thick and custardy. Remove from heat and continue to stir until custard cools slightly. Stir in ½ cup Cognac.

Chill the mixture in refrigerator (about 30 minutes).

Break up enough walnuts to measure ½ cup and set aside.

In medium-sized bowl beat 6 egg whites until stiff peaks form. Set aside in refrigerator.

In small bowl whip ½ cup heavy cream until it forms soft peaks. Fold in nuts.

Remove chilled custard and egg whites from refrigerator. Fold egg whites into custard. Fold in the whipped cream with nuts. Pour into parfait glasses or serving dish, cover, and freeze until firm (about 3 hours).

Let mousse ripen in refrigerator 10 minutes before serving.

PEACH MOUSSE

Makes 1 quart of a refreshing, light dessert welcome on a summer afternoon.

2 cups fresh peaches, cut up
Juice of ½ orange
3 Tbsp confectioners' sugar
⅓ cup egg whites
1 Tbsp confectioners' sugar
½ cup heavy cream

Wash, peel, and cut up enough peaches to measure 2 cups. Pour into medium-sized bowl. Squeeze juice from half an orange. Add orange juice and 3 Tbsp confectioners' sugar to peaches. Stir until fruit is well covered with sugar and juice. Set aside in refrigerator at least 1 hour.

Using medium-sized bowl beat ⅓ cup egg whites until soft peaks form. Add 1 Tbsp confectioners' sugar and beat until stiff, smooth, and glossy. Set aside in refrigerator.

Whip ½ cup heavy cream until stiff peaks form. Set aside in refrigerator.

Remove sugared peaches from refrigerator. Pour into blender and blend until puréed.

Take beaten egg whites and whipped cream out of refrigerator. Pour peach purée into chilled egg whites and fold one into the other. Then gently fold whipped cream into peach mixture. Scrape into freezer container or serving dish, cover, and freeze until firm (about 4 hours).

Allow mousse to ripen in refrigerator 15 minutes before serving.

PLUM MOUSSE

Makes 1 quart. Plum Mousse is plum good.

1 to 1½ cups California plums, cut up
¼ cup light-brown sugar, with lumps broken up
2 egg whites
Pinch of cream of tartar
1 Tbsp confectioners' sugar
½ cup heavy cream

Wash, peel, and cut into chunks enough plums to measure 1 to 1½ cups. Pour into medium-sized bowl, sprinkle in ¼ cup brown sugar with lumps broken up and stir until fruit is well coated. Set aside in refrigerator at least 1 hour.

Beat 2 egg whites with a pinch of cream of tartar until soft peaks form. Add 1 Tbsp confectioners' sugar and beat until thick, smooth, and glossy. Set aside in refrigerator.

Whip ½ cup heavy cream until stiff peaks form. Set aside in refrigerator.

Take sugared plums from refrigerator, pour into blender and blend until puréed. Pour back into medium-sized bowl. Remove beaten egg whites and whipped cream from refrigerator. First fold egg whites into the plum purée, then the whipped cream. Scrape mixture into freezer container or serving dish, cover, and freeze until firm.

Allow mousse to ripen in refrigerator 1 hour before serving.

RASPBERRY MOUSSE

Makes 1½ pints of a light, tart dessert, refreshing after a heavy meal. Oscar, Diana's husband, likes it best of all the ice creams.

2 cups ripe raspberries (1 pint)
¼ cup granulated sugar
⅓ cup egg whites
⅛ tsp salt
1 tsp grated lemon rind
1 cup heavy cream

Gently wash 2 cups raspberries. Drain and pour into medium-sized bowl. Add ¼ cup sugar and stir until berries are well covered. Set aside in refrigerator 1 hour so that sugar can penetrate berries.

Beat ⅓ cup egg whites with ⅛ tsp salt until stiff peaks form. Set aside in refrigerator.

Grate 1 tsp rind from lemon. Set aside.

Whip 1 cup heavy cream until soft peaks form and stir in lemon rind. Remove beaten egg whites from refrigerator and fold into whipped cream. Return to refrigerator while preparing raspberries.

Remove sugared raspberries from refrigerator and press through a fine sieve or put through a food mill into medium-sized bowl. A few crushed stones will come through mill. Should these disturb you, press purée through a fine sieve lined with cheesecloth.

Remove egg white mixture from refrigerator and scrape into raspberry purée. Fold one into the other. Gently scrape into freezer container or serving dish, cover, and freeze until firm.

Allow mousse to ripen 20 to 30 minutes in refrigerator before serving.

RHUBARB MOUSSE

Makes just under 1 quart of a tart dessert with a definite presence of rhubarb.

2 to 2½ cups rhubarb, cut into 1-inch chunks
¼ cup water
¼ cup granulated sugar
1 Tbsp lime juice
2 egg whites
1 Tbsp confectioners' sugar
1 cup heavy cream
1 Tbsp confectioners' sugar
1 Tbsp Kirschwasser

Cut off and discard leaves and small stems from rhubarb stalks. Wash and cut stalks into 1-inch chunks.

Combine rhubarb with ¼ cup water and ¼ cup sugar in a heavy pot. Cook over low heat until rhubarb is tender and starts to fall apart. Immediately remove from heat and chill in refrigerator.

Squeeze enough lime juice to measure 1 Tbsp. When rhubarb has chilled, remove from refrigerator and stir in the lime juice. Return to refrigerator while preparing egg whites and cream.

Beat 2 egg whites until soft peaks form. Add 1 Tbsp confectioners' sugar and beat until egg whites are smooth and glossy. Set aside.

Whip 1 cup heavy cream until soft peaks form. Add 1 Tbsp confectioners' sugar and 1 Tbsp Kirschwasser. Whip cream a moment longer.

Remove rhubarb from refrigerator and pour into medium-sized bowl. First fold in the beaten egg whites, then the whipped cream.

Leave in bowl or scrape into freezer container or serving dish. Cover tightly and freeze until firm.

Allow mousse to ripen in refrigerator 1 hour before serving.

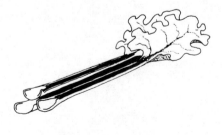

VANILLA MOUSSE

Makes 1 quart of a mild-flavored, very light-textured, semi-sweet dessert.

1/4 cup granulated sugar
1/2 cup water
1-inch piece of vanilla bean
3 egg yolks
1/4 tsp cornstarch
2 egg whites
1 tsp confectioners' sugar
1 1/2 cups heavy cream

Combine 1/4 cup sugar and 1/2 cup water in small saucepan. Heat to boiling and boil for 5 minutes over moderate heat.

Cut off a 1-inch piece of vanilla bean. Slice in half lengthwise, scrape out the black vanilla powder, and add to 3 egg yolks and 1/4 tsp cornstarch in medium-sized bowl. Beat with electric mixer or wire whisk until light yellow.

In a thin stream pour hot sugar water into egg yolks, beating all the while. Pour mixture into top of double boiler and cook over simmering water, stirring constantly, until custard is thick (about 20 minutes). Remove from heat and continue to stir until custard cools slightly. Set aside.

Beat 2 egg whites with 1 tsp confectioners' sugar until stiff peaks form and mixture is smooth and glossy.

Whip 1 1/2 cups heavy cream until stiff peaks form. First fold beaten egg whites into custard, then the whipped cream.

Scrape mixture into freezer container, serving dish, parfait glasses, or demi-tasse cups, cover, and freeze until firm (3 to 4 hours).

Dessert may be served directly from freezer if used within 3- to 4-hour period. Otherwise, it will be necessary to ripen mousse in refrigerator 20 to 30 minutes.

WILD BLACKBERRY MOUSSE

Makes 1 quart of a mildly tart dessert that more than compensates for the pricked fingers one suffers in gathering the berries. If you substitute cultivated blackberries you may want to reduce the sugar, since they are sweeter.

1 cup or more wild blackberries
1/4 cup granulated sugar
4 egg whites
1 Tbsp confectioners' sugar
1 cup heavy cream
1 Tbsp blackberry brandy (optional)
1/4 tsp lime juice

Carefully and gently wash 1 cup or more blackberries. Drain and pour into medium-sized bowl. Sprinkle 1/4 cup sugar over the berries and gently stir with fork until they are well covered. Set aside in refrigerator at least 1 hour.

Beat 4 egg whites until soft peaks form. Add 1 Tbsp confectioners' sugar and beat egg whites until stiff peaks form and mixture is smooth and glossy. Set aside in refrigerator.

Whip 1 cup heavy cream until soft peaks form. If you wish to use blackberry brandy, add 1 Tbsp and whip a moment longer. Set aside in refrigerator.

Remove sugared blackberries from refrigerator and press through a fine sieve or put through a food mill into another medium-sized bowl. A few crushed stones will come through food mill; should these disturb you, press purée through a fine sieve lined with cheesecloth. Squeeze enough lime juice to measure 1/4 tsp and add to blackberry purée.

Remove beaten egg whites and heavy cream from refrigerator. First fold the egg whites into the blackberry purée, then the whipped cream. Scrape into freezer container or serving dish, cover, and freeze until firm (about 3 hours).

If mousse is frozen longer, allow to ripen in refrigerator 30 to 45 minutes before serving.

Soufflés

The desserts in this section are extremely smooth and sweet. The texture is very light and the taste very rich; a large scoop is an ample serving. These desserts are among the favorites of Nancy's friends. Soufflés incorporate both beaten egg whites and whipped cream into an egg yolk base. The soufflé mixture is poured into a soufflé dish, with or without a collar.

Use heavy-duty aluminum foil to make a collar. Tear off a piece 12 inches wide and long enough to encircle soufflé dish with a couple of inches to spare. Fold foil in half twice ending with a piece of foil 3 inches wide and about 2 inches longer than the circumference of the dish. Attach collar to dish with sealing or masking tape. One inch of foil goes below the rim while the rest extends above, holding the soufflé in place.

Since the following recipes were written with the soufflé coming only to the top of the dish, to achieve a risen effect reduce the size of the container by 2 cups and attach collar.

To make soufflés we recommend using an electric mixer or hand-held electric beater. The smooth texture comes from properly beaten egg yolks, which should be at room temperature. To beat, place in medium-sized or smaller bowl of electric mixer. At highest speed beat

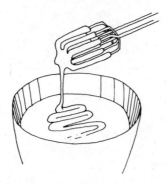

until yolks lighten in color and increase in volume. With beaters going still at high speed, add sugar in a slow stream. Beat yolks and sugar until mixture becomes very pale in color, and very thick and sticky. Ribbons trailing from raised beaters will remain visible on surface of mixture. Beating takes 5 minutes or longer. Underbeating will not give proper texture. Taste the mixture. If there are any grains of sugar, continue beating until sugar has completely dissolved.

Beat the egg whites, which should be at room temperature, until stiff peaks form. Taste a sample. If there are undissolved grains of sugar, continue beating until sugar has completely dissolved.

Beat heavy cream until soft peaks form.

Fold beaten egg whites into the egg yolks. Then fold in whipped cream. Scrape into soufflé dish with or without collar, and freeze until firm.

Another way to make soufflés is to cook a custard base, then fold in beaten egg whites and whipped cream.

Prepare custard base according to directions for cooking custard (see page 24). The egg yolks need be beaten only until they lighten in color, since the sugar will dissolve in the cooking. Place custard in refrigerator to cool while preparing other ingredients.

Beat egg whites according to preceding directions.

Whip heavy cream according to preceding directions.

Remove custard from refrigerator; it doesn't have to be very cold.

Fold the egg whites into the custard, then fold in whipped cream. Scrape into soufflé dish with or without collar and freeze until firm.

If you don't intend to serve the soufflé immediately, cover tightly after it is firmly frozen.

Remove collar, if used, and serve directly from the freezer, unless otherwise indicated in recipe.

APPLEJACK SOUFFLÉ

Makes 1½ quarts or serves 8. Light apple-flavored dessert laced with applejack, a distilled liquor made from fermented apples.

½ cup milk
2 egg yolks
3 Tbsp light-brown sugar, with lumps broken up
½ tsp cornstarch
6 Tbsp applejack
1½ cups applesauce
¾ tsp grated lemon rind
2 Tbsp butter
½ tsp cinnamon
3 egg whites
¼ tsp cream of tartar
3 Tbsp granulated sugar
¾ cup heavy cream

In top of double boiler heat ½ cup milk to lukewarm over simmering water.

While the milk is warming beat together with a wire whisk 2 egg yolks, 3 Tbsp light-brown sugar with lumps broken up, and ½ tsp cornstarch until yolks are light yellow in color.

Slowly pour warm milk into egg yolks, stirring all the while.

Scrape eggs and milk back into the top of double boiler and cook over simmering water until mixture thickens, stirring constantly. Remove from heat and continue to stir until custard cools slightly.

Stir in 6 Tbsp applejack and place custard in refrigerator to chill.

In a small saucepan, combine 1½ cups applesauce with ¾ tsp grated lemon rind, 2 Tbsp butter, and ½ tsp cinnamon. Simmer over medium heat until applesauce thickens. Chill applesauce in refrigerator.

Beat 3 egg whites with ¼ tsp cream of tartar until soft peaks form. Slowly beat in 3 Tbsp sugar and continue beating until the whites are smooth and glossy and hold very stiff peaks. Set aside.

Whip ¾ cup heavy cream until soft peaks form.

Remove custard and applesauce from refrigerator. Stir the applesauce mixture into custard. Fold in beaten egg whites, then the whipped cream.

Scrape mixture into a 6-cup soufflé dish and freeze for 3 hours or until firm.

Allow soufflé to ripen in refrigerator for 20 minutes before serving.

If soufflé is to be stored, cover tightly after firmly frozen. Soufflé will keep for 1 week.

CHOCOLATE SOUFFLÉ

Makes 2 quarts and serves 8. Bittersweet dessert with a hint of rum. This smooth dessert is a chocolate lover's delight.

4 oz semi-sweet chocolate
6 egg yolks
¼ cup granulated sugar
6 egg whites
¼ tsp cream of tartar
6 Tbsp granulated sugar
¼ cup Rumona, a Jamaican rum liqueur
1 cup heavy cream

Place 4 oz semi-sweet chocolate in a small saucepan. Melt chocolate on "warm" burner of an electric stove or place pan in a large bowl filled with very hot water.

Beat 6 egg yolks at high speed with an electric mixer for 5 minutes, or until yolks are very thick and pale yellow in color. While mixer is going at high speed, slowly pour in ¼ cup sugar; continue beating until ribbons trailing from lifted beaters remain visible on the surface. The sugar should be completely dissolved.

Stir in melted chocolate and continue to stir until chocolate is uniformly combined. Set aside.

Beat 6 egg whites with ¼ tsp cream of tartar until soft peaks form. Slowly beat in 6 Tbsp sugar and continue beating until smooth and glossy and very stiff peaks form. Add ¼ cup Rumona liqueur and beat a few moments longer. Set aside.

Whip 1 cup heavy cream until soft peaks form. Set aside.

Fold beaten egg whites into egg yolks. Then fold in the whipped cream.

Scrape mixture into an 8-cup soufflé dish and freeze for 5 hours or until firm. It can be served directly from the freezer.

If soufflé is to be stored, cover tightly after firmly frozen. It will keep for 2 weeks.

BANANA SOUFFLÉ

Makes 1½ quarts or serves 8. A delightful blend of Rumona, a Jamaican rum liqueur, and ripe bananas.

½ cup milk
2 egg yolks
3 Tbsp light-brown sugar, with lumps broken up
½ tsp cornstarch
6 Tbsp Rumona liqueur
1½ cups overripe bananas, mashed
2 Tbsp orange marmalade
3 egg whites
3 Tbsp granulated sugar
¾ cup heavy cream

In top of double boiler heat ½ cup milk to lukewarm over simmering water.

While milk is warming beat together 2 egg yolks, 3 Tbsp light-brown sugar with lumps broken up, and ½ tsp cornstarch until light in color.

Slowly pour warm milk into egg yolks, stirring all the while.

Scrape eggs and milk back into top of double boiler and cook over simmering water until mixture thickens, stirring constantly. Remove from heat and stir to cool.

Stir in 6 Tbsp Rumona liqueur and place custard in refrigerator to chill.

Mash 1½ cups bananas with 2 Tbsp orange marmalade. Set aside.

Beat 3 egg whites until soft peaks form. Slowly beat in 3 Tbsp sugar and continue beating until whites are smooth and glossy with very stiff peaks. Set aside.

Whip ¾ cup heavy cream until soft peaks form.

Remove custard from refrigerator. Stir in mashed bananas. Fold in beaten egg whites, then the whipped cream.

Scrape into 6-cup soufflé dish and freeze for 4 hours or until firm.

Before serving allow soufflé to ripen in refrigerator for 20 minutes.

If soufflé is to be stored, cover tightly after firmly frozen. Soufflé will keep for 1 week.

GRAND MARNIER SOUFFLÉ

Makes 2 quarts and serves 8. A very mild-flavored soufflé with a hint of orange liqueur.

3/4 cup milk
3 egg yolks
1/2 cup granulated sugar
3/4 tsp cornstarch
1 1/2 Tbsp grated orange rind
1/2 cup orange juice
3 Tbsp Grand Marnier
6 egg whites
1/4 tsp cream of tartar
6 Tbsp granulated sugar
1 1/2 cups heavy cream

In top of double boiler heat 3/4 cup milk to lukewarm over simmering water.

While the milk is warming beat together in medium-sized bowl with a wire whisk 3 egg yolks, 1/2 cup sugar, and 3/4 tsp cornstarch until egg yolks are light in color.

Slowly pour warm milk into egg yolks, stirring all the while.

Scrape the eggs and milk back into top of double boiler and cook over simmering water until the custard thickens, stirring constantly. Remove from heat and stir to cool.

Place custard in refrigerator to chill.

Grate enough orange rind to measure 1 1/2 Tbsp. Squeeze enough orange juice to measure 1/2 cup. Combine orange rind, orange juice, and 3 Tbsp Grand Marnier. Place in refrigerator to chill.

Beat 6 egg whites with 1/4 tsp cream of tartar until the whites hold soft peaks. Slowly beat in 6 Tbsp granulated sugar and continue beating until the whites are smooth and glossy and hold very stiff peaks. Set aside.

Whip 1 1/2 cups heavy cream until soft peaks form.

Remove custard and orange juice mixture from refrigerator. Stir juice into custard. Fold in beaten egg whites, then the whipped cream.

Scrape mixture into 8-cup soufflé dish and freeze for 4 hours or until firm. Serve directly from freezer.

If soufflé is to be stored, cover tightly after firmly frozen. It will keep for 1 week.

LEMON SOUFFLÉ

Makes 2 quarts and serves 8. Sweet, tangy dessert with a distinct lemon flavor.

> 9 egg yolks
> 1 cup granulated sugar
> 2 tsp grated lemon rind
> ½ cup lemon juice
> 4 egg whites
> 4 Tbsp granulated sugar
> ½ cup heavy cream

Beat 9 egg yolks at high speed, using an electric mixer, for 5 minutes or until yolks are very thick and increased in volume. With mixer still on high, slowly pour in 1 cup sugar and continue beating until mixture is very thick, and ribbons trailing from lifted beaters remain visible on the surface. The sugar should be completely dissolved.

Grate enough lemon rind to measure 2 tsp and squeeze enough lemon juice to measure ½ cup.

Stir lemon rind and lemon juice into beaten egg yolks and set aside.

In a large bowl beat 4 egg whites until soft peaks form. Slowly beat in 4 Tbsp sugar and continue beating until whites are smooth and glossy and hold very stiff peaks. Set aside.

Whip ½ cup heavy cream until soft peaks form. Set aside.

Fold beaten egg whites into beaten egg yolks and then fold in the heavy cream.

Scrape mixture into 8-cup soufflé dish and freeze until firm (about 4 hours). Serve directly from freezer.

If soufflé is to be stored, cover tightly after firmly frozen. It will keep for 2 weeks.

LIQUEUR SOUFFLÉ

Makes 6 servings. A very smooth, rich dessert flavored with your favorite liqueur.

2 egg whites
1/4 tsp cream of tartar
1/4 cup granulated sugar
4 egg yolks
2 Tbsp granulated sugar
1/2 cup heavy cream
2 Tbsp or more to taste of your favorite liqueur

Beat 2 egg whites with 1/4 tsp cream of tartar until they hold soft peaks. Slowly beat in 1/4 cup sugar and continue beating until mixture is smooth and glossy and very stiff peaks form. Set aside.

In a separate bowl, using an electric mixer, beat 4 egg yolks at high speed for 5 minutes or until yolks are very thick and increased in volume. At high speed slowly add 2 Tbsp sugar and continue beating until mixture is very thick and ribbons trailing from lifted beaters remain visible on the surface. The sugar should have completely dissolved. Set aside.

In another bowl whip 1/2 cup heavy cream until soft peaks form.

Fold beaten whites into beaten yolks. Stir in 2 Tbsp or more to taste of your favorite liqueur. Fold in the whipped cream.

Scrape soufflé into 6 individual serving dishes and freeze for 3 hours or until firm. Serve directly from the freezer.

If soufflé is to be stored, cover tightly after firmly frozen. It will keep for 1 week.

MOCHA SOUFFLÉ

Makes a little bit more than 1½ quarts (or serves 8) of a dessert with a rich coffee flavor.

   ½ cup extra strong coffee (page 21)
   2 oz semi-sweet chocolate
   6 egg yolks
   ½ cup granulated sugar
   3 egg whites
   5 Tbsp granulated sugar
   ½ cup heavy cream

Brew ½ cup extra strong coffee.

In a small metal bowl combine 2 oz semi-sweet chocolate with the coffee and place small bowl in large bowl containing very hot water to melt chocolate. Set aside.

Beat 6 egg yolks at high speed with electric mixer for about 5 minutes or until yolks are thick, pale yellow in color, and volume has increased. While mixer is going at high speed slowly pour in ½ cup sugar and continue beating until mixture is very thick and ribbons trailing from lifted beaters remain visible on the surface. The sugar should have completely dissolved.

Stir the melted chocolate and coffee until smooth. Fold into beaten egg yolks.

In a separate bowl beat 3 egg whites until soft peaks form. Slowly beat in 5 Tbsp sugar and continue beating until the whites are smooth and glossy and hold very stiff peaks. Set aside.

Whip ½ cup heavy cream until soft peaks form. Set aside.

Fold beaten egg whites into mocha mixture, and then fold in the whipped cream.

Scrape mixture into 8-cup soufflé dish and freeze until firm (about 4 hours). Serve directly from freezer.

If soufflé is to be stored, cover tightly after firmly frozen. It will keep for 1 week.

VANILLA SOUFFLÉ

Makes 1½ quarts of a soufflé good by itself or in combination with a fruit sherbet and a fruit sauce.

3 egg whites
¼ tsp cream of tartar
¼ cup granulated sugar
4 egg yolks
2 Tbsp granulated sugar
1 cup heavy cream
1 Tbsp vanilla extract

Beat 3 egg whites with ¼ tsp cream of tartar until they hold soft peaks. Slowly beat in ¼ cup sugar and continue beating until smooth and glossy. Set aside.

Beat 4 egg yolks at high speed for about 5 minutes or until very thick and increased in volume. With mixer still on high speed, slowly add 2 Tbsp sugar and continue beating until mixture is very thick and ribbons trailing from lifted beaters remain visible on the surface. The sugar should have completely dissolved.

Fold beaten whites into beaten yolks and set aside.

Whip 1 cup heavy cream and stir in 1 Tbsp vanilla extract.

Fold whipped cream into egg mixture.

Scrape mixture into 6-cup soufflé dish and freeze for 5 hours or until firm. Serve directly from freezer.

If soufflé is not to be used immediately, cover tightly after firmly frozen. It will keep 2 weeks.

Note: If soufflé is to be used as a layer with sherbet, leave in bowl, cover tightly, and place in freezer until partially frozen. Use as specified.

Sherbets
and Milk Sherbets

Sherbet is a light frozen dessert, much less rich than ice cream, and it's especially good in the summer.

These sherbets are good desserts for children because they are not excessively rich and contain nutritive ingredients. And for the diet-conscious, many sherbets are encouragingly low in calories.

There are two basic types of sherbet: those made with a milk and egg white base are generally called "milk sherbet," while those made with an egg white base alone are called "sherbet."

Unless specified in the recipe, sherbets should be served directly from the freezer.

APRICOT SHERBET

Makes 1 quart of a sherbet with an intense apricot flavor.

3/4 cup boiling water
12 dried apricots
3 Tbsp granulated sugar
A few drops almond extract
2 egg whites

In a small saucepan bring 3/4 cup water to a boil. Remove from heat and put in 12 dried apricots. Return to heat and simmer about 15 minutes over low heat until apricots are tender. Stir in 3 Tbsp sugar. Pour entire contents of saucepan into blender and blend at high speed until mixture is smooth. Add a few drops almond extract and blend a moment longer. Set aside.

Beat 2 egg whites until they hold soft peaks. Pour in apricot purée and fold it into the egg whites.

Leave in original container or pour into freezer container, cover tightly, and place in freezer for 1 hour, or until mixture is partially frozen around the edges.

Remove from freezer, uncover, stir to break up large pieces, and beat until sherbet lightens in color and increases in volume. Cover again and return to freezer. Repeat process 1 hour later. Scrape into freezer container or serving dish, cover, and freeze until firm (about 4 hours).

Serve directly from freezer.

BLUEBERRY-BRANDY SHERBET

Makes 1 quart of swirls of purple cow milk among fluffy clouds.

1 15-oz can blueberries in heavy syrup
Juice of ½ lemon
2 egg whites
2 Tbsp Turbinado sugar
½ cup heavy cream
2 Tbsp brandy
1 Tbsp Turbinado sugar

Drain the blueberries. Reserve liquid for eating with waffles or pancakes or for other use.

Squeeze juice of half a lemon and pour into blender with drained blueberries. Blend a few moments until puréed. Set aside.

In medium-sized bowl using electric mixer beat 2 egg whites until stiff peaks form. Add 2 Tbsp Turbinado sugar and beat until smooth and glossy. Pour in puréed blueberries and quickly fold them into egg whites. Cover bowl and freeze until mixture is frozen to a stiff mush (about 2 hours).

Remove from freezer, uncover, and beat at high speed until sherbet increases in volume and becomes very fluffy and lighter in color. Cover again and return to freezer for 2 hours.

In small container whip ½ cup heavy cream until it starts to hold soft peaks. Add 2 Tbsp brandy and 1 Tbsp Turbinado sugar. Whip a few moments longer and set aside in refrigerator.

Remove sherbet from freezer, uncover, and beat as before. Remove whipped cream from refrigerator and quickly fold into sherbet until marbled effect is observed.

Leave sherbet in original container or pour into serving dish, and freeze until firm (about 3 hours).

Before serving, allow sherbet to ripen in refrigerator for 10 minutes.

BANANA SHERBET

Makes 1 pint of heavy, creamy sherbet with a strong banana flavor.

    2 egg whites
    ¼ cup raw sugar
    3 overripe bananas
    2 tsp lemon juice
    1 Tbsp rum
    ½ cup heavy cream

In a medium-sized bowl beat 2 egg whites until soft peaks are formed. Slowly beat in ¼ cup raw sugar and continue beating until smooth and glossy and whites hold stiff peaks.

In a small bowl mash 3 overripe bananas. Squeeze enough lemon juice to measure 2 tsp and stir the juice and 1 Tbsp rum into bananas.

Fold banana mixture into beaten egg whites. Cover tightly, and place bowl in freezer until partially frozen around the edges.

Whip ½ cup heavy cream until soft peaks form. Remove sherbet from freezer, uncover, stir thoroughly to break up frozen pieces, and fold in the whipped cream. Scrape into freezer container or serving dish, cover again, and freeze for 3 hours or until firm.

Serve directly from freezer.

CANDIED GINGER SHERBET

Makes 1 quart of a spicy, sweet sherbet that will tickle the palate of the most sated epicure.

    1 tsp finely grated candied ginger
    2 egg whites
    6 Tbsp granulated sugar
    ¼ cup pineapple juice

Finely grate 1 tsp candied ginger.

Beat 2 egg whites until soft peaks are formed. Gradually beat in 6 Tbsp sugar and the grated candied ginger. Continue beating until egg whites are smooth and glossy and hold stiff peaks. Quickly stir in ¼ cup pineapple juice. Leave sherbet in bowl or scrape into freezer container, cover tightly, and place in freezer until partially frozen around the edges (about 1 hour).

Remove from freezer, uncover, and beat at high speed until sherbet is smooth and glossy. Scrape into freezer container or serving dish and freeze until firm (about 3 hours). This sherbet remains soft and can be served directly from the freezer.

This sherbet will keep in a tightly covered container for 1 month.

CHOCOLATE MILK SHERBET

Makes 1 quart of a light sherbet, a favorite of Nancy's children.

3 oz semi-sweet chocolate
1½ cups milk
¼ cup granulated sugar
2 egg whites
⅛ tsp cream of tartar
¼ cup granulated sugar

Place 3 oz of semi-sweet chocolate in top of double boiler and set over simmering water to melt. Add ½ cup milk to melted chocolate and stir until chocolate and milk are well combined. Continue heating so that chocolate does not form lumps. Add the other cup of milk and ¼ cup sugar and stir until mixture is smooth, the chocolate is well combined, and the sugar has dissolved. Remove from heat and place in freezer until mixture has started to freeze around the edges (about 1 hour).

Using medium-sized bowl beat 2 egg whites with ⅛ tsp cream of tartar until soft peaks form. Slowly beat in ¼ cup sugar and continue beating until whites are smooth and glossy and sugar has dissolved.

Remove chocolate milk from freezer, uncover, stir thoroughly to break up frozen pieces. Fold chocolate milk into beaten egg whites.

Scrape mixture into freezer container or serving dish, cover tightly, and place in freezer for 4 hours or until firm. Serve directly from freezer.

CRANBERRY SHERBET

Makes 2 quarts of a tart, light sherbet, pink and fluffy.

    2 cups fresh cranberries
    1/2 cup water
    2 Tbsp fresh orange juice
    1/2 cup granulated sugar
    2 egg whites
    1/2 cup granulated sugar

Place 2 cups cranberries and 1/2 cup water in small saucepan. Cook cranberries over medium heat for 5 minutes until berries pop open. Set aside to cool.

When berries are cool, force them through a sieve or food mill to remove skins. Squeeze enough orange juice to measure 2 Tbsp, then add it plus 1/2 cup sugar to cranberry purée. Stir to dissolve sugar and set aside.

In a large bowl beat 2 egg whites until soft peaks form. Slowly beat in 1/2 cup sugar and continue beating until whites are stiff, smooth, and glossy. Fold berry mixture into beaten egg whites. Leave in bowl or place in freezer container, cover tightly, and place in freezer for 1 1/2 hours or until partially frozen.

Remove sherbet from freezer, uncover, and beat at high speed until light in color and greatly increased in volume. Return sherbet to freezer container or scrape into serving dish, cover tightly, and freeze for 5 hours.

This sherbet remains very soft and can be served directly from the freezer.

This sherbet will keep in a tightly covered container in the freezer for 1 month.

FRESH PINEAPPLE MILK SHERBET

Makes 2 quarts of a very light sherbet with the taste of fresh pineapple, well worth the effort. An electric mixer is necessary for this dessert.

    1 fresh pineapple
    6 egg whites
    3/4 cup raw sugar
    1 cup milk

Split pineapple in half, peel it, and slice away core. Cut into small chunks. Place in blender and blend until puréed (do this in batches, if necessary). Set aside.

In a large mixing bowl beat 6 egg whites until soft peaks form. Slowly beat in ¾ cup raw sugar and continue beating until mixture is smooth, glossy, and holds stiff peaks. At low speed beat in 1 cup milk and the pineapple purée.

Cover and place mixture in freezer until partially frozen. Mixture will separate, with foam on top and liquid on bottom. Remove from freezer, uncover, and beat at high speed until smooth. Strings from pineapple will collect on beaters; scrape them off and discard. Cover and return bowl to freezer until frozen to a mush. Remove from freezer, uncover, and beat at high speed again, scraping off and discarding any more pineapple strings. Cover and return to freezer until a stiff mush. Remove, uncover, and beat once more. Sherbet should be well combined and may now be frozen to serve. Scrape into freezer container or serving dish, cover, and freeze for 4 hours or until firm. Serve directly from freezer.

GRAPEFRUIT MILK SHERBET

Makes 1 quart of slightly tart sherbet that is delightful with fresh fruit cocktail.

2 egg whites
⅛ tsp cream of tartar
½ cup granulated sugar
3 oz frozen concentrated grapefruit juice, thawed
1 cup milk

Beat 2 egg whites with ⅛ tsp cream of tartar until soft peaks form. Slowly beat in ½ cup sugar and continue beating until mixture is smooth and glossy.

Combine 1 cup milk and 3 oz grapefruit juice. Quickly stir into egg whites. Scrape mixture into freezer container, cover tightly, and freeze for 1 hour or until mixture is partially frozen.

Remove from freezer, uncover, and stir thoroughly to incorporate any liquid that may have settled to the bottom. Leave sherbet in original container or scrape into serving dish, cover again, and freeze until firm (about 4 hours).

This soft dessert should be served immediately from freezer and eaten quickly, since it melts fast.

LEMON MILK SHERBET

Makes 1 pint of a sweet milk sherbet that is particularly good with
Raspberry Sauce (page 181).

    2 egg whites
    ½ cup granulated sugar
    2 Tbsp lemon juice
    1 cup milk
    1 tsp candied lemon rind (page 23)

Beat 2 egg whites until soft peaks form. Slowly beat in ½ cup
granulated sugar and continue beating until stiff peaks form and the
whites are smooth and glossy.

Squeeze enough lemon juice to measure 2 Tbsp.

At very low speed beat into the egg whites the lemon juice, 1 cup
milk, and 1 tsp candied lemon rind.

Cover bowl and place in freezer until sherbet is mushy. Top will be
frozen foam, while bottom will be liquid.

Remove from freezer, uncover, and beat at high speed until
sherbet is uniformly mixed and smooth.

Scrape sherbet into freezer container or serving dish, cover
tightly, and freeze for 4 hours or until firm. Serve directly from
freezer.

LEMON SHERBET

Makes 1½ quarts. A flavor as pure as driven snow.

1½ tsp unflavored gelatin
¼ cup cold water
2 cups water
½ cup granulated sugar
Juice of 6 lemons
3 egg whites
¼ tsp cream of tartar
1 tsp confectioners' sugar

Sprinkle 1½ tsp gelatin over ¼ cup cold water in a small bowl. Stir and set aside to allow gelatin to soften.

Using 1-quart saucepan combine 2 cups water with ½ cup sugar. Bring to a boil and boil 5 minutes over moderate heat or until sugar has dissolved. Remove from heat and pour in gelatin; stir until it melts. Set aside in refrigerator to cool.

Squeeze juice from 6 lemons. Remove cooled sugar water from refrigerator. Pour in the lemon juice and stir until well mixed. Pour into bowl or freezer container, cover, and freeze 1 hour.

Beat 3 egg whites with ¼ tsp cream of tartar until soft peaks form. Add 1 tsp confectioners' sugar and beat until egg whites form stiff peaks and are smooth and glossy.

Remove lemon water from freezer, uncover, break up icy pieces, and beat until smooth. Scrape in beaten egg whites. Beat mixture together until smooth. Leave in bowl or pour into freezer container, cover, and freeze 2 hours. Remove from freezer, uncover, and beat as before. Cover again and freeze until firm.

Allow sherbet to ripen in refrigerator 10 minutes before serving.

LIME MILK SHERBET

Makes 1 pint of milk sherbet. Try it with Blueberry Sauce (page 178).

> 2 egg whites
> 6 Tbsp granulated sugar
> 1/4 cup lime juice
> 1 cup milk
> 1 tsp candied lime rind (page 23)

In a medium-sized mixing bowl beat 2 egg whites until soft peaks form. Slowly beat in 6 Tbsp sugar and continue beating until egg whites form stiff peaks and are smooth and glossy.

Squeeze enough lime juice to measure 1/4 cup.

At very low speed beat into the egg whites 1 cup milk, lime juice, and 1 tsp candied lime rind.

Cover bowl and place in freezer until sherbet is mushy. Top will be frozen foam, while bottom will be liquid.

Remove sherbet from freezer, uncover, and beat at high speed until it is uniformly mixed and smooth.

Scrape into freezer container or serving dish, cover tightly, and freeze for 4 hours or until firm.

Serve directly from freezer.

LINGONBERRY SHERBET

Makes 1 quart of sherbet slightly milder than the Cranberry Sherbet. The lingonberry is a northern European heath berry resembling a cranberry.

2 egg whites
4 Tbsp granulated sugar
1 cup lingonberry preserves

Beat 2 egg whites until soft peaks are formed. Gradually beat in 4 Tbsp sugar and continue beating until stiff peaks form that are smooth and glossy. Fold in 1 cup lingonberry preserves. Cover bowl tightly and place in freezer until partially frozen around the edges.

Remove sherbet from freezer, uncover, and beat at high speed until it lightens in color and increases in volume. Scrape into freezer container or serving dish, cover tightly, and freeze for 3 hours.

This sherbet remains soft and can be served directly from the freezer.

If kept tightly covered, this sherbet will keep about 1 month.

MANGO SHERBET

Makes 1 quart of a light, refreshing sherbet.

2 mangoes
2 egg whites
1/4 cup granulated sugar

Peel and cut 2 mangoes into small pieces. Put in blender and blend until fruit is puréed. Set aside.

Beat 2 egg whites until soft peaks form. Slowly beat in 1/4 cup sugar and continue beating until whites are smooth, glossy, and hold stiff peaks. Fold them into the mango purée.

Scrape mixture into freezer container, cover tightly, and freeze until firm around the edges of container (about 1 hour).

Remove sherbet from freezer, uncover, stir thoroughly, return to container or put in serving dish, cover again, and freeze until firm (about 2 hours). Serve directly from freezer.

MARBLED STRAWBERRY SHERBET

Makes about 1½ quarts of an attractive and light ice creamlike sherbet.

　　1 16-oz container whole frozen strawberries
　　　　in sugar syrup, thawed
　　1 Tbsp lemon juice
　　2 egg whites
　　2 Tbsp granulated sugar
　　½ cup heavy cream
　　1 Tbsp Kirschwasser
　　1 Tbsp granulated sugar

　　Drain strawberries. Save liquid for making strawberry topping or for another recipe. Purée whole strawberries and 1 Tbsp lemon juice in blender and set aside.
　　Beat 2 egg whites until soft peaks form. Slowly add 2 Tbsp sugar and continue to beat until thick, smooth, and glossy. Quickly fold in puréed strawberries. Cover bowl and place in freezer until frozen to a stiff mush (about 1 hour).
　　Remove from freezer, uncover, and beat until sherbet becomes very fluffy and much lighter in color. Cover again and return to freezer for another hour.
　　Whip ½ cup cream until soft peaks form. Add 1 Tbsp Kirschwasser and 1 Tbsp sugar and beat until stiff peaks begin to form. Set aside.
　　Remove sherbet from freezer, uncover, and beat as before. Quickly fold in whipped cream until a marbled appearance is obtained. Leave sherbet in bowl, or pour into freezer container or serving dish, cover, and freeze until firm.
　　Let sherbet ripen in refrigerator for 10 minutes before serving.

ORANGE MILK SHERBET

Makes 1 pint of a sweet, mild sherbet, a favorite of Nancy's children.

　　¼ cup fresh orange juice
　　1 Tbsp lemon juice
　　½ tsp candied orange rind (page 23)
　　2 egg whites
　　6 Tbsp granulated sugar
　　1 cup milk

Squeeze enough orange juice to measure ¼ cup and enough lemon juice to measure 1 Tbsp. Combine juices in small cup and add ½ tsp candied orange rind. Set aside.

In medium-sized bowl beat 2 egg whites until soft peaks form. Slowly beat in 6 Tbsp sugar and continue beating until mixture holds stiff peaks and egg whites are smooth and glossy.

Slowly beat in 1 cup milk and combined citrus juices.

Cover bowl and place in freezer until mushy. (Top will be frozen foam; bottom will be liquid.)

Remove from freezer, uncover, and beat at high speed until sherbet is uniform, light, and smooth.

Scrape sherbet into freezer container or serving dish, cover tightly, and freeze until firm.

Serve directly from freezer.

PINEAPPLE MILK SHERBET

Makes 1½ pints of a light, sweet, smooth sherbet that is easy to make and refreshing to eat.

2 egg whites
¼ tsp cream of tartar
¼ cup raw sugar
1 cup canned pineapple juice
½ cup milk

Beat 2 egg whites with ¼ tsp cream of tartar until soft peaks form. Slowly beat in ¼ cup raw sugar and continue beating until egg whites are smooth, glossy, and hold very stiff peaks. Quickly stir in 1 cup pineapple juice and ½ cup milk. Place sherbet in freezer container, cover tightly, and freeze for 1 hour.

This sherbet has a great tendency to settle. To correct, stir several times during the freezing process.

Remove sherbet from freezer, uncover, and stir thoroughly to incorporate the liquid that has settled to the bottom. Cover and return to freezer for 30 minutes, then stir again. Return for another 30 minutes, stir, freeze 30 minutes, then stir a third time. Cover and freeze for 3 hours or until firm. Serve directly from freezer.

PLUM SHERBET

Makes 1 quart of a light fruity sherbet particularly good after a poultry dinner.

    1 1-lb 1-oz can purple plums, drained and pitted
    2 Tbsp frozen concentrated orange juice
    2 egg whites
    1/3 cup granulated sugar

Drain and pit the canned plums. Put them with 2 Tbsp concentrated orange juice in blender and blend at high speed until plums are puréed.

In large bowl beat 2 egg whites until soft peaks form. Slowly beat in 1/3 cup sugar and continue beating at high speed until whites are smooth and glossy, and sugar has completely dissolved. Fold in plum purée. Leave mixture in bowl or place in freezer container, cover tightly, and place in freezer for 1 hour or until partially frozen.

Remove from freezer, uncover, and beat at high speed until mixture lightens and greatly increases in volume. Scrape sherbet into freezer container or serving dish, cover tightly, and freeze until firm (about 3 hours).

Serve directly from freezer.

RASPBERRY SHERBET

Makes 1 to 1½ quarts of a red, tangy dessert good by itself or as a layer in a parfait (page 198) or pie.

    Juice of 1/2 lemon
    1 10-oz container frozen raspberries, in sugar syrup, thawed
    3 egg whites
    2 Tbsp granulated sugar
    3/4 cup heavy cream (optional)
    2 Tbsp granulated sugar (optional)

Squeeze half a lemon into blender. Add thawed raspberries and their juice and blend until puréed. Set aside.

In 1½-quart bowl beat 3 egg whites until soft peaks form. Slowly add 2 Tbsp sugar and continue beating until egg whites are smooth and glossy.

Gently stir in the raspberry purée. Cover bowl tightly and place in freezer until frozen to a stiff mush.

Remove sherbet from freezer, uncover, and beat at high speed until it becomes very fluffy and much lighter in color. Cover and return to freezer for 1 hour.

Remove sherbet from freezer, uncover, and beat as before.* Pour into freezer container, cover tightly, and freeze until firm.

Allow sherbet to ripen in refrigerator 10 minutes before serving.

*For a richer dessert add whipped cream. Whip 3/4 cup heavy cream until soft peaks form. Add 2 Tbsp sugar and continue whipping until soft peaks begin to form. Quickly fold in whipped cream. If using sherbet as part of a layered dessert omit whipped cream.

STRAWBERRY SHERBET

Makes 1 quart of a light, delightful, low-calorie dessert.

1 pint fresh strawberries, mashed or finely chopped
1 Tbsp lemon juice (optional)
2 egg whites
1/2 cup granulated sugar

Wash, hull, and mash or finely chop 1 pint fresh strawberries. Add 1 Tbsp lemon juice if you want to; it brings out the flavor of the berries even more.

Beat 2 egg whites until soft peaks form. Slowly beat in 1/2 cup sugar and continue beating until whites hold stiff peaks and the sugar has completely dissolved. At low speed beat in the strawberries.

Scrape mixture into freezer container or serving dish, cover tightly, and freeze for approximately 4 hours. Sherbet remains fairly soft and can be served directly from freezer.

Serve with Strawberry Sauce (page 183).

STRAWBERRY SHERBET ICING

Makes 1 quart icing for Valentine Cake on page 232 or a layer in a parfait.

1 Tbsp lemon juice
1 16-oz container frozen whole strawberries
   in sugar syrup, thawed
2 egg whites
2 Tbsp granulated sugar

Squeeze lemon juice into blender and add the drained strawberries, reserving 6 or 8 berries to decorate top of cake. Blend until puréed.

In medium-sized bowl beat egg whites until soft peaks form. Add 2 Tbsp sugar and continue beating until egg whites are stiff, smooth, and glossy and the sugar has dissolved.

Quickly fold strawberry purée into egg whites, cover bowl tightly, and place in freezer until partially frozen (about 1 hour).

Remove from freezer, uncover, and beat until mixture lightens in color and increases in volume.

Sherbet is now ready to spread as icing or may be frozen further and served as a sherbet. Serve it directly from freezer.

VANILLA BUTTERMILK SHERBET

Makes 1 quart of a light sweet sherbet relatively low in calories. This sherbet was very popular during the 1930s; our updated and sweeter version makes a good luncheon dessert.

2 egg whites
1/8 tsp cream of tartar
1/2 cup granulated sugar
1 tsp vanilla extract
1 cup buttermilk

In a medium-sized bowl beat 2 egg whites with 1/8 tsp cream of tartar until soft peaks form. Slowly beat in 1/2 cup sugar and continue beating until egg whites hold stiff peaks and are smooth and glossy.

Add 1 tsp vanilla extract to 1 cup buttermilk. Fold buttermilk into beaten egg whites.

Place in freezer container or serving dish, cover tightly, and place in freezer until firm (about 3 hours). Serve sherbet directly from freezer.

YOGURT SHERBET

Makes 1 quart of a cool, refreshing dessert. Nancy's children eat it by the pint.

    2 egg whites
    ¼ tsp cream of tartar
    2 Tbsp granulated sugar
    2 8-oz containers of flavored yogurt or plain yogurt
        with 1 Tbsp sugar added to each container

Beat 2 egg whites with ¼ tsp cream of tartar until soft peaks form. Slowly beat in 2 Tbsp sugar and continue beating until egg whites hold stiff peaks. Quickly fold in the yogurt from 2 8-oz containers.

Scrape mixture into freezer container, cover tightly, and freeze for 1½ hours or until partially frozen.

Remove sherbet from freezer, uncover, and scrape into bowl. Beat for a few moments using either an electric mixer or hand-held beater. Scrape sherbet back into freezer container or serving dish, cover tightly, and freeze until firm.

Allow sherbet to ripen in refrigerator for 10 minutes before serving.

YOGURT CUPS

Makes 6 individual desserts. Save empty yogurt containers to make this treat for children. This idea was sent to Nancy by her godchildren in Seattle.

    3 egg whites
    1/4 tsp cream of tartar
    3 Tbsp granulated sugar
    3 8-oz containers flavored yogurt or plain yogurt
        with 1 Tbsp honey added to each container
    6 empty 8-oz yogurt containers with lids, thoroughly washed

Beat 3 egg whites with 1/4 tsp cream of tartar until soft peaks form. Slowly beat in 3 Tbsp sugar and continue beating until egg whites hold stiff peaks. Stir honey into yogurt. Quickly fold in yogurt from 3 8-oz containers.

Divide mixture among 6 empty thoroughly washed containers. Cover tightly and freeze until firm.

Allow cups to ripen in refrigerator for 10 minutes before serving.

As an added treat, empty contents of cup into a dessert dish and serve with sauce.

Water Ices

Water ices are similar to sherbets but have a coarser grain. They generally use gelatin as a stabilizer instead of egg whites, unless egg whites are specified in the recipe.

Water ices consist of fruit juice or purée and sugar water or syrup to which gelatin has been added to act as a stabilizer. They usually require a second beating to break up the larger ice crystals.

We recommend serving ices alone or using in combination with other ingredients in punches, granités, and bombes.

Serve water ices in sherbet glasses.

You will find many good ways of using water ices when you get to the sections on punches, granités, and bombes.

APRICOT ICE

Makes 1 to 1½ pints of a good, not very sweet restorative on a hot summer day.

1¼ cups water
¾ cup granulated sugar
1 tsp unflavored gelatin
⅓ cup cold water
1½ lbs fresh apricots, puréed
1 tsp lime juice

In small saucepan combine 1¼ cups water with ¾ cup sugar. Bring to a boil over high heat, stirring. Reduce heat and keep at slow boil for 5 minutes without stirring.

Sprinkle 1 tsp gelatin over ⅓ cup cold water in small bowl. Stir until gelatin starts to soften.

Remove sugar water from heat and pour in the gelatin water. Stir until gelatin has melted and water has slightly thickened. Chill in refrigerator 30 minutes.

Wash, peel, and pit 1½ lbs fresh apricots. Put through food mill or blend in blender until puréed. Pour into medium-sized bowl and squeeze in 1 tsp lime juice.

Remove chilled sugar water from refrigerator and pour it into the apricot purée. Beat mixture with wire whisk until smooth. Pour into freezer container or serving dish, cover, and freeze until firm.

Allow the ice to ripen in refrigerator 2 hours before serving.

BANANA ICE

Makes 1½ pints of a light-brown dessert, not very imposing looking, but fine tasting.

    1 cup water
    ¼ cup dark-brown sugar
    1 cup very ripe bananas
    1 Tbsp lime juice
    ⅓ cup egg whites
    2 Tbsp Kirschwasser

In small saucepan combine 1 cup water with ¼ cup brown sugar. Bring to a boil over high heat, stirring; lower heat and keep at slow boil for 5 minutes without stirring. Set aside.

Break up 2 ripe bananas (1 cup) into blender. Squeeze enough lime juice to measure 1 Tbsp and add to blender. Blend until a purée, then pour in the hot sugar water. Blend a moment and let stand at least 1 hour.

In medium-sized bowl beat ⅓ cup egg whites until stiff peaks form. Pour in banana mixture and fold one into the other. Stir in 2 Tbsp Kirschwasser.

Scrape mixture into freezer container, cover, and freeze 1½ hours.

Remove from freezer, uncover, and stir to break up any frozen pieces and reincorporate egg whites and banana. Cover again, and return to freezer until firm.

Allow to ripen 2 hours in refrigerator before serving.

CANTALOUPE ICE

Makes 1½ to 2 quarts of an ice with the strong flavor that makes you realize why cantaloupes are also called "muskmelons."

2 tsp unflavored gelatin
¼ cup cold water
1¾ cups water
½ cup honey
Handful of mint leaves
1 very ripe cantaloupe, cut up
Juice of 2 oranges
Juice of ½ lime
2 egg whites

In a small bowl sprinkle 2 tsp gelatin over ¼ cup cold water. Stir. Set aside to soften gelatin.

In a small saucepan combine 1¾ cups water with ¼ cup honey and a handful of fresh mint leaves. Heat to boiling over high heat, stirring; then reduce heat and keep at a slow boil for 5 minutes. Remove from heat and add the softened gelatin. Stir until gelatin has melted. Set aside in refrigerator to cool.

Cut cantaloupe in half, scoop out the seeds, and then scoop out the meat. Put in blender. Squeeze juice from half a lime and 2 oranges and add to blender. Purée the cantaloupe.

Remove chilled sugar water from refrigerator, strain out mint leaves, and pour into blender. Blend until evenly mixed. Pour into medium-sized bowl, cover, and freeze 1½ hours.

Beat 2 egg whites until soft peaks form. Remove ice from freezer, uncover, break up icy pieces, and beat until smooth. Fold in the softly beaten egg whites. Pour into freezer container or serving dish, cover, and freeze until firm.

Allow to ripen 2 hours in refrigerator before serving.

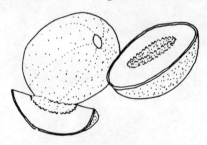

CHOCOLATE-ORANGE ICE

Makes 1 quart of a bittersweet ice that is best served in small portions and is as refreshing as afterdinner coffee.

3 oz unsweetened chocolate
1/4 cup cold water
1 1/2 tsp unflavored gelatin
Grated rind of 1 orange
Grated rind of 1 lemon
Juice of 1 orange, strained
2 cups water
1 cup light-brown sugar
1-inch piece of vanilla bean

In top of double boiler melt 3 oz chocolate over simmering water. Do not stir. Set aside.

Combine 1/4 cup cold water with 1 1/2 tsp gelatin in a small bowl. Stir. Set aside to soften.

Grate the orange and lemon. Squeeze the juice from the orange, strain, set aside.

In small saucepan combine 2 cups water with 1 cup sugar. Bring to a boil over high heat, stirring; then reduce heat and keep at slow boil until solution appears clear. Meanwhile, cut off a 1-inch piece of vanilla bean, split in half lengthwise, scrape out black powder, and add it and the bark to the sugar water. Boil rapidly for 5 minutes longer without stirring. Remove vanilla bean bark and take sugar water off heat.

Add grated orange and lemon rind and softened gelatin to sugar water. Stir and put in refrigerator to cool for 30 minutes.

Inspect the chocolate. If it has solidified a bit, heat it a few moments to soften.

Remove sugar water from refrigerator. Slowly pour it into the chocolate, beating with wire whisk to make mixture smooth. Then gradually beat in strained orange juice. If mixture isn't smooth enough, pour into blender and blend a few seconds.

Pour into freezer container, cover, and freeze until sides begin to harden. Take out of freezer, uncover, break up icy pieces, and return to bowl or blender and beat or blend until smooth. Pour back into freezer container or into sherbet glasses, cover, and freeze until firm.

This dessert may be served directly from freezer.

HONEYDEW ICE

Makes 1½ pints of a crisp, sweet ice.

1 tsp unflavored gelatin
¼ cup cold water
¾ cup water
½ cup granulated sugar
½ medium-sized honeydew melon
Juice of ½ lime
Juice of 1 orange

Sprinkle 1 tsp gelatin over ¼ cup cold water, stir, and set aside to soften gelatin.

In small saucepan combine ¾ cup water with ½ cup sugar. Bring to a boil over high heat, stirring. Reduce heat and keep at slow boil for 5 minutes without stirring. Remove from heat and add the softened gelatin. Stir until gelatin has melted. Set aside in refrigerator to cool.

Scoop out seeds from half a honeydew; put the meat in blender. Squeeze juice from half a lime and 1 orange into blender and blend honeydew until puréed.

Remove chilled sugar water from refrigerator, pour into blender, and blend until well mixed. Pour honeydew mixture into bowl or freezer container, cover, and freeze 2 hours or until icy.

Remove ice from freezer, uncover, break up icy chunks, and beat until smooth. Pour into serving dish or back into freezer container and freeze until firm.

Allow ice to ripen 2 to 2½ hours in refrigerator before serving.

KIWI ICE

Makes 1 pint of a light-green, bittersweet ice.

1 tsp unflavored gelatin
1/2 cup cold water
1 cup water
1/2 cup granulated sugar
3 kiwis
1/2 tsp lime juice
2 Tbsp granulated sugar

In small bowl sprinkle 1 tsp gelatin over 1/2 cup cold water. Stir and set aside to soften gelatin.

In small saucepan combine 1 cup water with 1/2 cup sugar. Bring to a boil over high heat, stirring. Lower heat and keep at slow boil 5 minutes without stirring. Remove from heat and add gelatin, stirring until it melts. Set aside to cool in refrigerator.

Wash, peel, and cut 3 kiwis into small pieces (makes about 1 cup). Put through food mill. If little black seeds have gone through mill, press purée through fine sieve into medium-sized bowl. Squeeze enough lime juice to measure 1/2 tsp. Add the juice and 2 Tbsp sugar to purée; stir.

Remove cooled sugar water from refrigerator. Stir it into kiwi purée, cover bowl, and set in freezer 2 hours.

Remove bowl from freezer, uncover, and stir to break up frozen pieces; then beat until smooth. Pour ice into freezer container, cover, and freeze until firm.

Allow ice to ripen 2 to 2 1/2 hours in refrigerator before serving.

LEMON ICE

Makes 1½ pints. Delightfully refreshing experience with just the right amount of sugar (a little) and lemon (lots of). Quite nice when served in lemon shells or by itself on a hot day. Try in iced tea as a substitute for lemon and sugar.

Grated rind of 1 lemon
Juice and shells of 5 lemons
1 tsp unflavored gelatin
½ cup cold water
½ cup light-brown sugar
1½ cups water

Wash and dry 6 lemons; grate the rind of 1 of them and put it aside. Reserve that peeled lemon for another use.

Cut remaining 5 lemons in half lengthwise and scoop out pulp into 2-cup measure, reserving lemon half-shells. Put lemon halves in freezer. Remove and discard seeds and white membrane from juice and pulp. (You should have about 1 cup depending on size of lemons. The juice of the grated lemon may also be added to create an even more lemony flavor.) Pour into blender and blend at high speed for 2 minutes. Put aside.

In a small bowl stir 1 tsp gelatin in ½ cup cold water and set aside to soften.

Bring ½ cup sugar and 1½ cups water to a boil over high heat, stirring. Lower heat and keep at slow boil for 5 minutes without stirring. Remove from heat and add softened gelatin. Stir until gelatin has melted. Then stir in grated lemon rind. Cool to lukewarm.

In medium-sized glass bowl combine cooled gelatin mixture with puréed lemon and beat until well blended and light in color. Cover bowl and set in freezer until mixture is partially frozen (about 1½ hours).

Remove ice from freezer, uncover, break up icy pieces, and beat until light in color and volume has increased.

Take frozen lemon halves out of freezer. Carefully spoon icy mixture into lemon halves, put on platter (a stuffed-egg serving dish is excellent), cover, and return immediately to freezer. Scrape rest of ice into glass or plastic container, cover, and refreeze.

Allow lemon halves to ripen in refrigerator 10 to 20 minutes before serving. Rest of lemon ice should be ripened 1 hour.

Note: Avoid freezing lemon ice in metal container, since the acidity of lemon may react with the metal and cause an off-taste.

FROZEN LEMON OR LIME ICE CUBES

Makes 10 ice cubes that are handy to use in iced tea or any iced drink that would benefit from the addition of lemon or lime. Diana uses 3 cubes per drink. If she needs more ice, she then uses plain ice.

1/4 cup lemon or lime juice
1 1/2 cups water
Plastic ice cube tray

Squeeze enough lemon or lime juice to measure 1/4 cup. Pour in 2-cup measure. Fill to 1 3/4 mark with water. Evenly distribute juice and water between 10 individual plastic ice cube molds.
Freeze and use as needed.

MANDARIN ORANGE ICE

Makes 1 quart of a light, very sweet orange ice that can be used in a baked Alaska (page 203).

2 Tbsp lemon juice
2 11-oz cans Mandarin oranges, well drained
2 egg whites
3 Tbsp granulated sugar

Squeeze enough lemon juice to measure 2 Tbsp and put in blender.
Drain liquid from the cans of Mandarin oranges. Put oranges in blender with lemon juice and blend until puréed. Set aside.
In a medium-sized bowl beat 2 egg whites until soft peaks are formed. Slowly beat in 3 Tbsp sugar and continue beating until stiff peaks form. Beat in Mandarin orange purée.
Cover bowl tightly and place in freezer for 1 hour or until partially frozen around the edges. Remove bowl from freezer, uncover, and beat at high speed until ice lightens in color.
Scrape ice into freezer container or serving dish, cover tightly, and freeze until firm, about 3 hours.
This ice may be served directly from freezer, or may be scooped out and made into a baked Alaska.

NECTARINE ICE

Makes 1½ to 2 pints. Next to nectar in excellence.

4 cups fresh nectarines, cut up
¼ cup granulated sugar
1 Tbsp lime juice
1½ tsp unflavored gelatin
½ cup cold water
1 cup water
⅓ cup granulated sugar

Wash, peel, and cut up into small pieces enough nectarines to measure 4 cups. Sprinkle ¼ cup sugar and 1 Tbsp lime juice over fruit. Stir until fruit is well coated with sugar. Set aside for at least 1 hour.

In a small bowl sprinkle 1½ tsp gelatin over ½ cup cold water. Stir and set aside for gelatin to soften.

In a small saucepan combine 1 cup water with ⅓ cup sugar. Bring to a boil over high heat, stirring. Lower heat and keep at slow boil for 5 minutes without stirring. Remove from heat and pour in softened gelatin. Stir until gelatin has melted. Set aside in refrigerator to cool.

Spoon the sugared fruit into blender and blend until puréed. Pour into medium-sized bowl. Remove sugar water from refrigerator, pour into fruit, and stir until well combined. Cover and freeze 1 hour or until mixture becomes icy.

Remove from freezer, uncover, stir to break up icy pieces, and beat until smooth. Pour into freezer container or serving dish, cover, and freeze until firm.

Allow ice to ripen in refrigerator 2 to 2½ hours before serving.

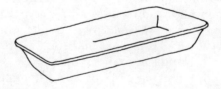

ORANGE ICE

Makes 1 quart. Refreshing to look at and to eat.

2 tsp unflavored gelatin
1/2 cup cold water
2 1/4 cups water
3/4 cup granulated sugar
Peel of 1 thick-skinned orange
Juice of 5 oranges
Juice of 1 lime

In a small bowl sprinkle 2 tsp gelatin over 1/2 cup cold water. Stir and set aside for gelatin to soften.

In 1-quart saucepan combine 2 1/4 cups water with 3/4 cup granulated sugar. Remove peel of orange and add it to sugar and water. Bring to a boil over high heat, stirring. Lower heat and keep at slow boil for 10 minutes without stirring. Turn off heat and pour in softened gelatin. Stir until gelatin has melted. Set aside in refrigerator to cool.

Squeeze juice from 5 oranges and 1 lime; set aside.

Remove sugar water from refrigerator. Combine with orange juice, then strain into freezer container, cover, and freeze for 1 1/2 hours or until mixture is frozen around the edges. Remove from freezer, uncover, scrape into bowl, stir to break up any icy chunks, and beat until smooth. Pour back into freezer container or into serving dish, cover, and freeze until firm.

Allow ice to ripen in refrigerator 2 to 2 1/2 hours before serving.

PINEAPPLE ICE

Makes 1 quart of an ice that hints much but says pineapple.

1½ cups water
½ cup light-brown sugar
½ cup cold water
2 tsp unflavored gelatin
Juice of 2 oranges
Juice of 1 lemon
2 cups canned pineapple chunks, drained
¼ cup Kirschwasser

In small saucepan combine 1½ cups water and ½ cup brown sugar. Bring to a boil over high heat, stirring. Lower heat and keep at slow boil for 5 minutes without stirring.

Sprinkle 2 tsp gelatin over ½ cup cold water; stir, and set aside for gelatin to soften.

When boiling sugar and water have become thick, remove from heat, and pour in softened gelatin. Stir until gelatin is melted. Set aside in refrigerator to cool.

Squeeze juice from 2 oranges and 1 lemon into blender. Drain and add 2 cups chunk pineapple. Blend until puréed. Pour into medium-sized bowl; fold in the cooled sugar water. Stir in ¼ cup Kirschwasser. Pour into freezer container or serving dish, cover, and freeze until firm.

Allow to ripen in refrigerator 2 to 2½ hours before serving.

RHUBARB ICE

Makes 1 pint of a delightful citrus-rhubarb concoction.

2 cups rhubarb, chopped
Juice of 1 orange
Juice of 1 lime
¼ cup granulated sugar
¼ cup water
1 tsp unflavored gelatin
¼ cup cold water

Cut off and discard the leaves and small stems from rhubarb stalks. Wash and cut enough stalks into small pieces to measure 2 cups. Put into heavy-gauge non-aluminum pot.

Add juice of 1 orange and 1 lime to rhubarb in pot. Add ¼ cup sugar, and ¼ cup water. Cook over low heat, stirring from time to time, until rhubarb falls apart (a little less than 10 minutes).

Sprinkle 1 tsp gelatin ouer ¼ cup cold water. Stir and set aside to soften gelatin.

When rhubarb is tender, remove from heat and stir in softened gelatin until gelatin has melted.

Chill mixture in refrigerator 30 minutes before freezing. Then pour into freezer container or serving dish, cover, and freeze until firm.

Allow to ripen in refrigerator 2½ hours before serving.

SAUTERNE ICE

Makes 1½ pints of a cool sweet ice that is particularly good with fresh pears.

    2 tsp unflavored gelatin
    ¼ cup cold water
    ½ cup sugar
    1 cup water
    1 cup Sauterne

Sprinkle 2 tsp gelatin over ¼ cup cold water, stir, and set aside to soften gelatin.

In small saucepan combine ½ cup sugar with 1 cup water. Heat to boiling, stirring to dissolve sugar. Remove from heat and add softened gelatin, stirring until it has melted. Stir in 1 cup Sauterne.

Pour into freezer container, cover tightly, and freeze for 2 hours or until mixture is partially frozen.

Remove ice from freezer, uncover, scrape into bowl, and beat until light in color and volume has increased.

Scrape into freezer container or serving dish, cover, and freeze ice until firm. Serve directly from freezer.

TANGY CITRUS ICE

Makes 1 quart. A tantalizing blend of citrus fruits, each enhancing the other's flavor.

2 tsp unflavored gelatin
1/2 cup cold water
1/2 cup light-brown sugar
1 cup water
Grated rind of 1 orange
Juice of 5 oranges
Juice of 1 grapefruit
Juice of 2 lemons

Sprinkle 2 tsp gelatin over 1/2 cup cold water, stir, and set aside to soften gelatin.

In small saucepan mix 1/2 cup light-brown sugar and 1 cup water. Bring to a boil over high heat, stirring. Lower heat and keep at slow boil for 5 minutes without stirring. Remove from heat and pour in softened gelatin. Stir until gelatin has melted. Set aside to cool.

Grate rind of 1 orange. Squeeze juice from 5 oranges, 1 grapefruit, and 2 lemons. Add grated rind to strained citrus juices.

In a plastic or glass container combine the cooled gelatin water and fruit juices. Cover tightly and freeze until mixture is partially frozen (2 to 3 hours). Remove from freezer, uncover, break up icy pieces, and beat until volume has increased slightly. Cover again and return to freezer until firm.

Allow to ripen 2 to 2 1/2 hours in refrigerator before serving.

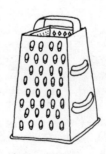

WATERMELON ICE

Makes 1½ pints of a sweet but refreshing dessert that Diana's Indian friends ate until it was all gone.

¾ cup water
½ cup Turbinado sugar
¼ cup cold water
1 tsp unflavored gelatin
2 cups ripe watermelon, chopped
3 oz frozen concentrated lemonade, thawed

In a small saucepan combine ¾ cup water with ½ cup sugar. Bring to a boil over high heat, stirring. Lower heat and keep at a slow boil for 5 minutes without stirring. Set aside.

In a small bowl stir 1 tsp gelatin into ¼ cup cold water until it starts to soften. When soft pour it into hot sugar water and stir until melted. Chill the sugar water in refrigerator for 30 minutes.

Peel, remove seeds, and chop 2 1-inch slices of watermelon, or enough to measure 2 cups. Pour into blender, add 3 oz lemonade, and blend until puréed.

Remove chilled sugar water from refrigerator and stir in the watermelon purée. Pour into freezer container or serving mold, cover, and freeze until firm.

Allow to ripen 30 to 45 minutes in refrigerator before serving.

Note: For a nice touch, garnish with a few pieces of fresh mint when serving.

WILD BLACKBERRY ICE

Makes 1 pint of an ice with a tart bramble sweetness worth the hunt among the briars of July and August.

1 cup wild blackberries
¼ cup granulated sugar
¾ cup water
½ cup granulated sugar
1 tsp unflavored gelatin
¼ cup cold water
Juice from ¼ lime

Gently wash and drain 1 cup blackberries. Put into medium-sized bowl, sprinkle ¼ cup sugar over berries, and gently stir until all berries are covered with sugar. Set aside in refrigerator 1 hour.

Put ¾ cup water and ½ cup sugar in small saucepan and bring to a boil over high heat, stirring. Lower heat and keep at a slow boil for 5 minutes without stirring.

Sprinkle 1 tsp gelatin over ¼ cup cold water in a small bowl, stir, and set aside to soften gelatin.

Remove sugar water from heat and pour in softened gelatin. Stir until gelatin has melted. Set aside to thicken and cool in refrigerator.

Take berries out of refrigerator. Press through fine sieve or put through food mill into medium-sized bowl. If a few crushed seeds remain and these disturb you, then press the juice through a fine sieve lined with cheesecloth as well. Squeeze juice from a quarter of a lime and add to berry juice.

Take sugar water out of refrigerator, pour into juice, and stir. Then pour into freezer container or serving dish, cover, and freeze until firm.

Allow ice to ripen 2 to 2½ hours in refrigerator before serving.

Popsicles

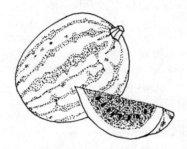

The discovery of the popsicle is reported to have been the result of an accident. Mr. Frank Epperson, who specialized in making lemonade, made up a batch one night in 1923 while visiting some friends in New Jersey. A glass had been left accidentally on the windowsill with a spoon in it. During the night the temperature dropped drastically. The next morning Mr. Epperson saw the glass, picked it up by the spoon handle, ran water over the glass, and out came the first epsicle. The name ultimately evolved to popsicle.

Popsicles are great favorites with children and adults have been known to enjoy them also. The following recipes are made of frozen concentrated fruit juices in some instances and of fresh fruit combinations in others. They exemplify the combinations you can try. The frozen concentrated fruit juice combinations are favorites of Nancy's children, David and Jonathan, while Diana and her son, Christopher, enjoy the fresh fruit combinations.

Popsicle mold kits are usually a seasonal item in some large department stores. There was a time when they were readily available, but not so today. They can, however, be ordered from Tupperware and from Maid of Scandinavia (see Sources of Supplies, page 275) all year around. The molds are usually a thin oval-like shape with a lid containing a stick. The kit includes a platform or stand in which the molds can be set upright.

Molds generally hold 2 oz of liquid or less. The recipes have been written to make 6 2-oz popsicles. Diana's molds are smaller and if she has any left over, she freezes it as she would an ice or makes a special drink from it. Fill the molds to within 1/4 inch of the top. Put on the top containing the stick, which goes into mold. Place in freezer.

To unmold popsicle, run mold under cold water, squeeze to let air in along the side of the popsicle, and out it will come. If the stick should also slip out, stick it back in.

Fresh Fruit Popsicles

APRICOT POPSICLES

$1/2$ tsp unflavored gelatin
3 Tbsp cold water
$3/4$ cup water
$1/2$ cup sugar
$3/4$ lb fresh apricots
$1/2$ tsp lime juice

Sprinkle $1/2$ tsp gelatin over 3 Tbsp cold water, stir, and set aside to soften gelatin.

Put $3/4$ cup water and $1/2$ cup sugar in small saucepan and bring to a boil over high heat, stirring. Lower heat and keep at a slow boil for 5 minutes without stirring. Remove from heat and pour in softened gelatin. Stir until gelatin has melted, then set aside to cool.

Peel and pit $3/4$ lb fresh apricots. Put in blender, squeeze over them enough lime juice to measure $1/2$ tsp, and blend until puréed. Add cooled sugar water and blend until well mixed. Pour into popsicle molds. Seal and freeze until firm. Unmold and serve immediately.

BLACKBERRY OR RASPBERRY POPSICLES

$1/2$ tsp unflavored gelatin
$1/4$ cup cold water
$2/3$ to 1 cup blackberries or raspberries
3 Tbsp granulated sugar
1 tsp lime juice
$3/4$ cup water
$1/4$ cup granulated sugar

Sprinkle ½ tsp gelatin over ¼ cup cold water, stir, and set aside to soften gelatin.

Wash and drain ⅔ to 1 cup blackberries or raspberries. Place in bowl and sprinkle with 3 Tbsp sugar and 1 tsp lime juice. Stir and set aside.

Put ¾ cup water and ¼ cup sugar in small saucepan and bring to a boil over high heat, stirring. Lower heat and keep at slow boil for 5 minutes without stirring. Remove from heat and pour in softened gelatin. Stir until gelatin has melted, then set aside to cool.

Press berries through fine sieve or put through food mill. If a few seeds remain and they disturb you, press juice through a fine sieve lined with cheesecloth as well.

Pour sugar water into berry juice. Stir and pour into popsicle molds. Seal and freeze until firm. Unmold and serve immediately.

FRUITY CHOCOLATE POPSICLES

½ tsp unflavored gelatin
¼ cup cold water
1-inch piece of vanilla bean
1 oz unsweetened chocolate
1 cup water
½ cup granulated sugar
Juice of 1 orange
¼ tsp lemon juice

Sprinkle ½ tsp gelatin over ¼ cup cold water in a small bowl, stir, and set aside for gelatin to soften.

Cut off a 1-inch piece of vanilla bean, split it in half lengthwise, and scrape out vanilla powder into top of double boiler. Add 1 oz chocolate, 1 cup water, and ½ cup sugar. Melt over simmering water. Do not stir.

Squeeze juice from 1 orange and enough lemon juice to measure ¼ tsp. Add to softened gelatin.

When chocolate has melted beat the mixture together vigorously with wire whisk until it is smooth. Remove from heat and add the gelatin juice; stir until gelatin is melted. Pour into 2-cup measure and refrigerate about 10 minutes until moderately cool.

Remove from refrigerator and pour mixture into popsicle molds. Seal and freeze until firm. Unmold and serve immediately.

LEMON-LIME POPSICLES

1/2 tsp unflavored gelatin
1/3 cup cold water
3/4 cup water
1/4 cup granulated sugar
Juice of 2 limes
Juice of 1 lemon

Sprinkle 1/2 tsp gelatin over 1/3 cup cold water. Stir. Set aside for gelatin to soften.

Pour 3/4 cup water and 1/4 cup sugar into a small saucepan. Bring to a boil over high heat, stirring. Reduce heat and keep at a slow boil for 5 minutes without stirring. Remove from heat and pour in softened gelatin. Stir until gelatin has melted and set aside to cool.

Squeeze juice from 2 limes and 1 lemon. Pour into 2-cup measure. Add sugar water and stir until well mixed. Pour into popsicle molds, seal, and freeze until firm. Unmold and serve immediately.

NECTARINE POPSICLES

1/2 tsp unflavored gelatin
1/4 cup cold water
1/2 cup water
1/4 cup dark-brown sugar
2 cups nectarines, cut into small pieces
2 Tbsp dark-brown sugar, with lumps broken up
1/2 tsp lime juice

Sprinkle 1/2 tsp gelatin over 1/4 cup cold water. Stir and set aside for gelatin to soften.

Pour 1/2 cup water and 1/4 cup dark-brown sugar into a small saucepan. Bring to a boil over high heat, stirring. Reduce heat and keep at a slow boil for 5 minutes without stirring. Remove from heat and pour in gelatin, stirring until it melts. Set aside in refrigerator to cool.

Wash, peel, and cut into small pieces enough nectarines to measure 2 cups. Pour into blender. Add 2 Tbsp dark-brown sugar, with the lumps broken up, and squeeze in 1/2 tsp lime juice. Blend until puréed. Remove sugar water from refrigerator and blend it into the purée.

Pour into popsicle molds, seal, and freeze until firm. Unmold and serve immediately.

Popsicles

ORANGE POPSICLES

1/2 tsp unflavored gelatin
1/4 cup cold water
3/4 cup water
1/3 cup granulated sugar
Juice of 2 oranges
1 1/2 tsp lime juice

Sprinkle 1/2 tsp gelatin over 1/4 cup cold water, stir, and set aside to allow gelatin to soften.

Pour 3/4 cup water and 1/3 cup sugar in a small saucepan. Bring to a boil over high heat, stirring. Reduce heat and keep at a slow boil for 5 minutes without stirring. Remove from heat and add softened gelatin, stirring until it melts.

Pour juice from 2 oranges and 1 1/2 tsp lime juice into 2-cup measure. Add sugar water. Stir and set aside to cool in refrigerator for 30 minutes.

Remove from refrigerator. Pour into popsicle molds, seal, and freeze until firm. Unmold and serve immediately.

PINEAPPLE-ORANGE POPSICLES

1/2 tsp unflavored gelatin
1/4 cup cold water
1/2 cup water
3 Tbsp light-brown sugar
Juice of 1 orange
1 tsp lemon juice
1 cup canned sweetened pineapple chunks, drained

Sprinkle 1/2 tsp gelatin over 1/4 cup cold water. Stir to soften gelatin and set aside.

Pour 1/2 cup water and 3 Tbsp light-brown sugar into a small saucepan. Bring to a boil over high heat, stirring. Reduce heat and keep at a slow boil for 5 minutes without stirring. Remove from heat and pour in gelatin water, stirring until it melts. Set aside to cool.

Squeeze juice from 1 orange and enough lemon juice to measure 1 tsp. Pour into blender, drain and add 1 cup pineapple chunks, and blend until puréed. Add cooled sugar water and blend until well mixed. Pour into popsicle molds, seal, and freeze until firm. Unmold and serve immediately.

WATERMELON POPSICLES

1/2 tsp unflavored gelatin
1/4 cup cold water
1/2 cup water
2 Tbsp light-brown sugar
1 cup watermelon
4 Tbsp frozen concentrated lemonade, thawed

Sprinkle 1/2 tsp gelatin over 1/4 cup cold water, stir, and set aside to soften gelatin.

Pour 1/2 cup water and 2 Tbsp light-brown sugar in a small saucepan. Bring to a boil over high heat, stirring. Reduce heat and keep at a slow boil for 5 minutes without stirring. Remove from heat and pour in softened gelatin, stirring until it melts. Set aside to cool.

Peel, remove seeds, and chop 1 1-inch slice of watermelon, or enough to fill a 1-cup measure. Pour into blender, add 4 Tbsp concentrated lemonade, and blend until puréed.

Pour cooled sugar water into blender and blend until well mixed with watermelon purée. Pour into popsicle molds, seal, and freeze until firm. Unmold and serve immediately.

YOGURT POPSICLES

These easy-to-prepare popsicles are superb mid-afternoon snacks for children.

1 tsp gelatin
1/2 cup cold whole milk
1 8-oz container flavored yogurt or plain
    yogurt with 1 1/2 Tbsp sugar added

Combine 1 tsp gelatin with 1/2 cup cold milk in a small enameled saucepan. Warm, stirring, until gelatin melts. Remove from heat. Stir in contents from an 8-oz container of yogurt. Pour mixture into popsicle molds, seal, and freeze until firm. Unmold and serve immediately.

Fruit Juice Popsicles

Using the instructions in the Cider-Grape Popsicle recipe as a model, make all the other fruit juice popsicles the same way.

CIDER-GRAPE POPSICLES

3/4 cup cold water
1 tsp unflavored gelatin
3/8 cup frozen concentrated apple cider, thawed
3/8 cup frozen concentrated grape juice, thawed

Combine 3/4 cup cold water with 1 tsp unflavored gelatin in small saucepan. Warm the water over medium heat, stirring, until gelatin melts. Remove from heat.

Combine 3/8 cup concentrated apple cider and 3/8 cup concentrated grape juice in 2-cup measure. Stir in melted gelatin. Pour mixture into popsicle molds, seal, and freeze until firm. Unmold and serve immediately.

CRANBERRY-CIDER POPSICLES

3/4 cup cold water
1 tsp unflavored gelatin
3/8 cup frozen concentrated cranberry juice, thawed
3/8 cup frozen concentrated apple cider, thawed

CRANBERRY-GRAPE POPSICLES

3/4 cup cold water
1 tsp unflavored gelatin
3/8 cup frozen concentrated cranberry juice, thawed
3/8 cup frozen concentrated grape juice, thawed

CRANBERRY-LEMON POPSICLES

³/₄ cup cold water
1 tsp unflavored gelatin
³/₈ cup frozen concentrated cranberry juice, thawed
³/₈ cup frozen concentrated lemonade, thawed

FRUIT FLAVOR POPSICLES

³/₄ cup cold water
1 tsp unflavored gelatin
3 Tbsp frozen concentrated cranberry juice, thawed
3 Tbsp frozen concentrated grape juice, thawed
3 Tbsp frozen concentrated apple cider, thawed
3 Tbsp frozen concentrated lemonade, thawed

GRAPE POPSICLES

³/₄ cup cold water
1 tsp unflavored gelatin
³/₄ cup frozen concentrated grape juice, thawed

LEMON-GRAPE POPSICLES

³/₄ cup cold water
1 tsp unflavored gelatin
³/₈ cup frozen concentrated grape juice, thawed
³/₈ cup frozen concentrated lemonade, thawed

ORANGE-GRAPEFRUIT POPSICLES

1 cup cold water
1 tsp unflavored gelatin
½ cup frozen concentrated orange juice, thawed
2 Tbsp frozen concentrated grapefruit juice, thawed

ORANGE-PINEAPPLE POPSICLES

1 cup plus 2 Tbsp pineapple juice
1 tsp unflavored gelatin
6 Tbsp frozen concentrated orange juice, thawed

PINEAPPLE-CRANBERRY POPSICLES

1 cup plus 2 Tbsp pineapple juice
1 tsp unflavored gelatin
6 Tbsp frozen concentrated cranberry juice, thawed

PINEAPPLE-GRAPE POPSICLES

1 cup plus 2 Tbsp pineapple juice
1 tsp unflavored gelatin
6 Tbsp frozen concentrated grape juice, thawed

Sauces, Syrups, and Toppings

We have divided this chapter into three parts: sauces, syrups, and toppings. There are deliciously unusual and sweet treats like Butterscotch Sauce and Honey Cream, plus delightful fruit sauces with blackberries, strawberries, apricots, pineapple. The syrups include the traditional (Caramel, Chocolate, and Vanilla) and the exotic (Rumona and Sambuka). Finally, the pièce de résistance, nut toppings.

These recipes have been prepared with a variety of uses in mind. We recommend using them as toppings for frozen desserts; as layers in cakes, parfaits, and bombes; as flavorings in baked Alaskas, sodas, milkshakes, and malteds.

Most sauces and syrups can be stored in tightly covered glass jars in the refrigerator for some time, unless otherwise indicated in the recipe, but their flavor is of course much better if they're fresh, particularly those containing butter and/or cream.

Sauces

APRICOT SAUCE

Makes 1 cup of a mildly sweet sauce with an emphasis on its fruit.

2 cups apricots, finely chopped
1/2 cup light-brown sugar
1 Tbsp Grand Marnier (optional)

Wash, peel, and finely chop enough apricots to fill a 2-cup measure. Pour into 3-quart heavy-bottomed pot, add 1/2 cup brown sugar, and bring to a boil. Reduce heat and simmer fruit for 10 minutes, stirring from time to time.

Remove sauce from heat. If you wish to add Grand Marnier, stir the sauce a few moments to cool it and then pour in the liqueur.

Allow sauce to cool completely before storing. Store in glass jar in refrigerator.

BLACKBERRY SAUCE

Makes 1/2 cup sauce. A very pleasant tart addition to Vanilla Ice Cream, Wild Blackberry Mousse, other bland desserts, or pancakes or waffles.

1 cup fresh blackberries
1/4 cup sugar

Gently wash 1 cup blackberries. Drain and pour into medium-sized bowl. Sprinkle 1/4 cup sugar over berries and stir gently until they all are covered. Set aside at least 1 hour.

Press the sugared berries and juice through a fine sieve or through a food mill into another medium-sized bowl. If any seeds go through and they bother you, press sauce through a fine sieve lined with cheesecloth.

Pour into pitcher to serve along with ice cream or into a covered jar and store in refrigerator until ready to use.

BLUEBERRY SAUCE

Makes 1 cup of tasty sauce for Blueberry Sherbet or Vanilla Ice Cream.

1 cup frozen blueberries
1 Tbsp lemon juice
3 Tbsp granulated sugar
1/4 cup water
1 tsp cornstarch

In a small enameled saucepan combine 1 cup frozen blueberries, 1 Tbsp lemon juice, 3 Tbsp sugar, 1/4 cup water, and 1 tsp cornstarch. Cook over medium heat, stirring constantly, until sauce thickens. Cool. Store in glass jar in refrigerator.

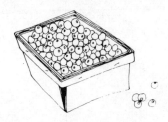

BUTTERSCOTCH SAUCE

Makes 3/4 cup of delicious traditional sauce.

 1/2 cup light-brown sugar
 1/4 cup light corn syrup
 1/4 cup butter
 1/2 cup evaporated milk

In a small enameled saucepan combine 1/2 cup light-brown sugar and 1/4 cup light corn syrup and stir over medium heat until brown sugar dissolves. Stir in 1/4 cup butter. Remove from heat and let cool slightly. Stir in 1/2 cup evaporated milk. Store in refrigerator in tightly covered glass jar.

CHERRY SAUCE

Makes 1/2 to 2/3 cup. A tasty addition to Vanilla, Chocolate, or Coffee Ice Cream and in sodas. Also works well using brandied Bing cherries.

 1 1/2 cups canned sweetened dark-red cherries with juice
 3 Tbsp granulated sugar
 1 Tbsp light corn syrup
 1/4 tsp ground cinnamon
 2 tsp lemon juice
 1 tsp arrowroot
 1 Tbsp water

Drain 1 1/2 cups canned cherries, reserving juice (about 2/3 cup). Set cherries aside.

In a 1-quart saucepan combine cherry juice, 3 Tbsp sugar, 1 Tbsp corn syrup, 1/4 tsp ground cinnamon, and 2 tsp lemon juice. Bring to a boil over high heat, stirring; then lower heat and simmer for 10 minutes. Remove from heat.

Mix together 1 tsp arrowroot and 1 Tbsp water until pasty. Add a little of cherry sauce to dilute the paste. Add a little more and then pour the mixture into the hot sauce. Return to heat and cook until sauce thickens, stirring constantly.

If sauce is to be used as a topping, stir in the cherries, allow to cool until lukewarm, and serve.

If sauce is to be used in making sodas or drinks, omit the cherries.

Cool and store in a glass jar in refrigerator.

FUDGE SAUCE

Makes 1½ cups of a delicious, rich, thick sauce, a must for sundaes.

2 oz unsweetened chocolate
3 Tbsp butter
¼ cup water
½ cup granulated sugar
½ cup light corn syrup
1 tsp vanilla extract

Melt 2 oz unsweetened chocolate with 3 Tbsp butter in small enameled saucepan over very low heat. When chocolate has melted, stir in ¼ cup water, ½ cup sugar, and ½ cup light corn syrup. Bring sauce to a boil, stirring to dissolve sugar. Remove pan from heat and allow sauce to cool before stirring in 1 tsp vanilla extract.

Store in tightly covered glass jar in refrigerator.

If using warmed sauce, pour the desired amount into a small saucepan and warm over very low heat, stirring often.

HONEY CREAM

Makes 1¼ cups of honey sauce that is pleasant with Honey Almond Ice Cream in a parfait glass.

½ cup honey
2 Tbsp butter
¾ cup heavy cream

Heat ½ cup honey and 2 Tbsp butter in a small enameled saucepan, stirring until butter melts. Stir in ¾ cup heavy cream. Cool.

Store in a glass jar in refrigerator. Sauce will keep about 1 week.

MELBA SAUCE

Makes 1 cup of a smooth, dark-red sauce to be used as a topping, parfait layer, or flavoring.

2 cups ripe red raspberries
1/3 cup granulated sugar
1/4 tsp lemon juice

Gently wash 2 cups red raspberries, drain, and pour into medium-sized bowl. Sprinkle on top 1/3 cup sugar and 1/4 tsp lemon juice; stir gently until berries are completely covered with sugar. Set aside for an hour for berries to steep in sugar and juice.

Press berries through a fine sieve lined with cheesecloth twice for a very smooth sauce.

Pour into pitcher to serve along with ice cream or into a covered jar and store in refrigerator.

NANCY'S RASPBERRY SAUCE

Makes 1 cup of a brilliant dark-red, tangy sauce good with Lemon, Strawberry, Raspberry Sherbet or Vanilla Ice Cream.

1 10-oz package raspberries frozen
  in sugar syrup, thawed
2 tsp cornstarch
Juice of 1/2 lemon
2 Tbsp granulated sugar

Drain juice from a 10-oz package frozen raspberries into a small enameled saucepan. Set berries aside.

Add 2 tsp cornstarch, juice of 1/2 lemon, and 2 Tbsp sugar to raspberry juice in saucepan. Cook over medium heat, stirring constantly, until sauce thickens.

Remove from heat and stir in reserved raspberries. Allow sauce to cool, scrape into a glass jar, cover, and store in refrigerator.

PEACH SAUCE

Makes 1 cup of ambrosial nectar good with soda or in a parfait.

6 ripe peaches
1/2 cup granulated sugar
1-inch piece of cinnamon bark

Wash, peel, and cut 6 peaches into very small pieces. Place in saucepan with 1/2 cup sugar and a 1-inch piece of cinnamon bark. Cook over very low heat until peaches fall apart and mixture becomes syrupy. Blend or put through a fine sieve.

Allow sauce to cool to lukewarm before using. Store in a glass jar in refrigerator.

PINEAPPLE-MINT SAUCE

Makes 1 cup thick, mint-flavored pineapple topping suggested for Pineapple Ice Cream (page 83).

1 8-oz can crushed unsweetened pineapple
1 Tbsp granulated sugar
1 Tbsp cornstarch
10 fresh mint leaves, crushed

Drain pineapple juice from an 8-oz can crushed unsweetened pineapple into a small enameled saucepan. Set fruit aside.

Add to the juice 1 Tbsp sugar, 1 Tbsp cornstarch, and 10 fresh mint leaves, crushed, to juice. Stir until cornstarch is uniformly distributed. Place saucepan over medium heat and, stirring constantly, cook until sauce is very thick.

Pour sauce through strainer and add reserved pineapple. Scrape into glass jar, cover tightly, and store in refrigerator.

STRAWBERRY SAUCE (FRESH)

Makes 1 cup of sauce. It is very good on Vanilla, Chocolate, Strawberry, and most other ice creams; as a layer in American parfaits; and as a topping on Belgian Waffles à la Mode (page 250).

    2 cups fresh, ripe strawberries
    1/2 cup granulated sugar
    1/2 tsp lemon juice

Wash, hull, and mince 2 cups fresh strawberries. Pour into bowl, sprinkle in 1/2 cup sugar, and stir gently until all berries are coated with sugar. Set aside at least 1 hour for sugar to penetrate berries.
    Stir 1/2 tsp lemon juice into strawberry sauce. Pour into pitcher and serve immediately. Store in refrigerator in a glass jar.

STRAWBERRY SAUCE (FROZEN)

2 cups of a sauce with chunks of berries. Try it with Strawberry Ice Cream.

    1 16-oz container whole frozen strawberries
      in sugar syrup, thawed
    1 tsp lemon juice
    1 Tbsp cornstarch
    2 Tbsp apricot jam

Thaw and drain juice from 1 16-oz container of frozen whole strawberries. Reserve juice for use later. Quarter the berries and set aside.
    Combine 1/2 cup juice from berries, 1 tsp lemon juice, and 1 Tbsp cornstarch in a small enameled saucepan. Cook over medium heat, stirring constantly, until sauce thickens.
    Remove sauce from heat and stir in 2 Tbsp apricot jam.
    Let sauce cool, then stir in reserved berries. Scrape into glass jar, cover tightly, and store in refrigerator.

Syrups

CARAMEL SYRUP

Makes 1/2 cup. To be used as directed in other recipes. Change proportions as necessary to produce amount needed.

2/3 cup granulated sugar
2 Tbsp water
1/2 cup water

In a small enameled saucepan combine 2/3 cup sugar and 2 Tbsp water. Over high heat swirl pan until the sauce turns a light amber color. Do not use a spoon.

Remove pan from heat and pour in 1/2 cup water. Now stir sauce over medium heat until all of the caramel sugar is dissolved in the water. Let syrup cool before using it. Syrup is best if freshly prepared.

CHOCOLATE SYRUP

Makes 1½ pints of a syrup that can be used as a topping or in parfaits, ice cream sodas, and malted milks.

    4 oz unsweetened chocolate
    1 cup boiling water
    1 cup granulated sugar
    1 tsp vanilla extract

In top of double boiler slowly melt 4 squares unsweetened chocolate. Add 1 cup boiling water, a little at a time, stirring all the while, until chocolate and water form a smooth mixture. Add 1 cup sugar and, continuing to stir, cook until sugar is completely dissolved.

Remove from heat. Continue to stir a few moments longer until syrup cools slightly. Then stir in 1 tsp vanilla extract.

Let cool completely before storing. Diana likes to store syrup in canning jars. This syrup can be stored in the cupboard and will keep several months.

COFFEE SYRUP

Makes ⅔ cup of a syrup that works very well as a topping but is particularly good in a soda.

    1 cup milk
    ¼ cup freshly ground coffee from Italian roast coffee beans
    ½ cup granulated sugar
    1½ tsp arrowroot

Bring 1 cup milk to a boil in a 1-quart saucepan. Add ¼ cup freshly ground coffee from Italian roast coffee beans. Stir and allow milk to boil up. Remove from heat and let steep 30 minutes.

In a small saucepan mix together ½ cup sugar and 1½ tsp arrowroot. Set aside.

Pour coffee milk through filter. Slowly add filtered coffee to sugar mixture, stirring all the while. Return to heat and cook until syrup thickens, stirring constantly.

Serve warm over ice cream or allow to cool and store in glass jar in refrigerator.

DIANA'S BLUEBERRY SYRUP

Makes 1 cup of syrup that is particularly good on Vanilla Ice Cream, but also fantastic on waffles, pancakes, and crêpes.

1 pint fresh blueberries
1/4 cup water
1/2 cup granulated sugar
Juice of 1/2 lemon

Carefully wash and remove stems from 1 pint blueberries. Pour into 3-quart pot with 1/4 cup water and 1/2 cup sugar. Bring to a boil, then reduce heat and simmer berries for 10 minutes, stirring from time to time. Press through a fine sieve to remove blueberry skin or use as is.

Squeeze juice from half a lemon and add to blueberry syrup. Cool. Store in a glass jar in refrigerator.

FRUIT JUICE SYRUP

Makes 1/2 cup of tangy syrup that goes well with sherbet.

1/4 cup frozen concentrated cranberry juice
1/4 cup frozen concentrated apple cider
1 tsp cornstarch

Combine 1/4 cup frozen cranberry juice and 1/4 cup frozen apple cider with 1 tsp cornstarch in a small enameled saucepan. Cook over medium heat, stirring constantly, until sauce thickens. Cool. Store in a glass jar in refrigerator.

GINGER SYRUP I

Makes 2/3 to 3/4 cup. An unusual topping for Vanilla or Banana Nut Ice Cream.

    1/2 cup light-brown sugar
    1 cup water
    3 Tbsp finely chopped candied ginger

Combine 1/2 cup light brown sugar, 1 cup water, and 3 Tbsp finely chopped ginger in small saucepan. Bring to a boil over high heat, stirring, then lower heat and simmer for 10 minutes or until slightly thick.

Cool and serve or store in a glass jar in the refrigerator.

GINGER SYRUP II

Makes 1 cup. A very sweet syrup with a tang of ginger—very good in sodas.

    1 cup granulated sugar
    1 cup water
    1 1/2 to 2 tsp powdered ginger

In a small saucepan combine 1 cup granulated sugar, 1 cup water, and 1 1/2 to 2 tsp powdered ginger, depending on how strong a taste you want.

Bring to a boil over high heat, stirring; then reduce heat and simmer for 10 minutes. Remove from heat. Cool and store in a glass jar in refrigerator.

RUM SYRUP

Makes ¼ cup rum syrup used to soak the sponge layers of ice cream cakes.

    ¼ cup rum
    ¼ cup granulated sugar

Combine ¼ cup rum and ¼ cup sugar in a small saucepan. Warm slightly and stir until sugar is dissolved.
Use immediately.

RUMONA SYRUP

Makes ½ cup, enough for 4 servings. This rich syrup is flavored with Rumona, a rum-based Jamaican liqueur. It is very good with Vanilla Ice Cream.

    ½ cup Rumona liqueur
    4 Tbsp granulated sugar
    4 Tbsp butter cut into small pieces

In a small enameled saucepan bring to a boil ½ cup Rumona liqueur with 4 Tbsp sugar over high heat, stirring. Continue to boil for 3 minutes. Remove from heat and stir in 4 Tbsp butter cut into small pieces.
Let sauce cool to room temperature before serving on ice cream.
Sauce may be stored in refrigerator in a tightly covered glass jar for 1 week.

SAMBUKA COFFEE SYRUP

Makes ½ cup syrup with an unusual licorice flavor; great with any coffee ice cream. Sambuka is an Italian liqueur flavored with licorice and elderberries, recently made available in this country. In Italy the liqueur is usually poured over a few coffee beans placed in the bottom of a cordial glass.

½ cup very strong freshly brewed coffee (page 21)
3 Tbsp granulated sugar
1½ tsp cornstarch
1 Tbsp Sambuka liqueur

Combine ½ cup coffee, 3 Tbsp sugar, and 1½ tsp cornstarch in a small enameled saucepan. Cook over medium heat, stirring constantly, until sauce thickens. Cool. Stir in 1 Tbsp Sambuka liqueur.

Store in a glass jar in refrigerator.

VANILLA SYRUP

Makes about ⅔ cup. Used primarily in sodas, milkshakes, and malteds.

1 cup water
½ cup granulated sugar
2-inch piece of vanilla bean
1 tsp arrowroot
1 Tbsp water

In small saucepan combine 1 cup water with ½ cup sugar. Cut off a 2-inch piece of vanilla bean, split in half lengthwise, scrape out black powder, and add to sugar and water along with remaining pieces of bark. Bring to a boil over high heat, stirring; then lower heat and simmer 10 minutes, until mixture becomes syrupy. Remove from heat.

Mix together 1 tsp arrowroot and 1 Tbsp water until pasty. Add a little of the sugar water to dilute the paste. Add a little more and then pour the mixture into the hot sugar water. Return to heat and cook until syrup becomes thick, stirring constantly. Remove vanilla bark.

Allow to cool and store in a glass jar in refrigerator.

Toppings

MAPLE TOPPING

Makes ¾ cup of a thick, maple-flavored syrup that is good with Vanilla Ice Cream.

½ cup maple syrup
2 Tbsp butter
4 Tbsp evaporated milk

In a small enameled saucepan boil ½ cup maple syrup over high heat for 4 minutes. Remove from heat and stir in 2 Tbsp butter. Then stir in 4 Tbsp evaporated milk. Place topping in a glass jar, cover tightly, and store in refrigerator.

PECAN TOPPING

1 cup crunchy pecans in caramel sauce to be used to decorate parfaits.

½ cup caramel syrup (page 184)
¼ cup light corn syrup
¾ cup pecans (chopped or whole)

Combine ½ cup caramel syrup, ¼ cup light corn syrup, and ¾ cup pecans.
If sauce is being used to decorate a mold, nuts should be left whole. If sauce is being used as a topping for ice cream, nuts should be chopped.
Store sauce in tightly covered glass jar in refrigerator.

SWEETENED WHIPPED CREAM

Makes 2 cups of sweetened whipped cream to be used as topping for parfaits and sundaes.

1 cup heavy cream
1 Tbsp granulated sugar

In a 1-quart mixing bowl, whip 1 cup heavy cream until soft peaks form. (It will whip very well if bowl, beaters, and cream are very cold.) Add 1 Tbsp sugar and whip a few moments longer.

Sweetened whipped cream may be stored in the refrigerator for several hours.

WALNUT TOPPING

Makes 1 cup of maple-flavored caramel sauce with walnuts to be used on sundaes and banana splits.

1/2 cup caramel syrup (page 184)
1/4 cup maple syrup
2/3 cup walnuts (chopped or whole)

Combine 1/2 cup caramel syrup, 1/4 cup maple syrup, and 2/3 cup chopped or whole walnuts.

If the sauce is being used to decorate a mold nuts should be left whole. If sauce is being used as a topping for ice cream nuts should be chopped.

Store sauce in tightly covered glass jar in refrigerator.

American Parfaits,
Baked Alaskas,
and Meringue Desserts

American Parfaits

American parfaits are a boon to the busy host or hostess. All you need are an ice cream, sauce, and topping, plus parfait or tall glasses and long spoons.

These desserts consist of layers of ripened ice cream, mousse, soufflé, sherbet, or water ice alternating with layers of sauce, syrup, or liqueur. The concoction is then returned to the freezer for a short time to firm up, topped with whipped cream and nuts, as desired, and served.

The Sherbet Bowl is a giant version of this dessert.

All the American parfaits are for 1 person, so the amount is not listed.

BLUEBERRY LIME PARFAIT

A cool, refreshing summer dessert.

Lime Sherbet (page 140)
Blueberry Sauce (page 178)

Spoon 1 small scoop of Lime Sherbet into bottom of parfait glass. Cover first layer of sherbet with 1 Tbsp Blueberry Sauce. Make 2 more layers of sherbet and sauce. Place in freezer until ready to serve. Serve directly from freezer.

CHERRY CREAM PARFAIT

1 Tbsp Brandied Cherry Sauce or Cherry Sauce (page 179)
3 Tbsp Vanilla Ice Cream (page 33)
2 Tbsp Pineapple-Mint Sauce (page 182)
3 Tbsp Chocolate Ice Cream (page 51)
2 Tbsp Blueberry Sauce (page 178)
3 Tbsp Strawberry Ice Cream (page 91)
Dollop of whipped cream
1 brandied cherry

In tall parfait glass place 1 Tbsp Brandied Cherry Sauce. Add 3 Tbsp Vanilla Ice Cream. Then add a 2-Tbsp layer of Pineapple-Mint Sauce. Top that layer with 3 Tbsp Chocolate Ice Cream. Add 2 Tbsp Blueberry Sauce. Top layer with 3 Tbsp Strawberry Ice Cream.

Place tall glass in freezer for 45 to 60 minutes until parfait has set. Add a dollop of whipped cream and a brandied cherry before serving.

CHOCOLATE FUDGE PARFAIT

Chocolate Ice Cream (page 51)
Fudge Sauce, chilled (page 180)
Whipped cream

Spoon 1 small scoop of softened Chocolate Ice Cream into bottom of parfait glass. Cover ice cream layer with 1 Tbsp chilled Fudge Sauce. Make 2 more layers of ice cream and sauce. Place in freezer until ready to serve.

When ready to serve remove parfait glasses from freezer and place a spoonful of whipped cream on top. Serve immediately.

LIQUEUR-FLAVORED PARFAITS

Special combinations of your own favorite flavors.

Ice cream or sherbet, your favorite flavor
3 Tbsp of your favorite liqueur
Sweetened Whipped Cream, optional (page 191)

Spoon 1 small scoop of ice cream or sherbet into bottom of parfait glass. Cover first layer with 1 Tbsp liqueur. Make 2 more layers of ice cream and liqueur. Place in freezer until ready to serve.

Remove parfait glasses from freezer and, if you wish, before serving, top with a spoonful of Sweetened Whipped Cream.

PINEAPPLE PARFAIT

Sweet, filling dessert with a chunky texture.

Vanilla Ice Cream (page 33)
Pineapple-Mint Sauce, chilled (page 182)
Whipped cream

Spoon 1 small scoop Vanilla Ice Cream into bottom of parfait glass. Cover with 1 Tbsp Pineapple-Mint Sauce. Make 2 more layers of ice cream and sauce. Place in freezer until ready to serve.

Remove parfait glasses from freezer and, before serving, top with a spoonful of whipped cream.

RASPBERRY SHERBET PARFAIT

Tangy, not too sweet dessert good after a heavy meal.

Raspberry Sherbet (page 144)
Raspberry Sauce, chilled (page 181)

Spoon 1 small scoop Raspberry Sherbet into bottom of parfait glass. Cover first layer of sherbet with 1 Tbsp Raspberry Sauce. Make 2 more layers of sherbet and sauce. Place in freezer until ready to serve.

Serve immediately from freezer.

SHERBET PARFAIT

A colorful refreshment for a hot summer night.

1 scoop Lemon Sherbet (page 138)
1 scoop Raspberry Sherbet (page 144)
1 scoop Lime Sherbet (page 140)
3 Tbsp Raspberry Sauce, chilled (page 181)

Spoon scoop of Lemon Sherbet into bottom of parfait glass. Cover with 1 Tbsp Raspberry Sauce. Add scoop of Raspberry Sherbet and cover with 1 Tbsp Raspberry Sauce. Add scoop of Lime Sherbet and top with 1 Tbsp Raspberry Sauce. Cover and place in freezer until ready to serve.
Serve directly from freezer.

SAMBUKA PARFAIT

Coffee ice cream enhanced with licorice-flavored liqueur is a very unusual dessert.

Coffee Ice Cream (page 59)
Sambuka Sauce (page 189)
Sweetened Whipped Cream (page 191)

Spoon 1 small scoop Coffee Ice Cream into bottom of parfait glass. Cover ice cream with 1 Tbsp Sambuka Sauce. Make 2 more layers of ice cream and sauce. Place in freezer until ready to serve.
Remove parfait glasses from freezer and, before serving, top with a spoonful of Sweetened Whipped Cream.

STRAWBERRY-LEMON PARFAIT

Very sweet with tart overtones.

> Lemon Sherbet (page 138)
> Strawberry Sauce, chilled (page 183)

Spoon 1 small scoop Lemon Sherbet into bottom of parfait glass. Cover sherbet with 1 Tbsp Strawberry Sauce. Make 2 more layers of sherbet and sauce. Place in freezer until ready to serve. Serve immediately from freezer.

RASPBERRY SUPREME

Serves 6. A colorful layered dessert, given to Nancy by a friend from Seattle.

> 1 quart Raspberry Sherbet (page 144; omit the heavy cream)
> 1½ pints Vanilla Soufflé (page 129)
> 1 cup Raspberry Sauce (page 181)

Prepare Raspberry Sherbet. When sherbet has been whipped for the second time, scrape into bottom of a 1½-quart glass bowl. Cover and freeze until firm.

While sherbet is freezing, prepare the Vanilla Soufflé. Leave soufflé in bowl, cover tightly, and place in freezer until ready to use.

Next prepare Raspberry Sauce. Chill.

Remove frozen Raspberry Sherbet mold from freezer. Spoon on half the sauce. Scrape Vanilla Soufflé on top of sauce and smooth with back of a spoon. Cover bowl tightly and place in freezer for 2 hours or until ready to serve.

Scoop dessert from bottom of bowl to include all of the layers. Serve rest of Raspberry Sauce separately.

SHERBET BOWL

Makes about 4 quarts of a very colorful summer dessert with a variety of flavors and textures. The dessert may be prepared in a glass punch bowl or individual parfait glasses. In addition, the layers may be varied with different flavors. The following flavors are Nancy's favorite combination of summer fruits and sherbets. Prepare the following:

    1 quart Lime Sherbet (page 140)
    1 cup Blueberry Sauce, chilled (page 178)
    ½ pint fresh blueberries
    1 quart Raspberry Sherbet (page 144)
    1 cup Raspberry Sauce, chilled (page 181)
    ½ pint fresh strawberries, sliced
    1 quart Vanilla Soufflé (page 129)
    ½ pint fresh blueberries
    ½ pint fresh strawberries, whole

Prepare all of the above sherbets, sauces, and soufflé at least 1 day before.

Assemble the dessert a few hours before serving. Place 1 quart Lime Sherbet in the bottom of a large glass bowl. Smooth with spoon or spatula. Cover sherbet with 1 cup Blueberry Sauce and ½ pint fresh blueberries. Add scoops of 1 quart Raspberry Sherbet. Cover with 1 cup Raspberry Sauce and ½ pint fresh sliced strawberries. Cover berries with 1 quart of Vanilla Soufflé. Smooth soufflé with the back of a spoon. Arrange ½ pint fresh blueberries and ½ pint fresh strawberries on top of soufflé.

Place dessert in freezer until ready to serve. Use a long-handled serving spoon to dish out dessert, making sure to dig down and get a little bit of everything.

Baked Alaskas

A baked Alaska is an attractive, elegant dessert that is relatively easy to prepare with a little practice. It is a combination of cake, ice cream or sherbet, and meringue that provides interesting taste and flavor contrasts and has the mystery of hot and cold combined.

A few days before, or at least the day before the dessert is to be served, make all of the parts necessary except the meringue—such as the ice cream or sherbet for the filling, the cake or crust for the bottom, and any sauce or glaze.

As soon as the parts are ready the dessert may be assembled. Place the cake on heatproof serving platter, cutting and arranging the pieces if the cake isn't the shape of the platter. Spread or spoon any sauce or glaze over cake.

Spoon the ice cream or sherbet on top of the cake, leaving a 1-inch border. The ice cream should be firm enough to hold its shape. Place platter in freezer.

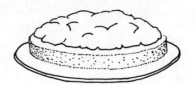

Next, prepare the meringue. Beat egg whites with cream of tartar until soft peaks form. Beat in granulated sugar 1 tablespoon at a time. Continue beating until egg whites hold stiff peaks and are smooth and glossy.

Remove platter from freezer. Spread meringue over ice cream either to edge of cake or down to platter. Be careful to cover ice cream completely.

The baked Alaska may now be placed in the freezer until ready to use. If Alaska is not going to be used immediately, cover loosely when firm. The dessert will keep 1 or 2 days. The only exceptions are Chocolate Pecan Baked Alaska and Strawberry Shortcake Baked Alaska.

When you are almost ready to serve dessert, preheat oven to 450°. Remove Alaska from freezer. For added insulation place platter on wooden board before putting Alaska in oven. Place in oven and bake approximately 5 minutes, or until meringue is lightly browned. Watch carefully and remove as soon as meringue is ready.

Serve immediately.

To slice the Alaska use a sharp 10-inch heavy-duty knife and serve with pie knife. If any dessert remains, place immediately in freezer. While not as good, because meringue and cake become soggy, leftovers can be eaten the next day by the family.

Proportions for Baked Alaskas

For 6 people

    One 8-inch round sponge cake layer
    3 to 4 Tbsp glaze or sauce
    1 quart ice cream or sherbet
    Meringue made with 5 egg whites, 1/2 tsp cream of tartar,
        and 5 Tbsp granulated sugar

For 8 people

    One 9-inch round sponge cake layer
    4 Tbsp glaze or sauce
    1 1/2 quarts ice cream or sherbet
    Meringue made with 5 egg whites, 1/2 tsp cream of tartar,
        and 5 Tbsp granulated sugar

For 12 people

    One 9-by-13-inch sponge cake layer cut to fit shape of platter
    6 Tbsp glaze or sauce
    2 quarts ice cream or sherbet
    Meringue made with 7 egg whites, 1/2 tsp cream of tartar,
        and 7 Tbsp granulated sugar

One serving or individual baked Alaska

    One 4-inch round or square piece sponge cake
    1 Tbsp glaze or sauce
    One large scoop of ice cream or sherbet
    Meringue made with 1 egg white, 1/8 tsp cream of tartar,
        and 1 Tbsp granulated sugar

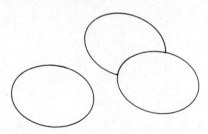

BAKED ALASKA WITH APRICOT SHERBET

Serves 10. Superb finale to any dinner.

    2 Tbsp brandy
    2 Tbsp water
    Meringue:
        2 Tbsp granulated sugar
        7 egg whites
        1/4 tsp cream of tartar
        7 Tbsp granulated sugar
    Chocolate Sponge Cake (page 236)
    2 quarts softened Apricot Sherbet (page 132)

To prepare Brandy Sauce combine 2 Tbsp brandy, 2 Tbsp water, and 2 Tbsp sugar in a small saucepan. Heat gently, stirring, until sugar dissolves. Set aside.

In large bowl beat 7 egg whites and 1/4 tsp cream of tartar until egg whites form soft peaks. Beat in 7 Tbsp sugar, 1 tablespoon at a time. Continue beating until egg whites are smooth and glossy and hold stiff peaks. Set aside.

To assemble Alaska, cut Chocolate Sponge Cake to fit a large ovenproof platter, leaving a 1½-inch border around the edge uncovered. Spoon Brandy Sauce over Chocolate Sponge Cake base.

Heap scoops of softened Apricot Sherbet (about 2 quarts) on top of chocolate cake, leaving a 1-inch border of cake. Cover sherbet with a 1-inch thick layer of meringue, making sure to bring meringue down to the cake layer to seal in sherbet. Alaska can be prepared in advance up to this stage and placed in freezer until ready to bake.

Preheat oven to 450°. Place platter on a wooden board for added insulation before putting Alaska in oven. Place Alaska in preheated oven until meringue is lightly brown (about 5 minutes).

Serve immediately.

To slice, use a sharp, heavy knife.

CHOCOLATE MINT BAKED ALASKA

Serves 8. A very colorful sweet dessert.

1 Nine-Inch Round Chocolate Sponge Cake (page 238)
1½ quarts Crème de Menthe Ice Cream (page 61)
3 Tbsp homemade Chocolate Syrup (page 185)
Meringue:
　　5 egg whites
　　½ tsp cream of tartar
　　5 Tbsp granulated sugar

Prepare Nine-Inch Round Chocolate Sponge Cake, 1½ quarts Crème de Menthe Ice Cream, and 3 Tbsp Chocolate Syrup. Store as directed until ready to use.

When ready to assemble dessert prepare meringue. Beat 5 egg whites with ½ tsp cream of tartar until soft peaks form. One at a time beat in 5 Tbsp sugar and continue beating until egg whites hold stiff peaks and are smooth and glossy. Set aside.

Arrange cake on ovenproof platter. Sparsely spread 3 Tbsp Chocolate Syrup on cake. Remove ice cream from freezer and heap scoops on top of cake, leaving a 1-inch border. Spread meringue over ice cream, covering completely. The dessert may now be frozen and stored for 1 or 2 days if you wish.

When ready to serve, preheat oven to 450°.

Remove baked Alaska from freezer, place platter on a wooden board, and bake until meringue is lightly browned (about 5 minutes).

Serve immediately. To slice, use a sharp, heavy knife.

DRAMBUIE BAKED ALASKA

Serves 8. Scotch-flavored ice cream gives an unusual taste to this dessert.

1 Nine-Inch Round Sponge Cake (page 238)
1½ quarts Drambuie Ice Cream (page 62)
Meringue:
　　5 egg whites
　　½ tsp cream of tartar
　　5 Tbsp granulated sugar

Prepare Nine-Inch Round Sponge Cake and the Drambuie Ice Cream. Store as directed until ready to use.

When ready to assemble dessert, remove Drambuie Ice Cream from freezer and allow to ripen at room temperature.

Prepare meringue. Beat 5 egg whites with ½ tsp cream of tartar until soft peaks form. One at a time beat in 5 Tbsp sugar and continue beating until egg whites hold stiff peaks and are smooth and glossy. Set aside.

Arrange cake on ovenproof platter. Heap scoops of ice cream on top of cake, leaving a 1-inch border. Spread meringue over ice cream, covering it completely. The dessert may now be frozen and stored for 1 or 2 days.

When ready to serve dessert preheat oven to 450°.

Remove baked Alaska from freezer, place platter on a wooden board, and bake until meringue is lightly browned (about 5 minutes).

Serve immediately. To slice, use a sharp, heavy knife.

CHOCOLATE PECAN BAKED ALASKA

Serves 6. A very chewy chocolate confection.

Pecan Meringue Crust (page 206)
1 quart Chocolate Pecan Ice Cream (page 56)
Meringue:
    5 egg whites
    ½ tsp cream of tartar
    5 Tbsp granulated sugar

Prepare Pecan Meringue Crust and Chocolate Pecan Ice Cream and store as directed.

This dessert must be assembled just before baking and then served immediately.

Preheat oven to 450°.

Prepare meringue. Beat 5 egg whites with ½ tsp cream of tartar until soft peaks form. One at a time beat in 5 Tbsp sugar and continue beating until egg whites hold stiff peaks and are smooth and glossy. Set aside.

Place Pecan Meringue Crust on round ovenproof platter. Heap scoops of Chocolate Pecan Ice Cream on top of crust, covering crust completely. Spread meringue over ice cream and crust to edge of platter.

Place platter on wooden board and bake in preheated oven until meringue is lightly browned (about 5 minutes).

Serve immediately. To slice, use a sharp, heavy knife.

PECAN MERINGUE CRUST

Crispy, nutty crust good under ice cream or in a baked Alaska.

½ cup finely chopped pecans
2 egg whites
½ cup granulated sugar
½ tsp vanilla extract

Cut two thicknesses of waxed paper into 8-inch circles and grease one side of each. Stick circles together and put on cookie sheet to form double thickness.

Finely chop enough pecans to fill ½ cup measure. Set aside.

Using medium-sized bowl beat 2 egg whites until soft peaks form. Slowly beat in ½ cup sugar and continue beating until mixture is smooth and glossy. Beat in ½ tsp vanilla extract. Fold in chopped pecans.

Spread prepared meringue onto 8-inch circles of wax paper. It does not matter if meringue does not exactly cover or overlap paper.

Bake at 250° for at least 2 hours, or until meringue is stiff and dried out, and can be easily removed from cookie sheet. Gently slide meringue onto a plate, invert onto a rack, and remove layers of waxed paper while still warm.

RASPBERRY BAKED ALASKA

Serves 8. Sherbet and meringue combine to form a tart but sweet treat.

    1 Nine-Inch Round Sponge Cake (page 238)
    1½ quarts Raspberry Sherbet (page 144)
    Meringue:
        5 egg whites
        ½ tsp cream of tartar
        5 Tbsp granulated sugar

Prepare Nine-Inch Round Sponge Cake and 1½ quarts Raspberry Sherbet. Store as directed until ready to use.

When ready to assemble dessert, remove Raspberry Sherbet from freezer and allow to ripen in refrigerator while preparing meringue.

Prepare meringue. Beat 5 egg whites with ½ tsp cream of tartar until soft peaks form. One at a time beat in 5 Tbsp sugar and continue beating until egg whites hold stiff peaks and are smooth and glossy. Set aside.

Arrange cake on ovenproof platter. Remove sherbet from refrigerator and heap scoops on top of cake, leaving a 1-inch border. Spread meringue over ice cream, covering completely. The dessert may now be frozen and stored for 1 or 2 days.

When ready to serve dessert preheat oven to 450°.

Remove baked Alaska from freezer, place platter on a wooden board, and bake until meringue is lightly browned (about 5 minutes).

Serve immediately. To slice, use a sharp, heavy knife.

RUM SPONGE BAKED ALASKA

Serves 8. A sweet, heavily rum-flavored dessert.

1 Nine-Inch Round Sponge Cake (page 238)
4 Tbsp Rum Syrup (page 188)
1½ quarts Rum Vanilla Ice Cream (French Vanilla
    Ice Cream made with 3 Tbsp rum, page 33)
Meringue:
    5 egg whites
    ½ tsp cream of tartar
    5 Tbsp granulated sugar

Prepare Nine-Inch Round Sponge Cake, the Rum Syrup, and Rum Vanilla Ice Cream. Store as directed until ready to use.

When ready to assemble dessert, remove Rum Vanilla Ice Cream from freezer and allow to ripen at room temperature.

Prepare meringue. Beat 5 egg whites with ½ tsp cream of tartar until soft peaks form. One at a time beat in 5 Tbsp sugar and continue beating until egg whites hold stiff peaks and are smooth and glossy. Set aside.

Arrange cake on ovenproof platter. Soak cake with 4 Tbsp Rum Syrup. Heap scoops of ice cream on top of cake, leaving a 1-inch border. Spread meringue over ice cream, being careful to cover completely. The dessert may now be frozen and stored for 1 or 2 days.

When ready to serve, preheat oven to 450°.

Remove baked Alaska from freezer, place platter on a wooden board, and bake until meringue is lightly browned (about 5 minutes).

Serve immediately. To slice, use a sharp, heavy knife.

STRAWBERRY SHORTCAKE BAKED ALASKA

Serves 8. An attractive dessert with a surprise in the middle.

1 Nine-Inch Round Sponge Cake (page 238)
1½ quarts French Vanilla Ice Cream (page 33)
½ pint fresh strawberries
Meringue:
    5 egg whites
    ½ tsp cream of tartar
    5 Tbsp granulated sugar

Prepare 1 Nine-Inch Round Sponge Cake and 1½ quarts French Vanilla Ice Cream. Store as directed.

The same day as serving dessert, wash, hull, and slice ½ pint fresh strawberries. Place in covered dish in refrigerator until ready to use.

This dessert must be assembled just before baking and then served immediately.

Preheat oven to 450°.

Remove French Vanilla Ice Cream from freezer and allow to ripen at room temperature.

Prepare meringue. Beat 5 egg whites with ½ tsp cream of tartar until soft peaks form. One at a time beat in 5 Tbsp sugar and continue beating until egg whites hold stiff peaks and are smooth and glossy. Set aside.

Arrange cake on ovenproof platter. Remove sliced strawberries from refrigerator and spoon over cake. Heap scoops of ice cream on top of cake, leaving a 1-inch border. Spread meringue over ice cream, covering completely.

Place platter on a wooden board and bake in preheated oven until meringue is lightly browned (about 5 minutes).

Serve immediately. To slice, use a sharp, heavy knife.

Meringue Desserts

A crisp meringue shell filled with ice cream is covered with sauce and topped with whipped cream. The crunchy sweet meringue blends beautifully with the cold ice cream. Chocolate sauce or strawberries add texture and flavor to these desserts. These lovely desserts are fun to serve to appreciative guests.

MERINGUE SHELL

Large round meringue shell to be filled with ice cream and topped with sauce.

> Prepared cookie sheet
> 5 egg whites
> 1/2 tsp cream of tartar
> 10 Tbsp granulated sugar
> 1 tsp vanilla extract
> Pastry bag

To prepare cookie sheet, cut two thicknesses of waxed paper into 11-inch circles. Grease the top of each circle. Stick these sides together to form a double layer and place on the cookie sheet.

Preheat oven to 250°.

In a large mixing bowl, using an electric mixer, beat 5 egg whites with 1/2 tsp cream of tartar until soft peaks form. While egg whites continue to beat, add 10 Tbsp sugar, 1 at a time. Add 1 tsp vanilla extract. Continue beating until egg whites are very smooth and glossy and hold stiff peaks.

Scrape meringue into pastry bag. Using pastry tube squeeze

meringue in a circle ¼ inch from edge of paper; then keep squeezing in smaller, spiraling circles to fill in the middle. Squeeze an extra layer of meringue on top of the outermost circle to form a rim.

Bake at 250° for 2 hours, or more if the day is humid, until meringue is stiff, dried out, and will slide easily off cookie sheet. Gently slide meringue onto a plate, invert onto a rack, and remove waxed paper.

To store meringue, wrap loosely in 2 layers of waxed paper and place in covered box. Meringue will keep several days in dry weather. In humid weather meringue may become soggy. To dry it out, place in a 250° oven until crispness returns.

CHOCOLATE FUDGE MERINGUE

Serves 8. Very sweet crunchy chocolate dessert with an interesting combination of textures.

> Prepared meringue shell (page 210)
> 1 quart homemade Chocolate Ice Cream (page 51)
> 1 cup Fudge Sauce (page 180)
> 1 cup heavy cream
> 1 Tbsp granulated sugar
> ½ tsp vanilla extract
> Semi-sweet chocolate curls

Prepare meringue shell and set aside. Make 1 quart Chocolate Ice Cream and set aside in freezer. Prepare 1 cup Fudge Sauce and pour into covered jar; place in refrigerator to chill. All these may be made a day in advance.

About 30 minutes before ready to serve, whip 1 cup heavy cream until soft peaks form. Add 1 Tbsp sugar and ½ tsp vanilla extract and whip a moment longer. Place in refrigerator until ready to use. Remove ice cream from freezer and place in refrigerator to ripen.

Just before serving, assemble dessert. Place meringue shell on a round platter. Place scoops of chocolate ice cream on top of meringue shell. Spoon Fudge Sauce over ice cream. Cover dessert to the edge of meringue with whipped cream. Decorate with chocolate curls made by scraping a solid piece of semi-sweet chocolate with a vegetable peeler.

To slice, use a sharp, heavy knife. Serve immediately.

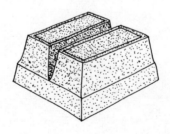

STRAWBERRY MERINGUE

Serves 8 generously. Elegant, pretty strawberry dessert.

Prepared meringue shell (page 210)
1 quart French Vanilla Ice Cream (page 33)
1 pint fresh strawberries
1 Tbsp granulated sugar
1 cup heavy cream
1 Tbsp granulated sugar
1/2 tsp vanilla extract

Prepare meringue shell and set aside.

Make 1 quart French Vanilla Ice Cream and store in freezer. Both of these may be made a day in advance.

Wash and hull 1 pint fresh strawberries. Set aside 4 or 5 whole berries. Slice remaining strawberries and sprinkle with 1 Tbsp sugar. Place strawberries in refrigerator until ready to use.

About 30 minutes before ready to serve, whip 1 cup heavy cream until soft peaks form. Add 1 Tbsp sugar and 1/2 tsp vanilla extract and whip a moment longer. Place in refrigerator until ready to use. Remove ice cream from freezer and put in refrigerator to ripen.

Just before serving, assemble dessert. Place meringue shell on round serving plate. Scoop the vanilla ice cream on top of meringue shell. Spoon sliced strawberries and any juice over ice cream. Cover dessert to the edge of meringue with whipped cream. Decorate with reserved whole berries.

To slice, use a sharp, heavy knife. Serve immediately.

Frozen Pies,
Ice Cream Cakes, and
Sponge Layers

Frozen Pies

Frozen ice cream pies are made using a crisp, tasty cookie crust and a velvety firm ice cream.

These pies are particularly attractive to serve. Nancy's guests have been enjoying them for years. One of the favorites, the Brandy Alexander Pie, combines a chocolate cookie crust with a rich, smooth brandy-flavored filling. The Chocolate Chocolate Chocolate Ice Cream Pie, a chocolate cookie crust, chocolate ice cream, and fudge sauce, is a must for any chocolate lover.

BANANA PUMPKIN PIE

This unusual combination makes an interesting dessert that serves 4.

    1 very ripe banana, mashed
    1/2 cup pumpkin purée (page 88)
    2 tsp lemon juice
    2 tsp unflavored gelatin
    1/4 cup milk
    3 egg yolks
    3 Tbsp light-brown sugar, with lumps broken up
    1/8 tsp nutmeg
    1/8 tsp powdered cloves
    1/4 cup heavy cream
    7 1/2-inch Graham Cracker Crust (page 222)

In a small bowl mash 1 banana. Add 1/2 cup pumpkin purée and 2 tsp lemon juice. Stir until well combined. Set aside.

In a small saucepan soften 2 tsp gelatin in 1/4 cup cold milk. Warm over low heat until gelatin melts.

In a medium-sized bowl beat 3 egg yolks until very thick and volume has increased (at least 5 minutes). Slowly add 3 Tbsp light-brown sugar with lumps broken up, and continue beating until mixture is very thick and resembles mayonnaise. Beat in 1/8 tsp nutmeg and 1/8 tsp powdered cloves. Stir in the melted gelatin and milk, then the banana and pumpkin mixture.

Place in refrigerator to chill.

Using a wire whisk, whip 1/4 cup heavy cream until soft peaks form. Remove chilled filling from refrigerator and fold into it the whipped cream. Scrape filling into prepared Graham Cracker Crust. Cover tightly and freeze for 3 hours.

Before serving, allow pie to sit at room temperature for about 10 minutes.

BRANDY ALEXANDER PIE

Makes 1 small pie, which is Nancy's favorite dessert.

2 Tbsp cold milk
4 Tbsp heavy cream
1 tsp unflavored gelatin
2 egg yolks
2 Tbsp granulated sugar
2 Tbsp brandy
3 Tbsp Crème de Cacao
1/2 cup heavy cream
1 Tbsp granulated sugar
7 1/2-inch Chocolate Cookie Crust (page 221)
    or your own favorite cookie crust

In a small saucepan combine 2 Tbsp cold milk, 4 Tbsp heavy cream, and 1 tsp gelatin. Stir to soften gelatin and then warm slowly until gelatin melts. Remove from heat and set aside.

Using medium-sized bowl beat together 2 egg yolks and 2 Tbsp sugar with wire whisk until mixture is thick and light yellow in color. Stir in 2 Tbsp brandy and 3 Tbsp Crème de Cacao. Then stir in gelatin and milk.

Chill in refrigerator about 20 minutes.

Whip 1/2 cup heavy cream until soft peaks form. Add 1 Tbsp sugar and whip a moment longer.

Remove chilled gelatin mixture from refrigerator and fold in the whipped cream. Pour filling into 7-1/2-inch prepared crust and place in freezer for several hours until firm.

CHOCOLATE CHOCOLATE CHOCOLATE ICE CREAM PIE

A rich, filling dessert with three different chocolate layers that serves 6 to 8.

> 9-inch Chocolate Cookie Crust (page 221)
> ¾ quart Chocolate Ice Cream (page 51)
> ¾ quart French Vanilla Ice Cream (page 33)
> 1 cup Fudge Sauce (page 180)

Prepare the Chocolate Cookie Crust, doubling recipe to make a 9-inch crust. When it's cool, place in freezer.

Make ¾ quart Chocolate Ice Cream and ¾ quart French Vanilla Ice Cream.

Prepare 1 cup Fudge Sauce and chill in refrigerator.

After the ice creams have partially frozen and have been stirred thoroughly, begin assembling the pie.

Remove pie crust from freezer. Spread chocolate ice cream on the crust. Next spread a thick layer of chilled Fudge Sauce. Cover fudge sauce with vanilla ice cream. Cover pie with plastic wrap and return to freezer until firm (about 2 hours).

Just before serving, decorate top of pie with some of the remaining Fudge Sauce.

Before slicing, allow pie to ripen at room temperature for 10 minutes. To slice the pie, use a sharp, heavy knife.

CREAM CHEESE PIE

Serves 6. Delicious, smooth almond-flavored pie resembling cheese cake.

> 2 3-oz packages cream cheese, at room temperature
> 4 egg yolks
> ¼ cup granulated sugar
> 1 tsp vanilla extract
> 1 tsp almond extract
> 2 egg whites
> ¼ cup granulated sugar
> 9-inch Graham Cracker Crust (page 222)

Whip 2 3-oz packages cream cheese until light and fluffy. Set aside.

Beat 4 egg yolks until thick and light and greatly increased in volume. Slowly beat in ¼ cup sugar and continue beating until yolks resemble mayonnaise. Add 1 tsp vanilla and 1 tsp almond extract. Add whipped cream cheese and beat a few moments longer. Set aside.

Beat 2 egg whites until soft peaks form. Slowly beat in ¼ cup sugar and continue beating until whites are smooth and glossy, and hold very stiff peaks. Fold egg whites into egg-and-cream-cheese mixture.

Scrape filling into the prepared 9-inch Graham Cracker Crust. Cover pie and freeze until firm.

Before serving, allow pie to ripen at room temperature for 10 minutes.

To slice pie use a sharp, heavy knife.

CRÈME DE MENTHE PIE

Reminiscent of a "Grasshopper."

2 Tbsp milk
4 Tbsp heavy cream
1 tsp unflavored gelatin
2 egg yolks
3 Tbsp granulated sugar
⅓ cup Crème de Menthe
1 Tbsp Crème de Cacao
½ cup heavy cream
1 Tbsp granulated sugar
7½-inch Chocolate Cookie Crust (page 221)
    or your own favorite cookie crust

In a small saucepan mix together 2 Tbsp milk, 4 Tbsp heavy cream, and 1 tsp gelatin. Slowly warm to melt gelatin. Remove from heat and set aside.

In medium-sized bowl beat together 2 egg yolks and 3 Tbsp sugar until thick, light yellow in color, and the sugar has completely dissolved. Beat in ⅓ cup Crème de Menthe and 1 Tbsp Crème de Cacao. Then slowly pour in warmed gelatin and milk, beating all the while.

Chill in refrigerator and allow to thicken slightly for 30 minutes.

Whip ½ cup cream until it forms soft peaks. Add 1 Tbsp sugar and whip a moment longer.

Remove chilled mixture from refrigerator. Fold in whipped cream. Scrape filling into 7½-inch prepared crust and place in freezer several hours until firm.

Dessert may be served directly from freezer.

ORANGE LIQUEUR PIE

Grand Marnier enthusiasts will particularly enjoy this frozen pie. The filling is also great alone in sherbet glasses.

    1/2 cup light cream
    1 tsp unflavored gelatin
    2 egg yolks
    1/4 cup light-brown sugar, with lumps broken up
    1/3 cup Grand Marnier
    1/2 cup heavy cream
    1 Tbsp light-brown sugar, with lumps broken up
    71/2-inch Chocolate Cookie Crust (page 221)
        or your own favorite cookie crust

In a small saucepan sprinkle 1 tsp gelatin over 1/2 cup light cream. Stir to soften. Slowly warm to melt gelatin. Remove from heat and set aside.

In medium-sized bowl with electric mixer beat together 2 egg yolks and 1/4 cup brown sugar with lumps broken up until mixture is thick, light in color, and the sugar has completely dissolved. Beat in 1/3 cup Grand Marnier. Slowly pour in the melted gelatin and cream, beating all the while.

Chill in refrigerator 30 minutes.

In small bowl whip 1/2 cup heavy cream until it forms soft peaks. Add 1 Tbsp brown sugar, with lumps broken up, and whip a moment longer.

Remove chilled custard from refrigerator and fold in the whipped cream. Pour filling into 71/2-inch prepared crust, cover, and place in freezer for several hours until firm. Or, if you want to try it without crust, pour filling into sherbet glasses, cover, and freeze until firm.

Pie can be served directly from freezer but it is better if allowed to ripen 15 minutes at room temperature.

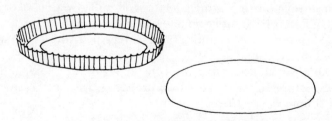

ORANGE-PINEAPPLE PIE

Delightful light but sweet pie that serves 4.

> 1 well-chilled Vanilla Cookie Crust (page 223)
> 1 quart Orange-Pineapple Ice Cream (page 79)

Prepare Vanilla Cookie Crust and place in freezer.

Make Orange-Pineapple Ice Cream. Fill crust with ice cream; there will be some left over. Wrap pie tightly and place in freezer.

This pie will keep for 1 month and may be served directly from freezer.

Slice with a very sharp, heavy knife.

CRUSTS

CHOCOLATE COOKIE CRUST

Ideal for Brandy Alexander Pie.

> 2 Tbsp melted butter
> 12 chocolate cookies (see below)
> 1 Tbsp granulated sugar

Preheat oven to 350°.

Melt 2 Tbsp butter and set aside.

In a small bowl crush 12 cookies to fine crumbs (about 1 cup). Add 1 Tbsp sugar and 2 Tbsp melted butter. Mix with fork. Press crumbs against bottom and sides of 7½-inch flan ring or pie tin.

Bake for 5 minutes at 350°. Remove from oven and allow pie shell to cool.

For 9-inch crust double all of the ingredients.

CHOCOLATE COOKIES

Makes about 2 dozen cookies, which are quite good by themselves but terrific for making Chocolate Pie Crust.

> 1/2 cup solid vegetable shortening
> 1/2 cup granulated sugar
> 1 egg
> 1/4 tsp vanilla extract
> 1/2 cup cocoa
> 1/2 cup unsifted white flour
> 1 tsp baking powder

Preheat oven to 350°.

Cream 1/2 cup shortening with 1/2 cup sugar. Add 1 egg and 1/4 tsp vanilla extract; beat with electric mixer or by hand until light and fluffy. Add 1/2 cup cocoa, 1/2 cup unsifted white flour, and 1 tsp baking powder. Beat until a comparatively smooth, stiff batter is formed.

Using a teaspoon drop spoonfuls of dough on well-greased cookie sheet, leaving 2 inches between drops.

Bake about 10 minutes at 350° or until cookies bounce back to the touch.

GRAHAM CRACKER CRUST

Crisp sweet crust good with cream cheese filling (pages 218-219).

> 2 Tbsp melted butter
> 3/4 cup graham cracker crumbs
> 5 tsp granulated sugar

Preheat oven to 350°.

Lightly butter 7 1/2-inch flan ring or pie plate.

Melt 2 Tbsp butter. Set aside.

Crush enough graham crackers to fill measuring cup to 3/4 mark.

In a small bowl combine graham cracker crumbs, 5 tsp sugar, and the melted butter. Press crumbs against bottom and halfway up sides of pan.

Place crust in preheated oven and bake for 5 minutes. Allow crust to cool before using.

Crust may be wrapped tightly and frozen for later use.

For 9-inch crust double all of the ingredients.

VANILLA COOKIE CRUST

Crisp, rich crust for an ice cream filling.

2 Tbsp melted butter
3/4 cup crushed Vanilla Wafers (see below)
2 Tbsp granulated sugar

Preheat oven to 400°.
Lightly butter 7½-inch flan ring or pie plate.
Melt 2 Tbsp butter. Set aside.
Crush enough vanilla wafers to fill measuring cup to 3/4 mark.
Combine cookie crumbs, 2 Tbsp sugar, and the butter in small bowl.
Press into buttered flan ring or pie plate, on bottom and sides.
Bake at 400° for 5 minutes.
Remove from oven and chill thoroughly or freeze before filling
with ice cream.
Crust may be wrapped tightly and frozen for later use.
For 9-inch crust double all of the ingredients.

VANILLA WAFERS

Makes about 3 dozen 2-inch cookies that are easy to make and taste
sweet and rich. The cookies are excellent for making Vanilla Cookie
Crust.

½ cup (1 stick) butter
⅓ cup sugar
1 egg
½ tsp vanilla extract
⅔ cup flour

Preheat oven to 375°. Grease cookie sheet.
Cream ½ cup butter with ⅓ cup sugar. Add 1 egg and ½ tsp vanilla
extract. Beat with electric mixer or by hand until light and fluffy. Add
⅔ cup flour and beat until smooth.
Using a teaspoon, drop spoonfuls of dough on well-greased cookie
sheet, leaving 2 inches between spoonfuls.
Bake at 375° for 10 minutes or until cookies are brown around the
edge. Remove cookies to rack to cool. Store in container with close-
fitting lid or use as directed in Vanilla Cookie Crust recipe.

Ice Cream Cakes

An ice cream cake is a special creation enjoyed and admired by guests and family alike. The combination of sponge cake, glaze, and ice cream produces an interesting contrast of textures.

The ice cream birthday cakes for children are cake layers filled with ice cream and frosted with whipped cream. The cake is then decorated with symbols of the birthday child's favorite fantasy.

The Valentine Cake looks like a great big candy heart. The pink frosting (made from Strawberry Sherbet Icing) produces an effect that is absolutely enchanting.

The Chocolate-Almond Ice Cream Cake, two layers of chocolate cake filled with Chocolate-Almond Ice Cream and frosted with whipped cream, is a crunchy, rich delicacy.

The sophisticated gourmet will enjoy the Frozen Walnut Cake, two rum-soaked cake layers filled and frosted with the heavenly combination of caramelized walnuts and whipped cream.

LEMON MERINGUE CAKE

Makes a tart-sweet yellow ice cream cake that is very pretty.

1 Nine-Inch Round Sponge Cake (page 238)
1⅓ cups lemon juice (about 6 to 8 large lemons)
½ cup granulated sugar
¾ cup very hot water
1 Tbsp unflavored gelatin
1 Tbsp candied lemon rind (page 23)
½ cup light corn syrup
6 egg whites
½ tsp cream of tartar

With a long serrated cake knife carefully slice the sponge cake in half lengthwise and place cut side up on platter. Set aside. (Reserve other half for later use.)

Squeeze enough lemon juice to measure 1⅓ cups. Set aside.

In small saucepan heat together ⅓ cup of the lemon juice and ½ cup sugar, stirring, until sugar dissolves. Remove from heat. Using large spoon slowly dribble glaze over each half of sponge cake, cut sides up. Set aside.

In a small bowl combine ¾ cup very hot water with 1 Tbsp gelatin and stir until gelatin melts. When gelatin has melted, stir in 1 cup lemon juice, 1 Tbsp candied lemon rind, and ½ cup corn syrup. Set aside.

In large bowl beat 6 egg whites with ½ tsp cream of tartar until egg whites hold stiff peaks. Slowly beat in lemon gelatin and continue beating until mixture is well combined.

Spread one third of the beaten egg-white-and-lemon mixture (the chiffon) over bottom layer of cake. Cover with second layer cut side down. Frost top and sides of the cake with remaining chiffon.

Place cake in freezer. When cake is frozen (about 4 hours), cover loosely, and store until ready to serve. Cake can be served directly from freezer.

BIRTHDAY ICE CREAM SHEET CAKE

Serves about 20 children. An absolutely delicious cake bound to please any child.

    1 quart ice cream, homemade, any flavor
    1 quart ice cream, homemade, any flavor
    Birthday Sponge Sheet Cake (see below)
    2 cups Whipped Cream Icing (page 234)

Prepare 2 quarts ice cream, 1 quart of each flavor to be used. For best results use ice creams with the same ripening time. One of Nancy's favorite combinations is Mocha Soufflé for the first layer and Vanilla Soufflé for the top layer. Soufflés make good fillings because they remain soft and do not need to ripen.

Prepare Birthday Sponge Sheet Cake:

    ²/₃ cup flour
    1 tsp baking powder
    ¹/₄ tsp salt
    4 eggs
    ²/₃ cup sugar

Preheat oven to 400°.

Grease and line with waxed paper a 9-by-13-inch pan. Grease top of waxed paper. Set aside.

Combine ²/₃ cup flour, 1 tsp baking powder, and ¹/₄ tsp salt in a small bowl. Set aside.

In a large bowl beat 4 whole eggs with an electric mixer until very thick and volume has increased. Slowly add ²/₃ cup sugar, beating all the while. Continue beating until ribbons falling from raised beaters remain visible on surface of batter (at least 5 minutes).

Using a rubber spatula quickly fold flour mixture into beaten eggs until ingredients are just barely combined.

Scrape batter into prepared pan. Bake at 400° for 10 minutes or until cake is lightly browned on top.

Remove cake from oven and quickly invert onto a cake rack. Peel off waxed paper and let cake cool.

After cake is cool slice into two layers using a long serrated cake knife. Set aside.

Prepare 2 cups Whipped Cream Icing. Place in refrigerator.

Remove prepared ice cream from freezer. Allow ice cream to ripen at room temperature if necessary until soft enough to scoop out.

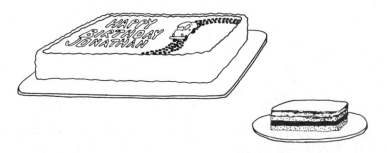

Place bottom layer of cake on cookie sheet, cut side up. Spread with 1 quart ice cream. Cover with second cake layer. Spread this with 1 quart ice cream.

Remove Whipped Cream Icing from refrigerator and frost the sides of the cake with the icing. Remaining icing can be colored with vegetable food coloring and squeezed through rolled waxed paper to decorate top of cake (page 30). In addition, top of cake can be decorated with purchased ornaments or toys. Nancy's children enjoy small cars on roads paved with chocolate chips. A tree made with raisins for trunk and branches and Lifesavers is another favorite.

FROZEN WALNUT CAKE

Makes an absolutely heavenly dessert for 12 to 14 people.

    2 Nine-Inch Round Sponge Cakes (page 238)
    4 Tbsp rum
    2 quarts Walnut Ice Cream (page 96)

Prepare 2 Nine-Inch Round Sponge Cakes. While still warm, sprinkle bottom of each layer with 2 Tbsp rum. Place layers in freezer while preparing ice cream.

Make 2 quarts Walnut Ice Cream. When ice cream is partially frozen, remove it and cake layers from freezer. Spread one third of ice cream on bottom layer. Place second layer on top and frost the entire cake with the remaining ice cream.

Place cake in freezer. When frozen, cover tightly.

This dessert may be made up to 2 weeks in advance.

CHOCOLATE-ALMOND ICE CREAM CAKE

Serves 10. Rich chocolate ice cream cake with almonds in the filling.

1 Nine-Inch Round Chocolate Sponge Cake (page 238)
1 quart Chocolate-Almond Ice Cream (page 53)
1 quart Whipped Cream Frosting (page 234)
1 oz semi-sweet chocolate

Slice Chocolate Sponge Cake in half lengthwise to make 2 layers. Place in freezer.

Prepare Chocolate-Almond Ice Cream. When ice cream is frozen enough to hold shape, but not frozen solid, scoop it onto 1 layer of frozen cake, cut side up. Cover ice cream with other layer cut side down.

Place cake in freezer until frosting is prepared.

Prepare Whipped Cream Frosting. Remove cake from freezer and frost it all over. Decorate with semi-sweet chocolate curls made by using a vegetable peeler to scrape the side of a 1-oz chocolate square. Store in freezer until ready to use.

To slice, use a sharp, heavy knife.

MOTHER MEERWARTH'S ICE CREAM ROLL

Serves 5 or 10 depending on how many people would like to have seconds, thirds, fourths . . .

3 cups Chocolate Velvet Ice Cream (page 57)
1 cup Strawberry Sauce (page 183)
Mother Meerwarth's Chocolate Roll Cake (page 237)

Make 3 cups Chocolate Velvet. Set aside in freezer to become slightly firm. If you make it a day or more in advance allow it to ripen 45 minutes to 1 hour in refrigerator before attempting to spread on cake.

Prepare 1 cup Strawberry Sauce. Set aside in refrigerator until ready for use.

Make Mother Meerwarth's Chocolate Roll Cake, leaving it rolled in sugared towel as directed in recipe. When cake has cooled, remove Chocolate Velvet from freezer. Unroll cake and gently spread soft ice cream on cake to within 1 inch of the edge.

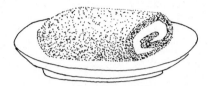

Lift up short side of towel, forcing filled cake to roll up jellyroll fashion on itself. Place on serving platter and put immediately in freezer until firm (4 hours or longer).

Allow dessert to ripen in refrigerator 30 minutes before serving. Pour 1 cup Strawberry Sauce on top. Cut with a long, sharp, thin-bladed knife and serve immediately.

ORANGE CAKE FILLED WITH SHERBET

Serves 8. Delightful citrus-flavored sponge cake with a sweet orange filling.

Orange Sherbet Filling (see below)
Orange Glaze (see below)
1 Nine-Inch Round Sponge Cake (page 283)
1 cup heavy cream
1 Tbsp granulated sugar

Prepare Orange Sherbet Filling and Orange Glaze. When filling is partially frozen and stiff enough to work with, proceed with assembly of cake.

Slice Nine-Inch Round Sponge Cake in half lengthwise to make 2 layers. Soak each layer with prepared glaze. Spread bottom layer (cut side up) with prepared filling. Cover with top layer (cut side down). Place cake in freezer.

Whip 1 cup heavy cream until soft peaks form; then whip in 1 Tbsp sugar.

Remove cake from freezer and frost the top and sides with whipped cream. Return cake to freezer, and after it has frozen, cover tightly.

To slice the cake, use a strong, sharp knife.

This cake should be eaten within a day after being made.

Orange Sherbet Filling

    2 tsp grated orange rind
    1 cup orange juice
    Juice from 1 lemon
    1/4 cup granulated sugar
    3 egg whites

    Grate 2 tsp orange rind and set aside. Squeeze enough orange juice to measure 1 cup and the juice from 1 lemon.
    In a small enameled saucepan combine the orange juice, grated orange rind, lemon juice, and 1/4 cup sugar. Boil over high heat until liquid is reduced to about 1/3 cup. Set aside.
    Beat 3 egg whites until soft peaks form. Pour in hot juice in a thin stream, beating all the while. Continue beating until egg whites are smooth and glossy.
    Place bowl in freezer until stiff enough to work with (about 1 1/2 hours). Stir thoroughly and proceed with Orange Cake.

Orange Glaze

    1/2 cup orange juice
    Juice from 1 lemon
    1/4 cup granulated sugar

    Squeeze enough orange juice to measure 1/2 cup and the juice from 1 lemon. Combine orange juice, lemon juice, and 1/4 cup sugar in a small enameled saucepan. Boil juices over high heat until reduced by half and slightly syrupy. Set aside until ready to spread on cake.

STRAWBERRY ICE CREAM CAKE

Serves 8. A colorful sweet cake, very attractive for a party.

    2 quarts Strawberry Filling (see below)
    1 Nine-Inch Round Sponge Cake (page 238)
    1/4 cup seedless raspberry jam
    2 Tbsp seedless raspberry jam (optional)

Prepare Strawberry Filling. When filling is partially frozen and stiff enough to work with, proceed with assembly of cake.

Slice Nine-Inch Round Vanilla Sponge Cake in half lengthwise to make 2 layers. Spread bottom layer with 1/4 cup seedless raspberry jam. Next spread bottom layer with 1 cup (one fourth) of the prepared Strawberry Filling, cover with top layer, and frost the top and sides of the cake with remaining Strawberry Filling. Place cake in freezer until firm.

When cake is frozen the top may be decorated with raspberry jam squeezed out of a pastry tube or rolled waxed paper (page 30). After cake is firmly frozen cover tightly until ready to serve.

Serve directly from freezer. To slice cake, use a strong sharp knife.

Strawberry Filling

Makes 1 quart filling for strawberry cake.

    1 pint fresh strawberries
    2 Tbsp granulated sugar
    2 egg whites
    4 Tbsp granulated sugar
    1 cup heavy cream

Wash and hull 1 pint fresh strawberries. Place in blender with 2 Tbsp sugar and blend until coarsely ground.

In a large bowl beat 3 egg whites until soft peaks form. Slowly beat in 4 Tbsp sugar and continue beating until egg whites are smooth and glossy.

Fold puréed berries into beaten egg whites.

In separate bowl whip 1 cup heavy cream until soft peaks form. Fold whipped cream into egg-white-and-berry mixture. Place bowl in freezer until filling is stiff enough to work with (approximately 2 hours).

VALENTINE CAKE

A lovely party dessert that serves 20 children.

> 2 Sponge Sheet Cakes 9 by 13 inches (page 239)
> 2½ quarts Vanilla Ice Cream (page 33)
> 1½ quarts Strawberry Sherbet Icing (page 146)
> 6 to 8 whole strawberries
> Cinnamon candies
> ¾ cup heavy cream
> 3 Tbsp confectioners' sugar
> ½ tsp vanilla extract

Cover a large sheet of cardboard (14 by 19 inches) with waxed paper. Place 2 Sponge Sheet Cakes side by side on cardboard. Cut off corners of cake according to diagram to produce a heart shape. Cover the cake layers, wrapping around cardboard too, and place in freezer.

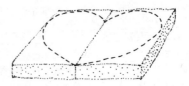

Make 2½ quarts of Vanilla Ice Cream. When ice cream is frozen around the edges of container, stir thoroughly to break up frozen pieces. Remove cake from freezer, uncover, and quickly spread ice cream over the top. Carefully cover cake and return to freezer. It should be thoroughly frozen before next spreading.

Make 1½ quarts Strawberry Sherbet Icing. After sherbet has been beaten a second time, remove cake from freezer, and spread sherbet on top of the firm vanilla ice cream. Decorate top of cake with extra strawberries and cinnamon candies. Return cake to freezer, uncovered, for 2 hours.

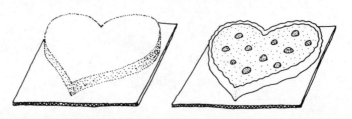

Whip ¾ cup heavy cream until soft peaks are formed. Whip in 3 Tbsp confectioners' sugar and ½ tsp vanilla extract and continue whipping until stiff peaks are formed.

Remove cake from freezer. Spread the sides with whipped cream and return cake to freezer. When whipped cream is frozen cover the cake and return to freezer until ready to serve.

If tightly covered, cake can be kept for 2 weeks.

VANILLA AND CHOCOLATE ICE CREAM CAKE

Makes enough to feed a birthday party of 8 two-year-olds and 12 adults (aout 20 slices) if you cut thin. Naturally, other flavors of ice cream can be used. Experiment with your favorite combinations.

> 4 frozen Sponge Cake Layers (page 240) or 2 9-inch layers of your favorite cake sliced in half to make 4 layers
> 4 cups softened French Vanilla Ice Cream (page 33)
> 2 cups softened Chocolate Ice Cream (page 51)
> Whipped Cream Icing (page 234)
> Decorative Chocolate Icing (page 234)

To assemble the cake, first place frozen sponge cake layer on serving plate cut side up. Spread with 2 cups softened French Vanilla Ice Cream. Cover with second cake layer and spread with 2 cups softened Chocolate Ice Cream. Cover with third cake layer and spread with 2 cups softened French Vanilla Ice Cream. Cover with fourth cake layer cut side down.

Cover cake carefully and place in freezer while preparing icing.

Remove from freezer. Spread Whipped Cream Icing over the top and sides of layered ice cream cake. Place in freezer for 1 hour. Remove and decorate with Decorative Chocolate Icing according to your whim.

ICINGS

WHIPPED CREAM ICING

Makes about 3½ cups of icing that can serve as a finishing touch to many ice cream desserts.

  2 cups heavy cream
  7 Tbsp confectioners' sugar
  1 tsp vanilla extract

Whip 2 cups heavy cream until it holds soft peaks. Add 7 Tbsp confectioners' sugar, a tablespoon at a time, whipping all the while. Add 1 tsp vanilla extract and whip until stiff peaks form.

Spread thickly over ice cream cake or use as topping for dessert.

Whipped Cream Icing will keep in the refrigerator for several hours.

DECORATIVE CHOCOLATE ICING

Makes about 3 Tbsp of icing that works very well for lettering and decorating.

  ½ oz unsweetened chocolate
  1 Tbsp sweet butter
  2 Tbsp confectioners' sugar

Using a double boiler melt ½ oz chocolate and 1 Tbsp butter over simmering water, stirring constantly. Remove from heat and quickly stir in 2 Tbsp confectioners' sugar. Place icing in a cone made from a double thickness of waxed paper (page 30) and squeeze out icing to decorate or letter a cake.

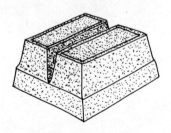

Sponge Layers

We use sponge cakes in our frozen desserts because their delicate, bland flavor blends well with ice cream. These cakes are firm in texture; they are easily cut into shapes, sliced, and/or rolled (see Mother Meerwarth's Chocolate Roll Cake); and they freeze well with little loss of flavor. They can also absorb liquid and paste flavorings without falling apart.

When preheating the oven, if using gas, raise the temperature 25° (except in Mother Meerwarth's Chocolate Roll Cake), since the recipe temperatures were written using an electric oven.

When preparing cake pan, grease bottom of pan with butter or, if you prefer, solid vegetable shortening; dust with flour. If pan does not have a removable bottom or is a large or irregular shape, line with waxed paper and then grease both sides of wax paper.

Before starting recipe, read it through carefully and measure out ingredients. Melt any butter or chocolate required by recipe. Measure out appropriate amount of sugar. In separate bowl measure out flour and other dry ingredients.

Sponge cakes rely mostly on air incorporated into beaten eggs for leavening. To achieve greatest volume, use eggs at room temperature. If eggs are taken from refrigerator, place them in a bowl of warm water 5 minutes before using. Then beat until very light and full of air.

Place whole eggs and any extra egg yolks in bowl. Using electric mixer or large wire whisk beat the eggs at high speed until they become thick and light yellow in color (about 5 minutes by machine; 15 minutes by large wire whisk). Slowly add the sugar in a thin stream, beating constantly. Continue beating until mixture is very thick, resembles mayonnaise, and ribbons falling from lifted beater remain visible on the surface of the batter. Using rubber spatula, quickly but gently fold in all other ingredients. Pour batter into prepared pan and spread evenly with spatula. Immediately place in preheated oven.

While the cake is baking, steam causes batter to rise or puff up. But as cake continues to bake the middle falls, leaving the sides slightly raised. A crust forms on top that then browns.

The cake is done when the crust is brown and a toothpick or cake tester inserted in the center comes out clean. It will also bounce back to the touch. Do not test cake until the end of the recommended cooking time or it may sink into a sticky mess.

Remove from oven, gently loosen cake from edges, place wire rack or towel on top, and carefully invert. If using waxed paper, remove while cake is still warm. Let cake cool on rack or towel, unless otherwise indicated in recipe, before proceeding.

When cake is cool, cut into desired shape or slice into layers. Carefully wrap and freeze for most uses; however, when making an ice cream roll the cake cannot be frozen, since it would then be too stiff to work with.

CHOCOLATE SPONGE CAKE

This cake, much firmer and crisper than following chocolate cake, makes a good base for baked Alaska. We recommend using an electric mixer when beating the eggs and sugar.

2 Tbsp melted butter
2 whole eggs, at room temperature
2/3 cup granulated sugar
1/3 cup cocoa, scant
2/3 cup cornstarch, scant

Preheat oven to 350°.

Grease with butter or shortening and lightly flour an oblong pan 9 by 13 by 2 inches.

Melt 2 Tbsp butter and set aside.

In medium-sized bowl using an electric mixer beat 2 eggs at high speed until mixture is very thick, light in color, and greatly increased in volume. Gradually add 2/3 cup sugar and continue beating until thick ribbons fall from lifted beaters and remain visible on the surface of the batter. This process takes about 15 minutes.

Very quickly fold in scant 1/3 cup cocoa and scant 2/3 cup cornstarch. Gently stir in melted butter. Quickly scrape batter into prepared pan and immediately place in upper third of preheated oven.

Bake at 350° for about 20 minutes, or until toothpick comes out clean when thrust into center of cake.

Remove from oven and let cake cool 5 minutes in pan. Loosen sides and bottom with spatula and invert onto cake rack to cool completely.

The cake is then ready to be used or it can be frozen for later use.

To freeze, cut cake in half, wrap each half in plastic, and put in freezer. Cake should not be stored longer than 2 months.

MOTHER MEERWARTH'S CHOCOLATE ROLL CAKE

Makes 1 flat cake that can be rolled easily. It works beautifully with any of the velvet ice creams.

5 egg whites
1/4 tsp cream of tartar
1 tsp confectioners' sugar
1 Tbsp flour
5 egg yolks
6 heaping Tbsp confectioners' sugar
1/8 tsp salt
2 heaping Tbsp cocoa
Linen tea towel dusted with 1/4 to 1/3 cup confectioners' sugar

Grease a jelly roll pan (15 1/2 by 10 1/2 by 5/8 inches) with butter. Set aside.

Beat 5 egg whites with 1/4 tsp cream of tartar until soft peaks form. Add 1 tsp confectioners' sugar and 1 Tbsp flour. Beat until thick, smooth, and glossy. Set aside in refrigerator.

Put in blender 5 egg yolks, 6 heaping Tbsp confectioners' sugar, and 1/8 tsp salt. Blend until smooth. Add 2 heaping Tbsp cocoa and blend a moment longer.

Preheat oven to 325°.

Remove beaten egg whites from refrigerator. Pour batter into egg whites and gently fold one mixture into the other.

Scrape mixture onto jelly roll pan. Spread to within 1 inch of edge of pan.

Bake in preheated 325° oven for 20 minutes. Cake will be very soft and spongy.

Dust a clean linen tea towel with confectioners' sugar.

Carefully loosen cake in pan with spatula. Gently lift or slide out onto sugared towel. Don't turn cake over. The bottom part of the cake will be the outside of the roll. Starting at narrow side, roll cake up in towel, and place on rack to cool until ready to use.

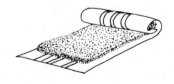

NINE-INCH ROUND SPONGE CAKE

A light, soft cake that is good for baked Alaska or with ice cream.

> 2 eggs, at room temperature
> 1/3 cup granulated sugar
> 1/3 cup flour
> 1/2 tsp baking powder
> 1/8 tsp salt

Preheat oven to 400°.

Grease a 9-inch round cake pan, line with waxed paper, and grease the top of the paper.

In medium-sized bowl beat 2 eggs with electric mixer until very thick and volume has increased. Gradually add 1/3 cup sugar, beating all the while. Continue to beat sugar and eggs until mixture is very thick and ribbons falling back from raised beaters remain visible on surface of batter (at least 5 minutes).

Combine 1/3 cup flour, 1/2 tsp baking powder, and 1/8 tsp salt in small bowl. Using a rubber spatula, quickly fold flour mixture into beaten eggs until ingredients are just barely combined.

Scrape batter into prepared pan. Bake at 400° for 11 minutes or until cake is lightly browned on top.

Remove cake from oven and quickly invert onto cake rack. Peel off waxed paper and let cake cool. Proceed with recipe or wrap tightly and freeze for later use.

This cake will keep frozen for 1 month.

NINE-INCH ROUND CHOCOLATE SPONGE CAKE

A light chocolate cake that, among other uses, complements Chocolate-Almond Ice Cream beautifully and makes a good base for a baked Alaska.

> 1 Tbsp melted butter
> 2 eggs, at room temperature
> 1/3 cup granulated sugar
> 3 Tbsp flour
> 3 Tbsp cocoa
> 1/2 tsp baking powder

Preheat oven to 350°.

Grease a 9-inch round cake pan. Line with waxed paper and grease the top of the paper.

Melt 1 Tbsp butter and set aside.

In medium-sized bowl beat 2 eggs with an electric mixer until very thick and volume has increased. Slowly add ⅓ cup sugar, beating all the while. Continue to beat sugar and eggs until mixture is very thick, like mayonnaise, and ribbons falling from raised beaters continue to remain visible on surface of batter (at least 5 minutes).

In a small bowl combine 3 Tbsp flour, 3 Tbsp cocoa, and ½ tsp baking powder.

Using a rubber spatula quickly fold flour mixture into beaten eggs until ingredients are just barely combined.

Scrape batter into prepared pan. Bake at 350° for 20 minutes or until cake bounces back when you press it gently.

Remove cake from oven and quickly invert onto cake rack. Peel off waxed paper and let cake cool. It is now ready to use or be wrapped tightly and frozen for later use.

This cake will keep frozen for 1 month.

SPONGE SHEET CAKE

Makes 1 cake sheet 1 inch deep that works very well in Valentine Cake or baked Alaska desserts.

½ cup flour
1 tsp baking powder
¼ tsp salt
3 eggs, at room temperature
½ cup granulated sugar

Preheat oven to 400°.

Grease and line with waxed paper a 9-by-13-inch pan. Grease the top of the waxed paper. Set aside.

Combine ½ cup flour, 1 tsp baking powder, and ¼ tsp salt in a small bowl. Set aside.

In a medium-sized bowl beat 3 whole eggs with an electric mixer until very thick and volume has increased. Slowly add ½ cup sugar, beating all the while. Continue beating until ribbons falling from raised beaters remain visible on surface of batter (at least 5 minutes).

Using a rubber spatula quickly fold flour mixture into beaten eggs until ingredients are just barely combined.

Scrape batter into prepared pan. Bake at 400° for 9 minutes or until cake is lightly browned on top.

Remove cake from oven and quickly invert onto cake rack. Peel off waxed paper and let cake cool. It is now ready to be used or wrapped and frozen. Cake will keep 1 month.

SPONGE LAYERS

Makes 4 layers of a delicately flavored cake good for birthday cakes. We recommend using an electric mixer when beating the eggs and sugar.

3 Tbsp melted butter
1 cup sifted white flour
3/4 cup sifted cornstarch
1 Tbsp soy flour
4 whole eggs, at room temperature
2 egg yolks, at room temperature
1½ cups granulated sugar
1½ tsp vanilla extract

Preheat oven to 350°.

Heavily grease with butter or shortening and dust with flour 2 9-inch round cake tins.

Melt 3 Tbsp butter. Set aside.

In a medium-sized bowl combine 1 cup sifted white flour, 3/4 cup sifted cornstarch, and 1 Tbsp soy flour.

Beat together 4 whole eggs, 2 egg yolks, and 1½ cups sugar in large bowl with an electric mixer until very thick, light in color, and greatly increased in volume. Thick ribbons should fall from raised beaters and remain visible on the surface of the batter. Add 1½ tsp vanilla extract and beat a moment longer.

Using a spatula, quickly fold flour mixture into the eggs and sugar. Then gently stir in the 3 Tbsp melted butter

Quickly scrape batter into prepared cake tins and immediately place on middle shelf of preheated oven.

Bake at 350° for 30 to 40 minutes or until toothpick comes out clean when thrust into center of cake.

Remove from oven and let cake layers cool in tins for a few minutes. Then invert onto cake rack and allow to cool completely.

With a long, thin serrated slicing knife carefully slice layers in half to make 4 layers. Wrap each layer individually with plastic wrap and freeze. Layers should not be stored longer than 2 months.

Bombes and Sundaes

Bombes

These desserts are fun, easy to make and an attractive way to serve your frozen delights. A bombe consists of 2 or more ice creams molded together. If you use a 1-quart mold (4 cups) you will need 1 pint each of two flavors; a 1½-quart mold (6 cups) will require 1 pint each of three flavors or 2 pints of one and 1 pint of another flavor. Should you have a larger or smaller mold, adjust the recipes accordingly. In choosing the ice creams you wish to use, consider their ripening times as well as the combination of flavors, colors, and textures. The ice cream with the longer ripening time should be on the outside and top or packed in first and last, while the softer ice cream should be in the middle. The best combination is an ice cream or fruit ice surrounding a mousse or velvet.

In this section we are assuming that the suggested ice creams have been prepared in advance.

Possible combinations using a 1½-quart, or 6-cup, mold are the following. Use the molding instructions below.

BOMBE CITRUS

1 pint Lemon Ice (page 156)
2 pints Raspberry Sherbet (page 144)

BOMBE FLORIDA

1 pint Orange Ice (page 159)
2 pints Vanilla Mousse (page 118) mixed with 2 Tbsp Curaçao
Whipped cream

BOMBE NOIRE

2 pints Chocolate-Almond Ice Cream (page 53)
1 pint Vanilla Mousse (page 118)

BOMBE BRAZILIAN

1½ pints Coffee Ice Cream (page 59)
1 pint Chocolate Mousse (page 108)
1 cup Whipped Cream mixed with 1 Tbsp brandy
   and ¼ cup pecan halves

BOMBE BLACKBERRY

2 pints Wild Blackberry Mousse (page 119)
1 pint Whipped Cream mixed with ½ cup roasted, crushed macaroons (page 106) and ½ cup chopped English walnuts

PISTACHIO DELIGHT

2 pints Pistachio Ice Cream (page 84)
1 pint French Vanilla Ice Cream (page 33)

PUCCI'S SPUMONI (USE 6-CUP MELON MOLD)

1½ pints French Vanilla Ice Cream (page 33)
1 pint Biscuit Tortoni (page 105)
1 cup Chocolate Mousse (page 108)

A possible combination using a 1-quart, or 4-cup, mold is:

BOMBE ORANGE

1 pint Orange Ice (page 159) mixed with 2 Tbsp Drambuie
1 pint Café Mousse (page 106)

To mold, ripen three quarters of the amount of ice cream chosen
for outside (first ice cream). Quickly spread a ¾- to 1-inch layer over
the bottom and sides of a chilled mold. Cover and freeze until firm.
Meanwhile ripen second ice cream. Remove mold from freezer,
uncover, and fill the middle cavity with softened second ice cream or
mousse. Quickly cover and return to freezer until firm. Then ripen
third ice cream or what is left of first ice cream. Remove mold from
freezer, uncover, and pack ripened ice cream on top filling to the brim.
Cover and freeze until firm or ready to use.
   The freezing time will vary depending on the type of ice cream

used and the capabilities of your freezing facility. An ideal unit for preparing this dessert is that which has a temperature range of 10° above 0° to 10° below 0°.

Unmold by dipping mold in lukewarm water up to 1 minute, depending on the thickness and composition of the mold. Place serving dish upside down on top of mold and invert. If dessert doesn't immediately unmold, repeat procedure. Quickly place unmolded dessert back in freezer to firm up, 10 minutes or longer. For a more complete discussion on unmolding see page 29.

Desserts can also be served directly from mold but be careful to reach far enough into container to serve a little bit of everything.

Another interesting way to prepare a bombe is in layers using a chilled 2-quart, or 8-cup, square or rectangular mold. Diana uses a large bread pan.

Below are two homemade versions of the familiar ice cream brick.

BOMBE NAPOLEON

1 pint Chocolate Ice Cream (page 51)
1 pint Vanilla Ice Cream (page 33)
1 pint Strawberry Ice Cream (page 91)

THREE-COLOR BOMBE

1½ pints Vanilla Ice Cream (page 33)
1 cup Kiwi Ice (page 155)
1 pint Strawberry Sherbet (page 145)

To mold, soften the first ice cream and press evenly over bottom of chilled mold. Cover and freeze until firm. Meanwhile, soften second ice cream. Remove mold from freezer, uncover, and quickly spread layer of second ice cream over first. Cover and freeze until firm. Then ripen third ice cream. Remove mold from freezer and firmly pack in ice cream. Cover and return to freezer until firm, or ready to use.

Thirty minutes before serving these desserts, unmold according to directions above and return to freezer 10 minutes before serving for ice cream to firm up.

Slice bombes with a long, thin-bladed knife.

Sundaes

The ice cream sundae appeared in the late 1890s and became popular around the turn of the century. During this period in American history the sale of soda was prohibited in many places on Sundays. To circumvent the law drugstore soda fountains got the idea of serving just ice cream with a syrup on Sundays, hence the name "Sunday" or "Soda-less Soda." The "y" evolved to "ae" as religious fanatics criticized the sacrilegious use of the name of the Sabbath. By removing the "y" and changing it to "ae" they changed the dish's Sunday-only connotation and were able to serve it every day.

The dish was traditionally ice cream with a sauce or syrup with nut topping served in a tulip-shaped dish. Our sundaes follow the tradition but they don't have to be in a tulip-shaped dish, though they are nice. These dishes are still available in many department stores.

The following recipes, unless otherwise noted, serve one and can be proportionately increased to serve more.

The pièce de résistance among the sundaes is Oscar's Delight or Waffles à la Mode.

Possible sundae combinations are the following:

BERRY SUNDAE

2 scoops Vanilla Ice Cream (page 33)
¼ cup Strawberry, Raspberry, Wild Blackberry, or
    Blueberry Sauce (see Sauces, pages 177-183)

BLACK AND WHITE SUNDAE

1 scoop Vanilla Ice Cream (page 33)
3 Tbsp Chocolate Syrup (page 185)
1 Tbsp Walnut Topping (page 191)

BROWNIE SUNDAE

1 3-inch square chocolate brownie
1 large scoop Vanilla Ice Cream (page 33)
Fudge Sauce (page 180), warmed
Pecan Topping, optional (page 190)

CARAMEL SUNDAE

1 scoop Vanilla Ice Cream (page 33)
3 Tbsp Warm Caramel Syrup (page 184)
2 Tbsp Pecan Topping (page 190)

CHOCOLATE SUNDAE

1 scoop Chocolate Ice Cream (page 51)
3 Tbsp Chocolate Syrup (page 185)
1 Tbsp salted peanuts, chopped

CHOCOLATE ALMOND SUNDAE

2 scoops Pistachio Ice Cream (page 84) or Pistachio-Almond Ice
   Cream (page 85)
¼ cup warm Chocolate Syrup (page 185)
1 Tbsp finely chopped almonds

COFFEE SUNDAE

1 large scoop French Vanilla Ice Cream (page 33) or Coffee Ice
   Cream (page 59)
½ cup warm strong black coffee or Coffee Syrup (page 185)

FUDGE SUNDAE

1 large scoop French Vanilla Ice Cream (page 33)
1/4 cup warm Fudge Sauce (page 180)
Whipped cream (optional)

GINGER SUNDAE

1 scoop Ginger Ale Ice Cream (page 64)
2 Tbsp Ginger Syrup I or II (page 187)
Whipped cream
1 tsp sesame seeds, toasted

HOT MAPLE SUNDAE

2 scoops French Vanilla Ice Cream (page 33)
1/4 cup hot maple syrup
2 Tbsp English walnuts, finely chopped

KAHLÚA SUNDAE

2 large scoops Coffee Ice Cream (page 59)
1/4 cup Kahlúa
Whipped cream (optional)

MACAROON SUNDAE

2 large scoops Chocolate Ice Cream (page 51)
1/4 cup almond macaroon crumbs
Whipped cream
1/4 cup Strawberry Sauce (page 183)

PEACH SUNDAE

2 scoops Peach and Cream Ice Cream (page 80)
1/2 fresh peach, peeled and sliced
Whipped cream
1/2 tsp nutmeg

PINEAPPLE SUNDAE

2 scoops Pineapple Ice Cream (page 83)
¼ cup Pineapple Mint Sauce (page 182)

STRAWBERRY SUNDAE

1 scoop Chocolate-Hazelnut Ice Cream (page 55)
3 Tbsp Strawberry Sauce (page 183)
2 Tbsp hazelnuts, finely chopped

STRAWBERRY–PEACH SUNDAE

2 scoops Strawberry-Peach Ice Cream (page 92)
½ peach, peeled and sliced
¼ cup Strawberry Sauce (page 183)

STRAWBERRY STRAWBERRY SUNDAE

1 scoop Strawberry Ice Cream (page 91)
Whipped cream
3 Tbsp Strawberry Sauce (page 183)

To make a sundae, place 1 or 2 scoops ice cream in a dessert dish. Top with sauce, syrup, or fresh fruit, liqueur, nuts, crumbs, whipped cream, or spice. Serve immediately.

BANANA SPLIT

Superb confection with a variety of tastes and textures.

1 ripe banana
4 scoops of ice cream, assorted flavors
4 sauces, assorted flavors
Nut topping of your choice
Whipped cream

Slice banana in half lengthwise and crosswise to produce 4 oblong pieces. In a large soup bowl arrange pieces to form an "x." Place 1 scoop of ice cream on top of each banana quarter. Cover each scoop of ice cream with a sauce. Cover each sauce with a teaspoon of nut topping. Place whipped cream on top of each mound. Serve with a long-handled spoon.

Nancy's favorite combination is a scoop of chocolate ice cream, strawberry ice cream, and two scoops of vanilla ice cream covered respectively with chocolate syrup, strawberry sauce, pineapple sauce, and blueberry sauce. The sauces are covered with pecan topping and whipped cream.

CANTALOUPE SURPRISE

1 half medium-sized cantaloupe
1 large scoop Vanilla Ice Cream (page 33)

Cut melon in half, reserving other half for other recipe. Scoop out seeds. Place 1 large scoop Vanilla Ice Cream in hollow. Serve immediately.

THREE-WAY SPLIT

3 brandied peach halves
1 large scoop French Vanilla Ice Cream (page 33)
2 Tbsp almonds, finely chopped and toasted

Arrange 3 brandied peach halves in a shallow bowl, round side down. Carefully place 1 large scoop French Vanilla Ice Cream in center of bowl. Top with 2 Tbsp almonds that have been finely chopped and toasted. Serve immediately.

OSCAR'S DELIGHT OR WAFFLES À LA MODE

Makes 7 round waffles. Wonderfully light and refreshing meal which can be served any time. Ingredients not available at grocery stores can be found in health food stores.

1 pint Vanilla Velvet (page 35)
Belgian waffles:
    1/4 cup melted butter
    1 Tbsp or pkg dry yeast
    1/2 cup lukewarm water
    2 Tbsp wheat germ
    1 Tbsp soy flour
    2 Tbsp whole-wheat flour
    About 1¾ sifted unbleached white flour
    1/4 cup light-brown sugar with lumps broken up
    1/4 tsp salt
    2 eggs, separated
    1 cup lukewarm milk
1 cup Strawberry Sauce (page 183)

Prepare 1 pint Vanilla Velvet.

Then make the waffle batter. In a small saucepan melt 1/4 cup butter. Set aside.

Sprinkle 1 Tbsp dry yeast over 1/2 cup lukewarm water. Set aside until yeast starts to foam up (about 10 minutes).

In a 2-cup measure place 2 Tbsp wheat germ, 1 Tbsp soy flour, 2 Tbsp whole-wheat flour and sift in enough white flour to make 2 cups. Pour into large bowl. Stir in 1/4 cup light-brown sugar, with lumps broken up, and 1/4 tsp salt.

Separate the eggs. Add the yolks to the flour mixture with 1 cup of lukewarm milk and softened yeast. Beat with a wire whisk until batter is smooth. Beat in melted butter.

Beat egg whites until stiff peaks form; then fold into batter. Set batter aside for at least 1 hour, stirring about every 15 minutes.

Prepare Strawberry Sauce.

Preheat waffle iron 10 minutes before you are ready to make waffles.

Follow waffle iron manufacturer's instructions for making waffles. Waffles are done when steam stops coming out of sides.

If ice cream has hardened, allow to ripen in refrigerator until waffles are ready.

Carefully remove waffle from iron with fork, put it on a plate, top with a scoop of Vanilla Velvet and some Strawberry Sauce. Serve immediately.

Milk Drinks

SODAS

According to Mr. Dickson in that fascinating book *The Great American Ice Cream Book*, Robert M. Green, a concessionaire at the semicentennial celebration of the Franklin Institute in Philadelphia, is reported to be the father of the ice cream soda.

During the exhibition Mr. Green ran out of cream, which was used in preparing a popular drink of the time, a mixture of sweet cream, syrup, and carbonated water, and he substituted vanilla ice cream. The ice cream soda was born and was an instant success.

The recipes in this section are traditional in that they are basically ice cream, syrup, and soda. There the similarity ends. We have traditional sodas, but many more unusual combinations too. The recipes were derived using club soda; but Diana likes to substitute ginger ale occasionally for a taste change. Should you have charged water, use it. Naturally, commercial ice cream and syrup can be used, but we prefer using our homemade concoctions.

We used a 14-oz glass to make these sodas. Should a larger or smaller container be used, reduce or increase the amounts suggested proportionately. The temperature of the ingredients is very important in making ice cream sodas. All ingredients should be very cold. Diana puts milk and soda in the freezer a half hour before making the drinks. The ice cream, of course, should be properly ripened, or, as Mr. Dickson, a former soda jerker, says, "dippable."

Nancy, however, doesn't believe the soda should be cold. She likes to use warm soda, which melts some of the ice cream, producing a thick, creamy, foamy drink.

Possible soda combinations are suggested below. Work out your own favorites and let your imagination fly!

All the recipes serve 1 person.

BERRY ICE CREAM SODA

1/3 cup Raspberry, Wild Blackberry, or Blueberry Sauce (see Sauces pages 177-183)
1/4 cup milk
Club soda
1 large scoop Raspberry, Wild Blackberry, Blueberry, or French Vanilla Ice Cream (see Ice Creams chapter)
Whipped cream

CHOCOLATE ICE CREAM SODA

2 Tbsp Chocolate Syrup (page 185)
1/3 cup milk
Club soda
1 large scoop Chocolate Ice Cream (page 51)
Whipped cream

COFFEE ICE CREAM SODA

3 Tbsp Coffee Syrup (page 185)
1/4 cup milk
1 large scoop Coffee Ice Cream (page 59) or Vanilla Ice Cream (page 33)
Whipped cream

PEACH ICE CREAM SODA

1/2 cup Peach Sauce (page 182)
1/4 cup heavy cream
Club soda
1 large scoop Peach and Cream Ice Cream (page 80)
Whipped cream (optional)

PINEAPPLE ICE CREAM SODA

1/4 cup Pineapple Mint Sauce (page 182)
1/4 cup milk
Ginger ale
1 large scoop French Vanilla Ice Cream (page 33) or Pineapple Ice Cream (page 83)

PINK LEMON ICE CREAM SODA

3 Tbsp frozen concentrated Pink Lemonade, thawed
Ginger ale
1 large scoop French Vanilla Ice Cream (page 33)

STRAWBERRY ICE CREAM SODA

¼ cup Strawberry Sauce (page 183)
¼ cup milk
Club soda
1 large scoop Strawberry Ice Cream (page 91) or Vanilla Ice
    Cream (page 33)
Whipped cream
1 strawberry

VANILLA ICE CREAM SODA

2 Tbsp Vanilla Syrup (page 189)
½ cup milk
Club soda
2 scoops French Vanilla Ice Cream (page 33)
Fresh cherry

YELLOW BLACK AND WHITE

3 Tbsp Chocolate Syrup (page 185)
¼ cup milk
Club soda
1 large scoop French Vanilla Ice Cream (page 33)

To make an ice cream soda, place syrup or sauce in bottom of a 14-oz
glass. Add milk or cream and stir. Fill glass three quarters full of soda,
stirring all the while. Gently slip in 1 or 2 scoops ice cream so that it
floats on top. Top with optional whipped cream and fruit, nuts, or
beans of your choice. Serve immediately.

FLOATS

A float is ice cream floated in your favorite drink. We have made a few suggestions, but the choice is really up to you.

COFFEE WITH FRENCH VANILLA ICE CREAM

Serves 1. A favorite of Diana's father.

     1 cup coffee
     1 to 2 heaping Tbsp French Vanilla Ice Cream (page 33)

     Brew 1 cup coffee to your taste. Gently slip in 1 to 2 Tbsp French Vanilla Ice Cream so that it floats on top. Serve immediately. As ice cream melts you sip the coffee through the cream.

COLA FLOAT

Serves 1.

     Coca-Cola
     1 scoop French Vanilla Ice Cream (page 33)

     Fill a glass three-quarters full of Coca-Cola. Gently slip in 1 small scoop French Vanilla Ice Cream. Serve immediately.

ROOT BEER FLOAT

Or Brown Cow, according to a friend of Nancy's from the Midwest. A filling but thirst-quenching drink.

     1 large scoop homemade vanilla ice cream
     8 oz carbonated root beer

     Place 1 large scoop vanilla ice cream in bottom of 12-oz glass. Fill glass with root beer and stir to cool the root beer. Serve immediately with a long-handled spoon.

MILKSHAKES

Milkshakes are very good afternoon snacks. The combination of milk, ice cream, and fruit is tasty and nourishing. And when your body clamors for sugar after a long, hot, exhausting hike, for instance, there is nothing on earth like a shake to satisfy.

In their 1960 book, *Front Runner, Dark Horse*, Ralph G. Martin and Ed Plaut describe John F. Kennedy's first Congressional race. As he walked the hot streets of Boston, every few blocks he stopped and had a milkshake to keep up his energy and good spirits. Later in New York, John V. Lindsay is reported to have done the same thing.

Below we have given you a few suggestions to try. Use your imagination and experiment with different combinations of sauces, syrups, ice creams, and fruits. The Orange Milkshake is a delicious complete breakfast.

BANANA MILKSHAKE

Makes 2 servings of a thick banana drink, filling and nutritious.

    1 cup milk
    1 large scoop homemade vanilla ice cream
    2 bananas, ripened to taste
    1 Tbsp light-brown sugar

Place 1 cup milk, 1 scoop vanilla ice cream, 2 bananas, and 1 Tbsp brown sugar in blender. Blend at high speed until smooth. Pour into 2 8-oz glasses and serve immediately.

Some of our traditional favorite combinations are:

CHOCOLATE MILKSHAKE

Serves 2.

    1 cup milk
    3 large scoops Chocolate Ice Cream (page 51)
       or Vanilla Ice Cream (page 33)
    4 Tbsp Fudge Sauce (page 180)

FRUIT MILKSHAKE

Serves 2.

> 1 cup puréed fruit (apples, peaches, pears, or any other fruit of
>   your choice, either fresh, frozen, or canned)
> 2 scoops Vanilla Ice Cream (page 33)
> 1 cup milk

VANILLA MILKSHAKE

Serves 2.

> 1 cup milk
> 3 scoops Vanilla Ice Cream (page 33)
> 1/8 tsp vanilla extract

ORANGE MILKSHAKE

Serves 1. Tasty combination any time of day. Oscar, Diana's husband,
calls this a breakfast drink; a friend of Nancy's calls this "almost Orange
Julius."

> 1 cup fresh orange juice
> 1/4 cup nonfat dry-milk solids
> 1 scoop Vanilla Ice Cream (page 33)
> 1 egg

Squeeze enough fresh orange juice to measure 1 cup.

Place orange juice, 1/4 cup nonfat dry-milk solids, 1 scoop Vanilla
Ice Cream, and 1 egg in blender. Blend until smooth. Pour into a 12-oz
glass and serve immediately.

STRAWBERRY SHAKE

Serves 1.

> 1 cup fresh strawberries
> 2 large scoops Vanilla Ice Cream (page 33)

Wash and hull 1 cup fresh strawberries. Pour into blender and
blend until puréed. Add 2 large scoops Vanilla Ice Cream and blend
until smooth. Pour into a 14-oz glass. Serve immediately with a long-
handled spoon.

MALTED MILKS

Malted milk is among Diana's husband, Oscar's, favorite drinks. It's simple to make, tasty, and quite nourishing. Below are several sample recipes. Make your own combinations. All you need is ³/₄ cup milk, 1 heaping Tbsp malted milk, your favorite ice cream, and an appropriate syrup, sauce, or flavoring.

Unflavored malted milk powder can usually be found around the dairy food section of your grocery store. After opening the jar, store it in the refrigerator.

Recipes serve 1 and make 14 ounces.

Possible malted milk concoctions are as follows:

CHOCOLATE MALTED MILK

³/₄ cup milk
1 heaping Tbsp malted milk
2 large scoops Chocolate Ice Cream (page 51)
2 Tbsp Chocolate Syrup (page 185)

STRAWBERRY MALTED MILK

³/₄ cup milk
1 heaping Tbsp malted milk
2 large scoops Strawberry Ice Cream (page 91)
¹/₄ cup Strawberry Sauce (page 183)

VANILLA MALTED MILK

³/₄ cup milk
1 heaping Tbsp malted milk
2 large scoops French Vanilla Ice Cream (page 33)
3 Tbsp Vanilla Syrup (page 189)

To make malted milks, place in a blender the milk, malted milk, ripened ice cream, and sauce or syrup. Blend 30 seconds to 1 minute or until smooth. Malted milk is usually served in an 8-oz glass, with remainder in a second one.

Cocktails and
Other Alcoholic Drinks

FROZEN ALCOHOLIC DRINKS

These icy refreshing drinks contain a fair amount of alcohol; therefore, beware.

FROZEN DAIQUIRI COCKTAIL

Serves 2 generously (2 cups). A sure sign of summer in the Collier household.

> Juice of 2 limes
> 2 rounded Tbsp granulated or confectioners' sugar
> 1/4 cup rum
> 10 or more medium-sized ice cubes, crushed

Squeeze juice of 2 limes. Pour into blender with 2 rounded Tbsp granulated or confectioners' sugar, 1/4 cup rum, and crushed ice from 10 or more ice cubes (use ice crusher). Blend until a smooth, icy mass.

Serve immediately in cocktail or champagne glasses. The blender pitcher could be put into refrigerator about 10 to 30 minutes if you're not ready to serve.

PIÑA COLADA

Serves 2 generously. This version was re-created in honor of friends of Diana's, Sue and Ken Garrison, who now live in California. Canned sweetened cream of coconut is available in specialty food stores and "gourmet" delicatessens.

> 1/4 cup sweetened cream of coconut
> 1/4 cup pineapple juice
> 1/4 cup rum
> 10 or more medium-sized ice cubes, crushed

Pour into blender 1/4 cup cream of coconut, 1/4 cup pineapple juice, and 1/4 cup rum. Crush 10 or more ice cubes with ice crusher and add to blender. Blend until a smooth, icy mass.

Serve immediately in cocktail or champagne glasses. The blender pitcher could be put into refrigerator 10 minutes or so if you're not ready to serve.

FROZEN PUNCHES

Originally frozen punches were served between courses of a dinner.
Now, however, we serve them as an iced apéritif or afterdinner drink.
These drinks resemble water ices with liqueur and/or wine added.
When the mixture is frozen, it becomes a mush.

The alcohol content is sufficiently high to prevent the mixture
from freezing into a solid mass. The mush melts quickly with ice
crystals remaining floating in the drink, making it powerfully cooling.

CARDINAL PUNCH

Makes 6 cups. A fantastic drink experience with which we recommend
serving food.

    4 cups water
    2 cups light-brown sugar
    12 cloves
    1 cup raspberries, fresh or frozen
    Peel of 2 oranges
    Juice of 4 oranges
    Juice of 2 limes
    1/3 to 1/2 cup brandy
    1/3 to 1/2 cup Curaçao

In a 3-quart stainless-steel pot combine 4 cups water with 2 cups
brown sugar, 12 cloves, and 1 cup raspberries. Peel 2 oranges and add
peel to the sugar water. Squeeze juice from peeled oranges and 2 more
oranges, and 2 limes; add juices to sugar water. Bring liquid to a boil
and simmer for 20 minutes. Remove from heat and cool. Press mixture
through a fine sieve into freezer container. Cover and freeze until a
hard mush.

Remove from freezer, uncover, stir, and add from 1/3 to 1/2 cup
brandy and 1/3 to 1/2 cup Curaçao, or to taste. Stir, cover, and freeze.
Mixture remains somewhat mushy.

Serve directly from freezer in champagne glasses.

MOTHER MEERWARTH'S FLORIDA SPECIAL

Makes about 2½ cups. Diana's mother devised this recipe and has been serving it to friends in Fort Lauderdale for many years. It has a strong citrus flavor and a pleasant icy consistency. In making her Florida Special Mrs. Meerwarth likes to use gin, but whisky or rum is perfectly acceptable.

> 1 6-oz can frozen concentrated lemonade, thawed
> ¾ cup orange juice or juice from 3 to 4 oranges
> ¾ cup ginger ale
> ¾ cup gin

Pour contents of a 6-oz can frozen concentrated lemonade, thawed, into a wide-mouthed quart jar. Add ¾ cup fresh orange juice or juice from 3 to 4 oranges, ¾ cup ginger ale, and ¾ cup gin. Stir with a long-handled spoon. Cover tightly and freeze for several hours or until mixture is partially frozen.

Remove from freezer, stir to mix liquor with other ingredients, cover again, and freeze until icy. Mixture never freezes up completely, but stays somewhat icy.

Drink may be served directly from freezer. To serve, remove mixture from freezer, briskly stir with long-handled spoon, and spoon icy mixture out into champagne or sherry glasses. Serve immediately.

ROMAN PUNCH

Makes 5 to 6 cups. A very strong, tasty fruit drink. A little bit goes a long way.

> Peel of 1 orange
> Peel of 1 lemon
> Juice of 4 oranges
> Juice of 4 lemons
> ½ cup raspberries or blackberries, fresh or frozen
> 1 cup granulated sugar
> 4 cups white wine or champagne
> 4 egg whites
> 1½ to 2 cups rum

Peel 1 orange and 1 lemon and place peels in 1½-quart saucepan. Squeeze juice from peeled orange and lemon into saucepan. Then squeeze juice from 3 more oranges and 3 more lemons into saucepan. Pour in ½ cup berries and 1 cup sugar. Bring to a boil and simmer 10 minutes. Remove from heat, cool, and strain mixture through a fine sieve into medium-sized bowl. Add 4 cups white wine or champagne, cover bowl, and freeze 2 hours or until a stiff mush.

Remove from freezer, uncover, and beat until frothy. Cover and return to freezer until fairly firm.

Beat 4 egg whites until soft peaks form. Remove ice from freezer, uncover, and fold in beaten egg whites; cover again and freeze 1½ hours. Remove from freezer, stir, cover, and freeze again until ready to serve.

Just before serving, stir in 1½ to 2 cups rum to taste. Serve in chilled sherbet or punch glasses.

MARQUISE

A *marquise* is an iced drink made with a fruit ice base, liqueur or wine, and whipped cream.

Prepare desired fruit ice mixture and choose an appropriate wine or liqueur. When fruit and sugar water mixture has cooled sufficiently in refrigerator, remove and add an equal amount of wine or liqueur to taste. Stir and pour into freezer container. Cover and freeze until partially frozen.

Measure out an amount of heavy cream equal to that of partially frozen mixture. Whip cream until soft peaks form. Remove mixture from freezer, uncover, and stir to break up large crystals. Scrape in whipped cream and fold one mixture into the other rather vigorously.

If serving almost immediately, spoon into sherbet or champagne glasses, cover, and return to freezer 10 minutes; or scrape into freezer container, cover, and freeze. If stored for any length of time, marquise should be allowed to ripen in refrigerator 30 minutes before serving.

Our favorite of these is the following champagne marquise, which can be counted on to get a rise out of even the most hardened non-gourmet.

CHAMPAGNE MARQUISE

Makes 2 quarts of an elusively flavored creamy ice that is a marvelous beginning or fitting finish to a great dinner.

1 tsp unflavored gelatin
1/4 cup cold water
3/4 cup water
1/2 cup granulated sugar
Juice of 1 orange
Juice of 1 lime
A split of chilled champagne (7 oz) or sparkling wine
1 1/2 cups heavy cream
1 Tbsp brandy
1 Tbsp confectioners' sugar

Soften 1 tsp gelatin in 1/4 cup cold water in a small bowl. Set aside.

Put 3/4 cup water and 1/2 cup sugar in a saucepan and bring to a boil over high heat, stirring. Lower heat and simmer without stirring for 5 minutes. Remove from heat and pour in softened gelatin. Stir until gelatin has melted. Set aside.

Squeeze juice from 1 orange and 1 lime. Add juices to gelatin and sugar water. Chill in refrigerator 1 hour.

Open split of champagne and pour into medium-sized glass or stainless-steel bowl. Remove chilled juices from refrigerator and pour into champagne. Stir. Cover bowl and set in freezer until almost firm (about 2 to 3 hours).

Whip 1 1/2 cups heavy cream until soft peaks form. Add 1 Tbsp brandy and 1 Tbsp confectioners' sugar. Whip a few moments longer.

Remove fruit ice from freezer, uncover, break up icy pieces, and beat with electric mixer a few seconds until smooth and icy. Fold in whipped cream. Spoon into sherbet or champagne glasses; then put them in the freezer 10 to 15 minutes to firm up. Remove from freezer and serve immediately.

Marquises may also be scraped into freezer container, covered, and frozen. Allow to ripen in refrigerator 20 to 30 minutes before serving.

GRANITÉ

A *granité* is a frozen drink with a rough and icy texture; it uses a fruit ice as a base.

Prepare the fruit ice, doubling the amount of gelatin, and remove it from freezer after first hour of freezing, or when mixture has become icy around the edges. Uncover, break up icy pieces and beat until smooth. Cover again and return mixture to freezer and allow it to freeze until almost firm. Remove again from freezer, uncover, and add approximately ¼ cup wine or 1 oz liqueur to 1 pint of fruit ice, depending on how strong a flavor you want.

When making granité, match the flavor of the fruit ice with the flavor of the wine or liqueur.

The added wine or liqueur gives its name to the granité, hence Curaçao Granité, Grand Marnier Granité, Mountain Rhine Granité, Rosé Granité, Champagne Granité.

Serve in a champagne glass.

CURAÇAO GRANITÉ

Serves 4. One drink transports you to Florida, two to Martinique, three to the South Seas.

    1 quart Orange Ice (page 159)
    ¼ cup Curaçao

Prepare 1 quart Orange Ice, doubling the amount of gelatin. Cover and place in freezer for 1 hour or until icy around the edges. Remove from freezer, uncover, stir to break up icy pieces, and beat until smooth. Cover and return mixture to freezer until almost firm. Take out of freezer, pour in ¼ cup Curaçao (or more, if you wish), stir, and freeze up mixture about 10 minutes if serving immediately or cover container and return to freezer until firm.

Spoon into champagne glasses 30 minutes before serving and place them in refrigerator.

SPOOMS

Spooms are iced drinks with a sherbet base, topped with wine or liquor, thus giving the particular drink its name: Whiskey Spoom, Brandy Spoom, Rum Spoom, Champagne Spoom, Burgundy Spoom.

When making a sherbet to use in a spoom, double the amount of egg whites used in the chosen recipe to produce a snowlike texture in the final product.

When sherbet is frozen, spoon into champagne glasses, and add 1 jigger, or 1½ oz, wine or liquor to 1 cup of sherbet in each glass.

WHISKEY SPOOM

Serves 6. Deceptively powerful despite its snowlike appearance.

    1½ quarts Lemon Sherbet (page 139)
    9 oz (6 jiggers) whiskey

Prepare Lemon Sherbet, doubling the amount of egg whites suggested in the recipe.

When sherbet is firm, spoon into goblets, allowing 1 cup sherbet for each glass. Pour 1 jigger, or 1½ oz, whiskey over the sherbet in each glass. Stir, allow to stand 10 minutes, and serve.

Carol Van Nattan told Diana that a traditional drink of her childhood among her friends was a *Cherry Heering Milkshake*. Mix one part Cherry Heering with 2 parts Vanilla Ice Cream in blender. Blend and serve. Parents knew it as a Strawberry Milkshake.

Another favorite of the same group was a Cherry Heering with Chocolate Ice Cream. Mix 1 part Cherry Heering with 2 parts Chocolate Ice Cream in blender. Blend and serve. Parents knew this one as a Chocolate Strawberry Milkshake.

Creating Your Own

You have mastered the techniques of beating egg yolks and egg whites to the proper consistency, whipping cream so that it doesn't become butter, melting chocolate without anxiety, unmolding without melting, making smooth, uncurdled custard.

You are now ready to create your own individual frozen delights.

When making your own creations you might find the following generalized recipes for basic custard ice cream, mousses, soufflés, sherbets, and ices helpful.

CUSTARD BASE

Makes 1½ quarts ice cream.

1½ cups combination of milk and cream or milk
4 egg yolks
1 tsp cornstarch
½ cup granulated sugar or equivalent sweetener
1½ cups heavy cream
1 cup fruit or moderate amount of other flavor

Place milk or milk and cream in top of double boiler and heat to lukewarm over simmering water.

In a small bowl using an electric mixer or a wire whisk beat together 4 egg yolks, 1 tsp cornstarch, and ½ cup sweetener until egg yolks are frothy and pale yellow in color.

Slowly pour in one third or all of the warmed milk and cream into egg mixture. Scrape eggs and milk back into top of double boiler and cook over simmering water until custard thickens, stirring constantly. Remove from heat and continue to stir until custard cools slightly.

Place custard in refrigerator to chill.

Whip 1½ cups heavy cream until soft peaks form. Remove custard from refrigerator. Fold in whipped cream and 1 cup of any fruits or flavor of your choice. Scrape mixture into freezer container, cover tightly, and freeze for approximately 1 hour or until frozen around edges of container.

Remove ice cream from freezer, uncover, and stir thoroughly to break up any large ice crystals. Cover and return to freezer until firm.

Before serving, allow ice cream to ripen in refrigerator until soft enough to serve. This time will vary, as explained in the introduction.

BASIC MOUSSE

Makes about 1 quart.

2 cups fruit, cut up; or 1 cup fruit purée
1/4 cup second fruit juice
1/2 to 1/3 cup sweetener
2 egg whites
1 Tbsp sweetener
1/2 to 1 cup heavy cream

Prepare chosen fruit. Pour 1/4 cup of second fruit juice, chosen to blend with main fruit, and sweetener, over fruit. Stir and set aside in refrigerator for 1 hour.

Beat 2 egg whites with 1 Tbsp sweetener until stiff peaks form. Whip the heavy cream.

Remove fruit from refrigerator and purée it. Pour purée into beaten egg whites and fold one into the other. Then fold in the whipped cream. Scrape into freezer container or serving dish, cover, and place in freezer until firm.

Allow mousse to ripen in refrigerator about 15 minutes before serving.

BASIC MILK SHERBET

Makes about 1 pint.

2 or more egg whites
1/2 cup or more to taste sweetener
1 cup milk
1/2 to 1 cup fruit juice or puréed fruit

Beat egg whites until soft peaks form. Slowly beat in sweetener and continue beating until mixture forms stiff peaks and egg whites are smooth and glossy.

At very low speed beat in 1 cup milk and puréed fruit or fruit juice.

Cover bowl and place in freezer until sherbet is mushy. Top will be frozen foam, while bottom will be liquid.

Remove from freezer, uncover, and beat at high speed until sherbet is uniformly mixed and smooth.

Scrape sherbet into freezer container, cover tightly, and freeze until firm.

Most sherbet combinations can be served directly from the freezer but test for ripening for your recipe.

BASIC SHERBET

Makes about 2 quarts.

  1 to 2 cups fruit purée
  2 or more egg whites
  ¼ cup sweetener (more or less depending on
      fruit used and its sweetness)
  1 cup heavy cream (optional)

Prepare chosen fruit.

Beat egg whites until soft peaks form. Slowly beat in sweetener and continue beating until whites are smooth, glossy, and hold stiff peaks. Fold in puréed fruit. Leave mixture in bowl or scrape into freezer container, cover tightly, and place in freezer for 1 hour or until partially frozen around the edges of container.

Remove sherbet from freezer, uncover, and beat at high speed until it lightens in color and increases in volume. Leave in bowl or scrape into freezer container, cover tightly, and return to freezer for 1 hour.

If a richer dessert is desired, whip 1 cup heavy cream until soft peaks form. Set aside.

Remove sherbet from freezer, uncover, and beat a second time until sherbet lightens in color and increases in volume. Fold in optional whipped cream. Scrape sherbet into freezer or serving container, cover tightly, and freeze until firm.

Serve sherbet directly from freezer.

BASIC SOUFFLÉ

Makes about 2 quarts and serves 8.

  6 egg yolks
  ¼ cup granulated sugar
  6 egg whites
  ¼ tsp cream of tartar
  ⅓ cup granulated sugar
  ½ to 1 cup heavy cream
  Any addition of fruit purée, juice, or flavor of your choice

Beat 6 egg yolks at high speed with an electric mixer for 5 minutes or until yolks are very thick and pale yellow in color. While mixer is going, slowly pour in ¼ cup sugar and continue beating until mixture is very thick and ribbons trailing from raised beaters remain visible on surface of mixture. The sugar should be completely dissolved. Set aside.

In a separate bowl beat 6 egg whites with ¼ tsp cream of tartar until soft peaks form. Slowly beat in ⅓ cup sugar and continue beating until smooth and glossy and very stiff peaks form. Set aside.

Whip ½ to 1 cup heavy cream until soft peaks form. Set aside.

First fold flavor or fruit of your choice into beaten egg yolks; then the beaten egg whites, and finally the whipped cream.

Scrape mixture into 8-cup soufflé dish and freeze for 5 hours or until firm.

Most soufflés remain soft enough to be served directly from the freezer.

BASIC WATER ICE

Makes about 1½ pints.

4 cups fruit, cut up into small pieces; or 2 cups fruit purée
¼ to ½ cup sweetener
1 Tbsp lemon or lime juice (optional)
2 tsp unflavored gelatin
½ cup cold water
1 cup water
⅓ to ¾ cup sweetener

Prepare chosen fruit. Pour sweetener, and lemon or lime juice, if used, over fruit. Stir and set aside for 1 hour.

Sprinkle 2 tsp gelatin over ½ cup cold water. Stir and set aside for gelatin to soften.

Pour 1 cup water and the sweetener into a small saucepan. Bring to a boil over high heat, stirring. Reduce heat and keep at a slow boil for 5 minutes without stirring. Remove from heat and pour in gelatin. Stir until gelatin is melted. Set aside in refrigerator to cool.

Pour fruit into blender and purée. Pour purée into a bowl. Remove sweetened water from refrigerator and stir into purée. Cover and freeze until mixture becomes icy.

Remove from freezer, uncover, stir to break up icy pieces, and beat until smooth. Pour into freezer container, cover, and freeze until firm.

Allow ice to ripen in refrigerator 2 to 2½ hours before serving.

FROZEN LIQUEUR-FLAVORED PIE

Serves 4.

1/2 cup cold light cream
1 tsp unflavored gelatin
2 egg yolks
3 to 4 Tbsp sweetener (depending on the sweetness of the liqueur)
4 to 6 Tbsp liqueur or combination of liqueurs
1/2 cup heavy cream
71/2-inch prepared Chocolate Cookie Crust (page 221) or Vanilla
    Cookie Crust (page 223) or Graham Cracker Crust (page 222)

In a small saucepan combine 1/2 cup cold light cream and 1 tsp gelatin. Stir to soften gelatin; then warm slowly to melt it. Remove from heat and set aside.

In a medium-sized bowl beat together 2 egg yolks and 3 or 4 Tbsp sweetener until mixture is thick, increased in volume, and ribbons from raised beaters remain visible on surface of mixture. The sugar should be completely dissolved. Stir in 4 to 6 Tbsp liqueur. Then stir in the gelatin and milk. Chill in refrigerator (about 20 minutes).

Whip 1/2 cup heavy cream until soft peaks form.

Remove chilled gelatin mixture from refrigerator and fold in the whipped cream. Pour filling into prepared crust and place in freezer for several hours until firm.

Before serving allow pie to ripen at room temperature for 10 minutes.

Creating Your Own

Appendices

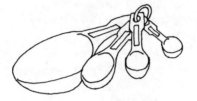

MEASUREMENTS

A pinch or dash = $1/8$ tsp
3 tsp = 1 Tbsp
2 Tbsp = 1 fluid ounce
4 Tbsp = $1/4$ cup
$51/3$ Tbsp = $1/3$ cup
6 Tbsp = $3/8$ cup
8 Tbsp = $1/2$ cup
$1/2$ cup + 2 Tbsp = $5/8$ cup
$102/3$ Tbsp = $2/3$ cup
12 Tbsp = $3/4$ cup
16 Tbsp = 8 fluid ounces = 1 cup
2 cups = 1 pint
2 pints = 4 cups = 1 quart
8 cups = 4 pints = 2 quarts = $1/2$ gallon
1 jigger = $11/2$ fluid ounces = 3 Tbsp

Solid Fats in sticks or pounds
1 pound = 2 cups
$1/2$ pound = 2 sticks = 1 cup
$1/4$ pound = 1 stick = $1/2$ cup = 8 Tbsp
$1/2$ stick = $1/4$ cup = 4 Tbsp

SUBSTITUTIONS

Don't feel frustrated if you don't have the exact ingredients suggested in the recipe. Below are substitutions that will work just as well.

1 Tbsp white granulated sugar = 1 Tbsp raw sugar = 1 Tbsp light- or dark-brown sugar = 2 Tbsp light corn syrup = $1/2$ Tbsp honey
3 oz unsweetened chocolate + 4 Tbsp sugar = 5 oz semi-sweet chocolate or 1 oz unsweetened chocolate + 4 tsp sugar = $12/3$ oz semi-sweet chocolate
1 oz, or 1 square, unsweetened chocolate = 3 Tbsp cocoa plus 1 Tbsp butter or oil

1 inch vanilla bean = 1 tsp vanilla extract
4 large egg yolks = 1/3 cup
5 medium egg yolks = 1/3 cup
2 large egg whites = 1/4 to 1/3 cup
3 medium egg whites = 1/3 cup
1 Tbsp cornstarch = 2 tsp arrowroot
1 pint whole milk = 1 cup evaporated milk + 1 cup water
1 pint light cream (butterfat 18%) + 1 pint Half and Half
  (butterfat 18%) = 1 cup milk + 1 cup heavy cream

SOURCES OF SUPPLIES

Most of the equipment and ingredients used in ice creammaking can be found in housewares departments of your local stores and grocery stores, supermarkets, or specialty stores. Some items, however, are not always readily available, so we have included a list of mail order sources that will send out catalogues or price lists on request describing their products, which range from high-quality cooking and baking equipment to tea, coffee, and vanilla beans.

Hammacher Schlemmer (mail order)
3925 Skillman Avenue, Long Island City, New York 11104
　　Extensive line of equipment and gadgets, some one of a kind items, including refrigerator trays with lids, coffee grinders, and filters.

Maid of Scandinavia Company
3244 Raleigh Avenue, Minneapolis, Minnesota 55416
　　Complete line of baking equipment, pastry bags, standard and unusual molds (including popsicle), scoops (one with anti-freeze handle) . . .

McNulty's Tea and Coffee Co.
109 Christopher Street, New York, New York 10014
　　Specializing in coffee and tea plus associated products such as coffee grinders, filters, teapots . . .

Paprikas Weiss
1546 Second Avenue, New York, New York 10028
   Excellent line of imported cooking and baking equipment, including molds and pans; limited but good selection of coffee beans, teas, spices.

Tupperware Home Parties
North High-441, Kissimmee, Florida, 32741
   Extensive catalogue of containers, including standard molds, popsicle molds, unusual storage containers. Check telephone directory for local distributor or write to home office in Kissimmee, a suburb of Orlando.

Walnut Acres, Inc.
Penns Creek, Pa. 17862
   Carefully described organic and nonorganic products; excellent source of nuts, vanilla beans, honey, unusual jams and jellies, syrups, etc.; also equipment such as coffee grinders.

Index